DATA STRUCTURES

IN C

Noel Kalicharan

Senior Lecturer, Computer Science
The University of the West Indies
St. Augustine, Trinidad

First published July 2008
Revised 2015, 2019

© Noel Kalicharan, 2008, 2015, 2019
noel.kalicharan@sta.uwi.edu
noelkali@gmail.com

To the delightful Vaishnavi

Preface

Data *Structures in C* is the third book in a sequence following *C Programming – A Beginner's Course* and *C Programming – An Advanced Course.*

Data structures is concerned with the storage, representation and manipulation of data in a computer. In this book, we discuss some of the more versatile and popular data structures used to solve a variety of useful problems. Many books on data structures tend to go for over-kill and the student gets lost in complexity; such books are better used as references.

This books presents a wealth of basic knowledge in a simplified form. It is based on the premise that it is better to learn a few concepts well than many concepts poorly. As a result, it restricts itself to what can be reasonably covered in a one-semester course in data structures. The emphasis is on treating material in such a way that the student is comfortable without being overwhelmed by complexity and analysis.

The approach is practical rather than theoretical. With this in mind, we show *how* to implement the data structures and operations on them using C. We also show how to write programs to solve problems using these structures. A basic knowledge of C is assumed. This includes writing functions that use *if...then...else*, *while* and *for* loops. You should also be comfortable working with strings and arrays.

In order to be as self-contained as possible, some material from *C Programming – An Advanced Course* is repeated here.

Chapter 1 shows how to define and work with structures in C.

Chapter 2 is devoted to pointers, one of the more difficult concepts for C programmers to master.

Chapter 3 deals with linked lists. It covers basic operations such as building, searching, insertion into and deletion from a linked list. The chapter ends with the merging of two sorted linked lists.

Chapter 4 covers stacks and queues. It shows how to implement these useful structures using linked lists and arrays. An important step in evaluating an arithmetic expression is converting it to postfix form. This chapter shows how.

Chapter 5 deals with that most versatile of data structures—the binary tree. It shows how to build and traverse a binary tree. The *binary search tree* is a special kind of tree that facilitates quick searching. We show how to build and manipulate such trees, and use one to produce a cross-reference listing of words in the input. We also show how to represent a binary tree compactly using an array.

Chapter 6 discusses several sorting methods, starting with a revision of the 'simple' ones— selection and insertion sort. This is followed by the faster methods—heapsort, quicksort and mergesort. The chapter ends with a discussion of Shell (diminishing increment) sort.

Chapter 7 deals with graphs. A very large number of problems/situations can be modelled using graphs. So learning about graphs is fundamental to solving many kinds of problems. Topics include how to represent, build and traverse a graph, topological sorting, finding shortest paths and minimum spanning trees.

Chapter 8 is devoted to *hashing*, one of the fastest ways to search. It covers hashing fundamentals and discusses several ways to resolve collisions.

Chapter 9 deals with matrices, in particular the storage requirements of matrices and how this storage can be reduced. It covers triangular matrices, symmetric and skew-symmetric matrices, band matrices and sparse matrices.

All the programs in the book have been tested using *Code::Blocks* (www.codeblocks.org). Code::Blocks is an Integrated Development Environment (IDE) that uses the GCC compiler. It is available for Windows, Linux and Mac OS X. To get up and running quickly, go to

http://www.codeblocks.org/downloads/binaries

and download the version you wish to use. The *User Manual* is available here:

http://www.codeblocks.org/user-manual

We also recommend the Tiny C compiler. This compiler is small and fast. It is freely available at

http://bellard.org/tcc/.

Our goal is to provide a good, basic understanding of important data structures and how they can be implemented in C. We hope that this will whet your appetite for deeper study of this exciting area of computer science.

Noel Kalicharan

Notes on Revised Edition, 2015

Since its publication in 2008, many readers have submitted comments and suggestions. While the changes are largely cosmetic (different cover, traditional programming font, improved program layout and removal of page references more compatible with electronic devices), we took the opportunity to make some small but meaningful changes. Among these are: saving a linked list, a more detailed comparison of using arrays and linked storage to hold a list of items, how to store a linked list using arrays, circular and doubly-linked lists, and an improved topological sort.

The original book contained many complete programs. However, in a few of the programming examples, we wrote the functions but did not provide a complete listing of the program in one place. We do so now.

Some readers requested that the source code for the programs be made available online. It can be found here:

https://onedrive.live.com/?authkey=%21AAMYL7b58wzbeBM&id=8ACA1678C859BCF7%21 278&cid=8ACA1678C859BCF7

Finally, we wish to thank those who have contributed to the success of this book. It is now the first choice for many computer science students and many others who prefer to learn about data structures on their own. Thank you all.

Noel Kalicharan

Contents

CHAPTER 1

▪ ▪ ▪

Structures

In this chapter, we will explain the following:

- What a structure is
- How to declare a structure
- How to use `typedef` to work with structures more conveniently
- How to work with an array of structures
- How to search an array of structures
- How to sort an array of structures
- How to declare *nested* structures
- How to use structures to manipulate fractions
- How to use structures to solve a "voting" problem
- How structures can be passed to a function

1.1 The Need for Structures

In C, a structure is a collection of one or more variables, possibly of different types, grouped together under a single name for convenient handling.

There are many situations in which we want to process data about a certain entity or object but the data consists of items of various types. For example, the data for a student (the *student record*) may consist of several *fields* such as a name, address and telephone number (all of type string), number of courses taken (integer), fees payable (floating-point), names of courses (string), grades obtained (character), and so on.

The data for a car may consist of manufacturer, model and registration number (string), seating capacity and fuel capacity (integer), and mileage and price (floating-point). For a book, we may want to store author and title (string), price (floating-point), number of pages (integer), type of binding—hardcover, paperback, spiral (string)—and number of copies in stock (integer).

Suppose we want to store data for 100 students in a program. One approach is to have a separate array for each field and use subscripts to link the fields together. Thus, `name[i]`, `address[i]`, `fees[i]`, and so on, refer to the data for the ith student.

1

The problem with this approach is that if there are many fields, the handling of several parallel arrays becomes clumsy and unwieldy. For example, suppose we want to pass a student's data to a function via the parameter list. This will involve the passing of several arrays. Also, if we are sorting the students by name, say, each time two names are interchanged, we have to write statements to interchange the data in the other arrays as well. In such situations, C structures are convenient to use.

1.2 Declare a Structure

Consider the problem of storing a date in a program. A date consists of three parts: the day, the month, and the year. Each of these parts can be represented by an integer. For example, the date "September 14, 2006" can be represented by the day, 14; the month, 9; and the year 2006. We say that a date consists of three *fields*, each of which is an integer.

If we want, we can also represent a date by using the *name* of the month, rather than its number. In this case, a date consists of three fields, one of which is a string and the other two are integers.

In C, we can declare a *date type* as a *structure* using the keyword `struct`. Consider this declaration:

```
struct date {int day, month, year;};
```

It consists of the word `struct` followed by some name we choose to give to the structure (`date`, in the example); this is followed by the declarations of the fields enclosed in left and right braces. Note the semicolon at the end of the declaration just before the right brace—this is the usual case of a semicolon ending a declaration. The right brace is followed by a semicolon, ending the `struct` declaration.

We could also have written the declaration as follows, where each field is declared individually:

```
struct date {
    int day;
    int month;
    int year;
};
```

This could be written as follows, but the style above is preferred for its readability:

```
struct date {int day; int month; int year;};
```

Given the `struct` declaration, we can declare variables of type `struct date`, as follows:

```
struct date dob; //to hold a "date of birth"
```

This declares `dob` as a "structure variable" of type `date`. It has three fields called `day`, `month`, and `year`. This can be pictured as follows:

We refer to the day field as `dob.day`, the month field as `dob.month`, and the year field as `dob.year`. In C, the period (`.`), as used here, is referred to as the *structure member operator*.

In general, *a field is specified by the structure variable name, followed by a period, followed by the field name.*

We could declare more than one variable at a time, as follows:

```
struct date borrowed, returned; //for a book in a library, say
```

Each of these variables has three fields: day, month, and year. The fields of borrowed are referred to by borrowed.day, borrowed.month, and borrowed.year. The fields of returned are referred to by returned.day, returned.month, and returned.year.

In this example, each field is an int and can be used in any context in which an int variable can be used. For example, to assign the date "November 14, 2019" to dob, we can use this:

```
dob.day = 14;
dob.month = 11;
dob.year = 2019;
```

This can be pictured as follows:

	day	month	year
dob	14	11	2019

We can also read values for day, month, and year with the following:

```
scanf("%d %d %d", &dob.day, &dob.month, &dob.year);
```

If today was a struct date variable holding a date, we could assign all the fields of today to dob, say, with the following:

```
dob = today;
```

This one statement is equivalent to the following:

```
dob.day = today.day;
dob.month = today.month;
dob.year = today.year;
```

We can print the "value" of dob with this:

```
printf("The party is on %d/%d/%d\n", dob.day, dob.month, dob.year);
```

For this example, the following will be printed:

```
The party is on 14/11/2019
```

Note that each field has to be printed individually. We *could* also write a function printDate, say, which prints a date given as an argument. For example, suppose we write this:

```
void printDate(struct date d) {
    printf("%d/%d/%d \n", d.day, d.month, d.year);
}
```

Then the call

```
printDate(dob);
```

will print this:

14/11/2019

We note, in passing, that C provides a date and time structure, `tm`, in the standard library. In addition to the date, it provides, among other things, the time to the nearest second. To use it, your program must be preceded by the following:

```
#include <time.h>
```

The construct `struct date` is a bit cumbersome to use, compared to single-word types such `int` or `double`. Fortunately, C provides us with `typedef` to make working with structures a little more convenient.

1.2.1 typedef

We can use `typedef` to give a name to some existing type, and this name can then be used to declare variables of that type. We can also use `typedef` to construct shorter or more meaningful names for predefined C types or for user-declared types, such as structures. For example, the following statement declares a new type-name `Whole`, which is synonymous with the predefined type `int`:

```
typedef int Whole;
```

Note that `Whole` appears in the same position as a variable would, not right after the word `typedef`. We can then declare variables of type `Whole`, as follows:

```
Whole amount, numCopies;
```

This is exactly equivalent to

```
int amount, numCopies;
```

For those accustomed to the term `real` of languages like Pascal or FORTRAN, the following statement allows them to declare variables of type `Real`:

```
typedef float Real;
```

In this book, we use at least one uppercase letter to distinguish type names declared using `typedef`.

We could give a short, meaningful name, `Date`, to the date structure shown earlier with the following declaration:

```
typedef struct date {
    int day;
    int month;
    int year;
} Date;
```

Recall that C distinguishes between uppercase and lowercase letters so that `date` is different from `Date`. We could, if we wanted, have used any other identifier, such as `DateType`, instead of `Date`.

We could now declare "structure variables" of type `Date`, such as the following:

```
Date dob, borrowed, returned;
```

Notice how much shorter and neater this is compared to the following:

```
struct date dob, borrowed, returned;
```

Since there is hardly any reason to use this second form, we could omit date from the earlier declaration and write this:

```
typedef struct {
    int day;
    int month;
    int year;
} Date;
```

Thereafter, we can use Date whenever the struct is required. For example, we can rewrite printDate as follows:

```
void printDate(Date d) {
    printf("%d/%d/%d \n", d.day, d.month, d.year);
}
```

To pursue the date example, suppose we want to store the "short" name—the first three letters, for example Aug—of the month. We will need to use a declaration such as this:

```
typedef struct {
    int day;
    char month[4]; //one position for \0 to end string
    int year;
} Date;
```

We can represent the date "November 14, 2019" in a Date variable dob with the following:

```
dob.day = 14;
strcpy(dob.month, "Nov");
dob.year = 2019;
```

And we can write printDate as follows:

```
void printDate(Date d) {
    printf("%s %d, %d \n", d.month, d.day, d.year);
}
```

The call

```
printDate(dob);
```

will print this:

```
Nov 14, 2019
```

Suppose we want to store information about students. For each student, we want to store their name, age, and gender (male or female). Assuming that a name is no longer than 30 characters, we could use the following declaration:

```
typedef struct {
    char name[31];
    int age;
    char gender;
} Student;
```

We can now declare variables of type Student, as follows:

```
Student stud1, stud2;
```

Each of stud1 and stud2 will have its own fields—name, age, and gender. We can refer to these fields as follows:

```
stud1.name    stud1.age    stud1.gender
stud2.name    stud2.age    stud2.gender
```

As usual, we can assign values to these fields or read values into them. And, if we want, we can assign all the fields of stud1 to stud2 with one statement:

```
stud2 = stud1;
```

1.3 Array of Structure

Suppose we want to store data on 100 students. We will need an array of size 100, and each element of the array will hold the data for one student. Thus, each element will have to be a structure—we need an "array of structures."

We can declare the array with the following, similar to how we say "int pupil[100]" to declare an integer array of size 100:

```
Student pupil[100];
```

This allocates storage for pupil[0], pupil[1], pupil[2], ..., up to pupil[99]. Each element pupil[i] consists of three fields that can be referred to as follows:

```
pupil[i].name    pupil[i].age    pupil[i].gender
```

First we will need to store some data in the array. Assume we have data in the following format (name, age, gender):

```
"Jones, John" 24 M
"Mohammed, Lisa" 33 F
"Singh, Sandy" 29 F
"Layne, Dennis" 49 M
"END"
```

Suppose the data are stored in a file input.txt and in is declared as follows:

```
FILE * in = fopen("input.txt", "r");
```

If str is a character array, assume we can call the function getString(in, str) to store the next data string in quotes in str without the quotes. Also assume that readChar(in) will read the data and return the next non-whitespace character.

Exercise: Write the functions getString and readChar.

We can read the data into the array pupil with the following code:

```
int n = 0;
char temp[31];
getString(in, temp);
while (strcmp(temp, "END") != 0) {
   strcpy(pupil[n].name, temp);
   fscanf(in, "%d", &pupil[n].age);
   pupil[n].gender = readChar(in);
   n++;
   getString(in, temp);
}
```

At the end, n contains the number of students stored, and pupil[0] to pupil[n-1] contain the data for those students.

To ensure that we do not attempt to store more data than we have room for in the array, we should check that n is within the bounds of the array. Assuming that MaxItems has the value 100, this can be done by changing the while condition to the following:

```
while (n < MaxItems && strcmp(temp, "END") != 0)
```

or by inserting the following just after the statement n++; inside the loop:

```
if (n == MaxItems) break;
```

1.4 Search an Array of Structures

With the data stored in the array, we can manipulate it in various ways. For instance, we can write a function to search for a given name. Assuming the data is stored in no particular order, we can use a sequential search as follows:

```
int search(char key[], Student list[], int n) {
   //search for key in list[0] to list[n-1]
   //if found, return the location; if not found, return -1
   for (int h = 0; h < n; h++)
      if (strcmp(key, list[h].name) == 0) return h;
   return -1;
} //end search
```

Given the previous data, the call

```
search("Singh, Sandy", pupil, 4)
```

will return 2, and the following call will return -1:

```
search("Layne, Sandy", pupil, 4)
```

1.5 Sort an Array of Structures

Suppose we want the list of students in alphabetical order by name. It will be required to sort the array pupil. The following function uses an insertion sort to do the job. The *process* is identical to sorting an int array, say, except that the name field is used to govern the sorting.

```
void sort(Student list[], int n) {
   //sort list[0] to list[n-1] by name using an insertion sort
   Student temp;
   int k;
   for (int h = 1; h < n; h++) {
      Student temp = list[h];
      k = h - 1;
      while (k >= 0 && strcmp(temp.name, list[k].name) < 0) {
         list[k + 1] = list[k];
         k = k - 1;
      }
      list[k + 1] = temp;
   }
} //end sort
```

Observe this statement:

`list[k + 1] = list[k];`

This assigns *all* the fields of `list[k]` to `list[k+1]`.

If we want to sort the students in order by age, all we need to change is the `while` condition. To sort in *ascending* order, we write this:

`while (k >= 0 && temp.age < list[k].age) //move smaller numbers to the left`

To sort in *descending* order, we write this:

`while (k >= 0 && temp.age > list[k].age) //move bigger numbers to the left`

We could even separate the list into male and female students by sorting on the `gender` field. Since *F* comes before *M* in alphabetical order, we can put the females first by writing this:

`while (k >= 0 && temp.gender < list[k].gender) //move Fs to the left`

And we can put the males first by writing this:

`while (k >= 0 && temp.gender > list[k].gender ) //move Ms to the left`

1.6 Read, Search, and Sort a Structure

We illustrate the ideas discussed earlier by writing Program P1.1. The program performs the following:

- Reads data for students from a file, `input.txt`, and stores them in an array of structures
- Prints the data in the order stored in the array
- Tests `search` by reading several names and looking for them in the array
- Sorts the data in alphabetical order by `name`
- Prints the sorted data

The program also illustrates how the functions `getString` and `readChar` may be written. `getString` lets us read a string enclosed within *any* "delimiter" characters. For example, we could specify a string as `$John Smith$` or `"John Smith"`. This is a very flexible way of specifying a string. *Each* string can be specified with its own delimiters, which could be different for the next string. It is particularly useful for specifying strings that may include special characters such as the double quotes without having to use an escape sequence like \".

Program P1.1

```
#include <stdio.h>
#include <stdlib.h>
#include <string.h>
#include <ctype.h>
#define MaxStudents 100
#define MaxNameLength 30
#define MaxNameBuffer MaxNameLength+1
typedef struct {
   char name[MaxNameBuffer];
   int age;
   char gender;
} Student;

int main() {
    Student pupil[MaxStudents];
    char aName[MaxNameBuffer];
    void getString(FILE *, char[]);
    int getData(FILE *, Student[]);
    int search(char[], Student[], int);
    void sort(Student[], int);
    void printStudent(Student);
    void getString(FILE *, char[]);

    FILE * in = fopen("input.txt", "r");
    if (in == NULL) {
       printf("Error opening file: %s.\n", strerror(errno));
       exit(1);
    }

    int numStudents = getData(in, pupil);
    if (numStudents == 0) {
       printf("No data supplied for students");
       exit(1);
    }

    printf("\n");
    for (int h = 0; h < numStudents; h++) printStudent(pupil[h]);
    printf("\n");

    getString(in, aName);
    while (strcmp(aName, "END") != 0) {
       int ans = search(aName, pupil, numStudents);
       if (ans == -1) printf("%s not found\n", aName);
       else printf("%s found at location %d\n", aName, ans);
       getString(in, aName);
    }

    sort(pupil, numStudents);
    printf("\n");
    for (int h = 0; h < numStudents; h++) printStudent(pupil[h]);
} //end main
```

```
void printStudent(Student t) {
      printf("Name: %s Age: %d Gender: %c\n", t.name, t.age, t.gender);
} //end printStudent

int getData(FILE *in, Student list[]) {
   char temp[MaxNameBuffer];
   void getString(FILE *, char[]);
   char readChar(FILE *);

   int n = 0;
   getString(in, temp);
   while (n < MaxStudents && strcmp(temp, "END") != 0) {
      strcpy(list[n].name, temp);
      fscanf(in, "%d", &list[n].age);
      list[n].gender = readChar(in);
      n++;
      getString(in, temp);
   }
   return n;
} //end getData

int search(char key[], Student list[], int n) {
   //search for key in list[0] to list[n-1]
   //if found, return the location; if not found, return -1
   for (int h = 0; h < n; h++)
      if (strcmp(key, list[h].name) == 0) return h;
      return -1;
} //end search

void sort(Student list[], int n) {
   //sort list[0] to list[n-1] by name using an insertion sort
   Student temp;
   int k;
   for (int h = 1; h < n; h++) {
      temp = list[h];
      k = h - 1;
      while (k >= 0 && strcmp(temp.name, list[k].name) < 0) {
         list[k + 1] = list[k];
         k = k - 1;
      }
      list[k + 1] = temp;
   } //end for
} //end sort

void getString(FILE * in, char str[]) {
   //stores, in str, the next string within delimiters
   // the first non-whitespace character is the delimiter
   // the string is read from the file 'in'
   char ch, delim;
   int n = 0;
   str[0] = '\0';
   // read over white space
   while (isspace(ch = getc(in))) ; //empty while body
   if (ch == EOF) return;

   delim = ch;
   while (((ch = getc(in)) != delim) && (ch != EOF))
      str[n++] = ch;
   str[n] = '\0';
} // end getString
```

```
char readChar(FILE * in) {
    char ch;
    while (isspace(ch = getc(in))) ; //empty while body
    return ch;
} //end readChar
```

Suppose the file `input.txt` contains the following data:

```
"Jones, John" 24 M
"Mohammed, Lisa" 33 F
"Singh, Sandy" 29 F
"Layne, Dennis" 49 M
"Singh, Cindy" 16 F
"Ali, Imran" 39 M
"Kelly, Trudy" 30 F
"Cox, Kerry" 25 M
"END"
"Kelly, Trudy"
"Layne, Dennis"
"Layne, Cindy"
"END"
```

The program prints this:

```
Name: Jones, John Age: 24 Gender: M
Name: Mohammed, Lisa Age: 33 Gender: F
Name: Singh, Sandy Age: 29 Gender: F
Name: Layne, Dennis Age: 49 Gender: M
Name: Singh, Cindy Age: 16 Gender: F
Name: Ali, Imran Age: 39 Gender: M
Name: Kelly, Trudy Age: 30 Gender: F
Name: Cox, Kerry Age: 25 Gender: M

Kelly, Trudy found at location 6
Layne, Dennis found at location 3
Layne, Cindy not found

Name: Ali, Imran Age: 39 Gender: M
Name: Cox, Kerry Age: 25 Gender: M
Name: Jones, John Age: 24 Gender: M
Name: Kelly, Trudy Age: 30 Gender: F
Name: Layne, Dennis Age: 49 Gender: M
Name: Mohammed, Lisa Age: 33 Gender: F
Name: Singh, Cindy Age: 16 Gender: F
Name: Singh, Sandy Age: 29 Gender: F
```

1.7 Nested Structures

C allows us to use a structure as part of the definition of another structure—a structure within a structure, called a *nested* structure. Consider the Student structure. Suppose that, instead of age, we want to store the student's date of birth. This might be a better choice since a student's date of birth is fixed, whereas his age changes, and the field would have to be updated every year.

We could use the following declaration:

```
typedef struct {
    char name[31];
    Date dob;
    char gender;
} Student;
```

If `mary` is a variable of type `Student`, then `mary.dob` refers to her date of birth. But `mary.dob` is *itself* a `Date` structure. If necessary, we can refer to *its* fields with `mary.dob.day`, `mary.dob.month`, and `mary.dob.year`.

If we want to store a name in a more flexible way, for example, first name, middle initial, and last name, we could use a structure like this:

```
typedef struct {
    char first[21];
    char middle;
    char last[21];
} Name;
```

The `Student` structure now becomes the following, which contains two structures, `Name` and `Date`:

```
typedef struct {
    Name name;
    Date dob;
    char gender;
} Student;
```

If `st` is a variable of type `Student`,

`st.name` refers to a structure of the type `Name`,
`st.name.first` refers to the student's first name, and
`st.name.last[0]` refers to the first letter of her last name.

Now, if we want to sort the array `pupil` by last name, the `while` condition becomes this:

```
while (k >= 0 && strcmp(temp.name.last, pupil[k].name.last) < 0)
```

A structure may be nested as deeply as you want. The dot (.) operator associates from left to right. If a, b and c are structures, the construct

`a.b.c.d`

is interpreted as

`((a.b).c).d`

1.8 Work with Fractions

Consider the problem of working with fractions, where a fraction is represented by two integer values: one for the numerator and the other for the denominator. For example, $\frac{5}{9}$ is represented by the two numbers 5 and 9.

We will use the following structure to represent a fraction:

```
typedef struct {
    int num;
    int den;
} Fraction;
```

If f is variable of type Fraction, we can store $\frac{5}{9}$ in f with this:

```
f.num = 5;
f.den = 9;
```

This can be pictured as follows:

	num	den
f	5	9

We can also read two values representing a fraction and store them in f with a statement such as this:

```
scanf("%d %d", &f.num, &f.den);
```

We can write a function to print a fraction. For example, the following will print 5/9 when called with printFraction(f):

```
void printFraction(Fraction f) {
    printf("%d/%d", f.num, f.den);
} //end printFraction
```

1.8.1 Manipulate Fractions

We can write functions to perform various operations on fractions. For instance, since

$$\frac{a}{b} + \frac{c}{d} = \frac{ad + bc}{bd}$$

we can write a function to add two fractions as follows:

```
Fraction addFraction(Fraction a, Fraction b) {
    Fraction c;
    c.num = a.num * b.den + a.den * b.num;
    c.den = a.den * b.den;
    return c;
}
```

Similarly, we can write functions to subtract, multiply and divide fractions.

```
Fraction subFraction(Fraction a, Fraction b) {
    Fraction c;
    c.num = a.num * b.den - a.den * b.num;
    c.den = a.den * b.den;
    return c;
} //end subFraction
```

```
Fraction mulFraction(Fraction a, Fraction b) {
    Fraction c;
    c.num = a.num * b.num;
    c.den = a.den * b.den;
    return c;
} //end mulFraction

Fraction divFraction(Fraction a, Fraction b) {
    Fraction c;
    c.num = a.num * b.den;
    c.den = a.den * b.num;
    return c;
} //end divFraction
```

To illustrate their use, suppose we want to find

$$\frac{2}{5} \text{ of } \left\{ \frac{3}{7} + \frac{5}{8} \right\}$$

We can do this with the following statements:

```
Fraction a, b, c, sum, ans;
a.num = 2; a.den = 5;
b.num = 3; b.den = 7;
c.num = 5; c.den = 8;
sum = addFraction(b, c);
ans = mulFraction(a, sum);
printFraction(ans);
```

Strictly speaking, the variables sum and ans are not necessary, but we've used them to simplify the explanation. Since an argument to a function can be an expression, we could get the same result with this:

```
printFraction(mulFraction(a, addFraction(b, c)));
```

When run, this code will print the following, which is the correct answer:

```
118/280
```

However, if you want, you can write a function to reduce a fraction to its lowest terms. This can be done by finding the highest common factor (HCF) of the numerator and denominator. You then divide the numerator and denominator by their HCF. For example, the HCF of 118 and 280 is 2 so 118/280 reduces to 59/140. Writing this function is left as an exercise.

1.9 A Voting Problem

This example will be used to illustrate several points concerning the passing of arguments to functions. It further highlights the differences between array arguments and simple-variable arguments. We will show how a function can return more than one value to a calling function by using a structure.

Problem: In an election, there are seven candidates. Each voter is allowed one vote for the candidate of their choice. The vote is recorded as a number from 1 to 7. The number of voters is unknown beforehand, but the votes are terminated by a vote of 0. Any vote that is not a number from 1 to 7 is an invalid (spoiled) vote.

A file, votes.txt, contains the names of the candidates. The first name is considered as candidate 1, the second as candidate 2, and so on. The names are followed by the votes. Write a program to read the data and evaluate the results of the election. Print all output to the file, results.txt.

Your output should specify the total number of votes, the number of valid votes, and the number of spoiled votes. This is followed by the votes obtained by each candidate and the winner(s) of the election.

Suppose the file votes.text contains the following data:

```
Victor Taylor
Denise Duncan
Kamal Ramdhan
Michael Ali
Anisa Sawh
Carol Khan
Gary Olliverie

3 1 2 5 4 3 5 3 5 3 2 8 1 6 7 7 3 5
6 9 3 4 7 1 2 4 5 5 1 4 0
```

Your program should send the following output to results.txt:

```
Invalid vote: 8
Invalid vote: 9

Number of voters: 30
Number of valid votes: 28
Number of spoilt votes: 2

Candidate        Score

Victor Taylor      4
Denise Duncan      3
Kamal Ramdhan      6
Michael Ali        4
Anisa Sawh         6
Carol Khan         2
Gary Olliverie     3

The winner(s):
Kamal Ramdhan
Anisa Sawh
```

We now explain how we can solve this problem using C structures. Consider these declarations:

```c
typedef struct  {
   char name[31];
   int numVotes;
} PersonData;

PersonData candidate[8];
```

Here, candidate is an array of structures. We will use candidate[1] to candidate[7] for the seven candidates; we will not use candidate[0]. This will allow us to work more naturally with the votes. For a vote (v, say), candidate[v] will be updated. If we use candidate[0], we would have the awkward situation where for a vote v, candidate[v-1] would have to be updated.

An element candidate[h] is not just a single data item but a structure consisting of two fields. These fields can be referred to as follows:

candidate[h].name and candidate[h].numVotes

To make the program flexible, we will define the following symbolic constants:

```
#define MaxCandidates 7
#define MaxNameLength 30
#define MaxNameBuffer MaxNameLength+1
```

We also change the earlier declarations to the following:

```
typedef struct  {
    char name[MaxNameBuffer];
    int numVotes;
} PersonData;

PersonData candidate[MaxCandidates+1];
```

The solution is based on the following outline:

```
initialize
process the votes
print the results
```

The function initialize will read the names from the file in and set the vote counts to 0. The file is passed as an argument to the function. We will read a candidate's name in two parts (first name and last name) and then join them together to create a single name that we will store in person[h].name. Data will be read for max persons. Here is the function:

```
void initialize(PersonData person[], int max, FILE *in) {
    char lastName[MaxNameBuffer];
    for (int h = 1; h <= max; h++) {
        fscanf(in, "%s %s", person[h].name, lastName);
        strcat(person[h].name, " ");
        strcat(person[h].name, lastName);
        person[h].numVotes = 0;
    }
} //end initialize
```

Processing the votes will be based on the following outline:

```
get a vote
while the vote is not 0
    if the vote is valid
        add 1 to validVotes
        add 1 to the score of the appropriate candidate
    else
        print invalid vote
        add 1 to spoiltVotes
    endif
    get a vote
endwhile
```

After all the votes are processed, this function will need to return the number of valid and spoiled votes. But how can a function return more than one value? It can, if the values are stored in a structure and the structure returned as the "value" of the function.

We will use the following declaration:

```
typedef struct {
   int valid, spoilt;
} VoteCount;
```

And we will write processVotes as follows:

```
VoteCount processVotes(PersonData person[], int max, FILE *in, FILE *out) {
   VoteCount temp;
   temp.valid = temp.spoilt = 0;

   int v;
   fscanf(in, "%d", &v);
   while (v != 0) {
      if (v < 1 || v > max) {
         fprintf(out, "Invalid vote: %d\n", v);
         ++temp.spoilt;
      }
      else {
         ++person[v].numVotes;
         ++temp.valid;
      }
      fscanf(in, "%d", &v);
   } //end while
   return temp;
} //end processVotes
```

Next, we write main, preceded by the compiler directives and the structure declarations.

```
#include <stdio.h>
#include <string.h>
#define MaxCandidates 7
#define MaxNameLength 30
#define MaxNameBuffer MaxNameLength+1

typedef struct {
   char name[MaxNameBuffer];
   int numVotes;
} PersonData;
PersonData candidate[MaxCandidates];

typedef struct {
   int valid, spoilt;
} VoteCount;

int main() {
   void initialize(PersonData[], int, FILE *);
   VoteCount processVotes(PersonData[], int, FILE *, FILE *);
   void printResults(PersonData[], int, VoteCount, FILE *);

   PersonData candidate[MaxCandidates+1];
```

```
    VoteCount count;
    FILE *in = fopen("votes.txt", "r");
    FILE *out = fopen("results.txt", "w");

    initialize(candidate, MaxCandidates, in);
    count = processVotes(candidate, MaxCandidates, in, out);
    printResults(candidate, MaxCandidates, count, out);

    fclose(in);
    fclose(out);
} //end main
```

The declarations of `PersonData` and `VoteCount` come before `main`. This is done so that other functions can refer to them, without having to repeat the entire declarations. If they were declared in `main`, then the names `PersonData` and `VoteCount` would be known only in `main`, and other functions would have no access to them.

Now that we know how to read and process the votes, it remains only to determine the winner(s) and print the results. We will delegate this task to the function `printResults`.

Using the sample data, the array `candidate` will contain the values shown in Figure 1-1 after all the votes have been tallied (remember, we are not using `candidate[0]`).

	name	numVotes
1	Victor Taylor	4
2	Denise Duncan	3
3	Kamal Ramdhan	6
4	Michael Ali	4
5	Anisa Sawh	6
6	Carol Khan	2
7	Gary Owen	3

Figure 1-1. The array candidate after votes are processed

To find the winner, we must first find the largest value in the array. To do this, we will call a function `getLargest` with the following, which will set `win` to the *subscript* of the largest value in the `numVotes` field from `candidate[1]` to `candidate[7]` (since `MaxCandidates` is 7):

```
int win = getLargest(candidate, 1, MaxCandidates);
```

In our example, `win` will be set to 3 since the largest value, 6, is in position 3. (6 is also in position 5, but we just need the largest value, which we can get from either position.)

Here is `getLargest`:

```
int getLargest(PersonData person[], int lo, int hi) {
    //returns the index of the highest vote from person[lo] to person[hi]
    int big = lo;
    for (int h = lo+1; h <= hi; h++)
        if (person[h].numVotes > person[big].numVotes) big = h;
    return big;
} //end getLargest
```

Now that we know the largest value is in `candidate[win].numVotes`, we can "step through" the array, looking for those candidates with that value. This way, we will find all the candidates, if there is more than one, with the highest vote and declare them as winners.

An outline of `printResults` is as follows:

```
printResults
    print the number of voters, valid votes and spoilt votes
    print the score of each candidate
    determine and print the winner(s)
```

The details are given in the function `printResults`:

```
void printResults(PersonData person[], int max, VoteCount c, FILE *out) {
    int getLargest(PersonData[], int, int);
    fprintf(out, "\nNumber of voters: %d\n", c.valid + c.spoilt);
    fprintf(out, "Number of valid votes: %d\n", c.valid);
    fprintf(out, "Number of spoilt votes: %d\n", c.spoilt);
    fprintf(out, "\nCandidate        Score\n\n");

    for (int h = 1; h <= max; h++)
        fprintf(out, "%-15s %3d\n", person[h].name, person[h].numVotes);

    fprintf(out, "\nThe winner(s)\n");
    int win = getLargest(person, 1, max);
    int winningVote = person[win].numVotes;
    for (int h = 1; h <= max; h++)
        if (person[h].numVotes == winningVote) fprintf(out, "%s\n", person[h].name);
} //end printResults
```

Putting all the pieces together, we get Program P1.2, the program to solve the voting problem using structures.

Program P1.2

```
#include <stdio.h>
#include <string.h>
#define MaxCandidates 7
#define MaxNameLength 30
#define MaxNameBuffer MaxNameLength+1

typedef struct  {
   char name[MaxNameBuffer];
    int numVotes;
} PersonData;

PersonData candidate[MaxCandidates];

typedef struct {
   int valid, spoilt;
} VoteCount;

int main() {
   void initialize(PersonData[], int, FILE *);
   VoteCount processVotes(PersonData[], int, FILE *, FILE *);
   void printResults(PersonData[], int, VoteCount, FILE *);
```

```
      PersonData candidate[MaxCandidates+1];
      VoteCount count;
      FILE *in = fopen("votes.txt", "r");
      FILE *out = fopen("results.txt", "w");

      initialize(candidate, MaxCandidates, in);
      count = processVotes(candidate, MaxCandidates, in, out);
      printResults(candidate, MaxCandidates, count, out);

      fclose(in);
      fclose(out);
} //end main

void initialize(PersonData person[], int max, FILE *in) {
      char lastName[MaxNameBuffer];
      for (int h = 1; h <= max; h++) {
         fscanf(in, "%s %s", person[h].name, lastName);
         strcat(person[h].name, " ");
         strcat(person[h].name, lastName);
         person[h].numVotes = 0;
      }
} //end initialize

VoteCount processVotes(PersonData person[], int max, FILE *in, FILE *out) {
      VoteCount temp;
      temp.valid = temp.spoilt = 0;

      int v;
      fscanf(in, "%d", &v);
      while (v != 0) {
         if (v < 1 || v > max) {
            fprintf(out, "Invalid vote: %d\n", v);
            ++temp.spoilt;
         }
         else {
            ++person[v].numVotes;
            ++temp.valid;
         }
         fscanf(in, "%d", &v);
      } //end while
      return temp;
}   //end processVotes

int getLargest(PersonData person[], int lo, int hi) {
      //returns the index of the highest vote from person[lo] to person[hi]
      int big = lo;
      for (int h = lo+1; h <= hi; h++)
         if (person[h].numVotes > person[big].numVotes) big = h;
      return big;
} //end getLargest

void printResults(PersonData person[], int max, VoteCount c, FILE *out) {
      int getLargest(PersonData[], int, int);
      fprintf(out, "\nNumber of voters: %d\n", c.valid + c.spoilt);
      fprintf(out, "Number of valid votes: %d\n", c.valid);
      fprintf(out, "Number of spoilt votes: %d\n", c.spoilt);
      fprintf(out, "\nCandidate        Score\n\n");

      for (int h = 1; h <= max; h++)
         fprintf(out, "%-15s %3d\n", person[h].name, person[h].numVotes);
```

```
        fprintf(out, "\nThe winner(s)\n");
        int win = getLargest(person, 1, max);
        int winningVote = person[win].numVotes;
        for (int h = 1; h <= max; h++)
            if (person[h].numVotes == winningVote) fprintf(out, "%s\n", person[h].name);
} //end printResults
```

Suppose it were required to print the names of the candidates in *descending* order by numVotes. To do this, the structure array candidate must be sorted in descending order using the numVotes field to control the sorting. This could be done by the following function call:

```
sortByVote(candidate, 1, MaxCandidates);
```

sortByVote uses an insertion sort and is written using the formal parameter person (any name will do), as shown here:

```
void sortByVote(PersonData person[], int lo, int hi) {
    //sort person[lo..hi] in descending order by numVotes
    PersonData insertItem;
    for (int h = lo+1; h <= hi; h++) { // process person[lo+1] to person[hi]
        // insert person h in its proper position
        insertItem = person[h];
        int k = h -1;
        while (k >= lo && insertItem.numVotes > person[k].numVotes) {
            person[k+1] = person[k];
            --k;
        }
        person[k+1] = insertItem;
    }
} //end sortByVote
```

Observe that the structure of the function is pretty much the same as if we were sorting a simple integer array. The major difference is in the while condition where we must specify which field is used to determine the sorting order. (In this example, we also use >, rather than <, since we are sorting in descending order rather than ascending order.) When we are about to process person[h], we copy it to the temporary structure, insertItem. This frees person[h] so that person[h-1] may be shifted into position h, if necessary. To shift an array element to the right, we use the following simple assignment:

```
person[k+1] = person[k];
```

This moves the entire structure (two fields, in this example).

If we need to sort the candidates in alphabetical order, we could use the function sortByName:

```
void sortByName(PersonData person[], int lo, int hi) {
    //sort person[lo..hi] in alphabetical order by name
    PersonData insertItem;
    for (int h = lo + 1; h <= hi; h++) { // process person[lo+1] to person[hi]
        // insert person j in its proper position
        insertItem = person[h];
        int k = h -1;
```

```
        while (k > 0 && strcmp(insertItem.name, person[k].name) < 0) {
            person[k+1] = person[k];
            --k;
        }
        person[k+1] = insertItem;
    }
} //end sortByName
```

The function `sortByName` is identical to `sortByVote` except for the `while` condition. We now compare the `name` fields and use < for sorting in ascending order.

Note the use of the standard string function, `strcmp`, for comparing two names. If `strcmp(s1, s2)` is negative, it means that the string `s1` comes before the string `s2` in alphabetical order.

As an exercise, rewrite the program for solving the voting problem so that it prints the results in descending order by votes and in alphabetical order.

1.10 Pass Structures to Functions

In the voting problem, we saw examples where candidate, an array of structures, was passed to various functions. We now discuss some other issues that arise in passing a structure to a function.

Consider a structure for a "book type" with the following fields:

```
typedef struct {
    char author[31];
    char title[51];
    char binding;      //paperback, hardcover, spiral, etc.
    double price;
    int quantity;      //quantity in stock
} Book;
Book text;
```

This declares a new type called Book, and text is declared as a variable of type Book.

We could pass individual fields to functions in the usual way; for a simple variable, its value is passed, but, for an array variable, its address is passed. Thus:

```
fun1(text.quantity);   // value of text.quantity is passed
fun2(text.binding);    // value of text.binding is passed
fun3(text.price);      // value of text.price is passed
```

but,

```
fun4(text.title);      // address of array text.title is passed
```

We could even pass the first letter of the title, as follows:

```
fun5(text.title[0]);     // value of first letter of title is passed
```

To pass the entire structure, we use this:

```
fun6(text);
```

Of course, the header for each of these functions must be written with the appropriate parameter type.

In the last example, the fields of text are copied to a temporary place (called the *run-time heap*), and the copy is passed to fun6; that is, the structure is passed "by value". If a structure is complicated or contains arrays, the copying operation could be time-consuming. In addition, when the function returns, the values of the structure elements must be removed from the heap; this adds to the overhead—the extra processing required to perform a function call.

To avoid this overhead, the *address* of the structure could be passed. We could do this with the following statement:

```
fun6(&text);
```

However, further discussion requires a knowledge of pointers which will be covered in the next chapter.

EXERCISES 1

1. Write a program to read names and phone numbers into a structure array. Request a name and print the person's phone number. Use binary search to look up the name.

2. Write a function that, given two date structures, d1 and d2, returns -1 if d1 comes before d2, 0 if d1 is the same as d2, and 1 if d1 comes after d2.

3. Write a function that, given two date structures, d1 and d2, returns the number of days that d2 is ahead of d1. If d2 comes before d1, return a negative value.

4. A time in 24-hour clock format is represented by two numbers; for example, 16 45 means the time 16:45, that is, 4:45 p.m.

   (a) Using a structure to represent a time, write a function that, given two time structures, t1 and t2, returns the number of minutes from t1 to t2. For example, if the two given times are 16 45 and 23 25, your function should return 400.

   (b) Modify the function so that it works as follows: if t2 is less than t1, take it to mean a time for the next day. For example, given the times 20:30 and 6:15, take this to mean 8.30 p.m. to 6.15 a.m. of the next day. Your function should return 585.

5. A length, specified in meters and centimeters, is represented by two integers. For example, the length 3m 75cm is represented by 3 75. Using a structure to represent a length, write functions to compare, add, and subtract two lengths.

6. A file contains the names and distances jumped by athletes in a long-jump competition. Using a structure to hold a name and distance (which is itself a structure as in Exercise 5), write a program to read the data and print a list of names and distance jumped in order of merit (best jumper first).

7. A data file contains registration information for six courses—CS20A, CS21A, CS29A, CS30A, CS35A, and CS36A. Each line of data consists of a seven-digit student registration number followed by six (ordered) values, each of which is 0 or 1. A value of 1 indicates that the student is registered for the corresponding course; 0 means the student is not. Thus, 1 0 1 0 1 1

means that the student is registered for CS20A, CS29A, CS35A, and CS36A, but not for CS21A and CS30A.

You may assume that there are no more than 100 students and a registration number 0 ends the data.

Write a program to read the data and produce a class list for each course. Each list consists of the registration numbers of those students taking the course.

8. At a school's bazaar, activities were divided into stalls. At the close of the bazaar, the manager of each stall submitted information to the principal consisting of the name of the stall, the income earned, and its expenses. Here are some sample data:

```
Games 2300.00 1000.00
Sweets 900.00 1000.00
```

(a) Create a structure to hold a stall's data

(b) Write a program to read the data and print a report consisting of the stall name and net income (income - expenses), in order of decreasing net income (that is, with the most profitable stall first and the least profitable stall last). In addition, print the number of stalls, the total profit or loss of the bazaar, and the stall(s) that made the most profit. Assume that a line containing xxxxxx only ends the data.

CHAPTER 2

▨ ▨ ▨

Pointers

In this chapter, we will explain the following:

- What is a C pointer
- How to declare pointer variables
- How to dereference a pointer
- How a function can change the value of a variable in a "calling" function
- Some issues involved in passing an array as an argument to a function
- How to work with character pointers
- The meaning of pointer arithmetic
- How to use pointers to structures
- How to use pointers to functions to write general-purpose routines
- What are `void` pointers and how to use them

2.1 Define Pointers

In C, arguments to functions are passed "by value". Suppose the function `test` is called with the variable `num` as an argument.

`test(num);`

The value of `num` is copied to a temporary location, and this location is passed to `test`. In this scenario, `test` has no access whatsoever to the original argument `num` and, hence, cannot change it in any way.

Does this mean that a function can never change the value of a variable in another function? It can, but in order to do so, it must have access to the address of the variable—the location in memory where the variable is stored.

If a computer has 1 million bytes of memory, its memory locations range from 0 to 999,999. Among other things, memory locations are used for storing the values of variables. Suppose a variable `num` has the value 36 and this value is stored at memory location 5000. We say the storage address (or, simply, the *address*) of `num` is 5000.

The operator &, when applied to a variable, returns the address of the variable. For example, suppose num is stored at address 5000. Then the value of &num is 5000.

The term *pointer* is used to refer to an address in memory. A pointer variable is one that can hold the address of a memory location.

If ptr is a pointer variable, we can assign a value to it, as in

```
ptr = &num;
```

This statement stores the *address* of num (whatever it may be) in ptr. We say that ptr "points to" num.

But how do we declare ptr to be a pointer variable? First, we observe that, in C, a given pointer variable can "point to" values of one type only (but see section "2.8 Void Pointers"). The declaration of the pointer variable specifies the type.

For example, the following declaration is read as "int pointer iPtr" and declares iPtr to be a *pointer* variable, which can "point to" (hold the address of) int values only:

```
int *iPtr;
```

Of course, since iPtr can assume only one value at a time, it can point to only one integer at any given time. The declaration could also have been written as

```
int* iPtr;
```

or

```
int * iPtr;
```

Caution: If you want to declare three pointers to int, it might be tempting to use this:

```
int* a, b, c;   //wrong
```

However, this would be wrong. As written, only a is a pointer variable; b and c are just ints. This might be more obvious had it been written like this:

```
int *a, b, c;
```

The correct way to declare a, b, and c as pointers is

```
int *a, *b, *c;
```

Suppose the *address* of num is 5000 and the *value* of num is 17. This statement assigns the value 5000 to iPtr:

```
iPtr = &num;
```

Assuming iPtr is stored at location 800, this can be pictured as follows:

ptr	800		num	5000
	5000			17

We use *iPtr to refer to "the value pointed at by iPtr" (in effect, the value of num), and it can be used in any context that an integer can. (Getting the value pointed to is called *dereferencing* the pointer.) For example, the following assigns the value 24 (17 + 7) to m:

```
int m = *iPtr + 7;
```

It is sometimes helpful to think of * and & as cancelling out each other. For instance, if iPtr = &num, then the following holds:

```
*iPtr ≡ *(&num) ≡ num;
```

An interesting assignment is this:

```
num = *iPtr + 1;
```

This is exactly equivalent to

```
num = num + 1;
```

It could even be written like this:

```
 (*iPtr)++;
```

This says to increment whatever iPtr is pointing at. The brackets around *iPtr are necessary. Without the brackets, *iPtr++ would mean "take the value pointed to by iPtr and then increment the value of iPtr" (see section "2.5 Pointer Arithmetic" for what it means to increment a pointer).

To increment num by a value other than 1 (5, say), you could write this:

```
 (*iPtr) += 5;
```

In many respects, iPtr is just like any other variable, and we can change its value if necessary. For example, the following assigns the address of m to iPtr:

```
iPtr = &m;
```

The old value of iPtr is lost. Now iPtr points to the value of m rather than num.

2.2 Pass Pointers as Arguments

Consider the problem of getting a function to change the value of a variable in the "calling" function. Specifically, we will attempt to write a function to add 6 to its integer argument. A naive attempt might be Program P2.1. The comments are for reference only.

Program P2.1

```
#include <stdio.h>
int main() {
    void test(int);
    int n = 14;
    printf("%d\n", n);    //before calling test
    test(n);
    printf("%d\n", n);    //after return from test
} //end main

void test(int a) {
    a = a + 6;
    printf("%d\n", a);    // within test
} //end test
```

When run, this program will print the following:

```
14        (before calling test)
20        (within test)
14        (after return from test)
```

At the end, the value of n is still 14. Clearly, test was unable to change the value of n.

As written, there is no way for test to change the value of n (declared in main) since it has no access to n; it has access to a *copy* of n. The only way test can change the value of n is if the address of n is passed to test. This can be achieved by calling test with this:

```
test(&n);
```

But now, since the actual argument is a pointer, we must change the definition of the formal parameter in test so that it is also a pointer. Program P2.2 incorporates the changes.

Program P2.2

```
#include <stdio.h>
int main() {
    void test(int *);
    int n = 14;
    printf("%d\n", n);     // before calling test
    test(&n);
    printf("%d\n", n);     // after return from test
} //end main

void test(int *a) {
    *a = *a + 6;
    printf("%d\n", *a);  // within test
} //end test
```

The following function prototype indicates that the argument to test is an integer pointer:

```
void test(int *);
```

The formal parameter a is declared accordingly. The integer value "pointed at" by a is denoted by *a. When test is called with the following, the address of n (5000, say) is passed to it:

```
test(&n);
```

test, therefore, has access to whatever value is stored at this address and may change it if desired. In this case, it adds 6 to the value at location 5000, effectively adding 6 to the value of n.

When run, Program P2.2 will print the following:

```
14        (before calling test)
20        (within test)
20        (after return from test)
```

At the end, the value of n in main has been changed to 20 by the function test.

Perhaps we can now understand why it is necessary to put the ampersand (&) in front of variables when we use the standard input function scanf(...) to read data. The only way scanf(...) can put a value into an actual argument is if its address is passed to it.

For example, in the following statement, the address of n is passed to scanf:

```
scanf("%d", &n);
```

This enables scanf to store the value read in the location occupied by n.

For the cognoscenti: even with pointers, it is still true that, in C, arguments are passed by value and a function *cannot* change the value of an original argument passed to it. Suppose ptr = &n and consider the following call:

```
test(ptr);
```

The value of the argument, ptr, is determined. Suppose it is 5000. This value is copied to a temporary location, and this location is passed to test where it is known as a. Thus, the value of a is 5000.

When interpreted as an address, this is the address of the variable n, in main. Thus, the function has access to n and can change it, if desired. But note that test cannot change the value of the *original* argument ptr since only a copy of ptr was passed. However, as we have seen, it can change the value *pointed to* by ptr.

2.3 Pass an Array as an Argument

We have learned that when an array name is used as an actual argument, the address of its first element is passed to the function. Consider Program P2.3.

Program P2.3

```
#include <stdio.h>
int main() {
    void test(int val[], int max);
    int list[5];

    for (int h = 0; h < 5; h++) list[h] = h;
    test(list, 5);
    for (int h = 0; h < 5; h++) printf("%d ", list[h]);
    printf("\n");
} //end main

void test(int val[], int max) {
// add 25 to each of val[0] to val[max - 1]
    for (int h = 0; h < max; h++) val[h] += 25;
} //end test
```

When run, this program prints the following:

```
25 26 27 28 29
```

In main, the elements list[0] to list[4] are set to 0, 1, 2, 3, and 4, respectively.

When the following call is made, the address of list[0] is passed to test where it becomes known as val[0]:

```
test(list, 5);
```

The function adds 25 to each of val[0] to val[4]. But since val[0] to val[4] occupy the same storage as list[0] to list[4], the function effectively adds 25 to list[0], list[1], list[2], list[3], and list[4].

The following call

```
test(list, 5);
```

could be replaced by the following since, in both cases, the address of the first element of list is passed to the function:

```
test(&list[0], 5);
```

In other words, an array name *is* a pointer—the address of the first element of the array.

An interesting variation is the following call:

```
test(&list[2], 3);
```

Here, the address of element list[2] is passed to test. In the function, this address is matched with val[0]. The net effect is the following:

```
val[0]    matches with    list[2];
val[1]    matches with    list[3];
val[2]    matches with    list[4];
```

These elements are incremented by 25 so that the program prints this:

```
0   1   27   28   29
```

In case you are wondering, it would be invalid to attempt something like this:

```
test(&list[2], 5);
```

This implies that, starting at list[2], there are at least five elements in the array, and, in our case, there are only three. In the function, val[3] and val[4] would be associated with the locations in memory immediately following list[4]. The contents of these locations would be altered with unpredictable consequences.

2.4 Character Pointers

Suppose word is declared as an array of characters.

```
char word[20];
```

We have emphasized that the array name word is a synonym for the address of its first element, word[0]. Thus:

```
word ≡ &word[0]
```

In effect, word "points to" the first character of the array and is, in fact, a pointer—a *character* pointer, to be more precise. However, word is not a pointer variable but, rather, a pointer *constant*. We can't change its value, which is the address of word[0].

Whenever a string constant appears in a program, the characters without the quotes are stored somewhere in memory; \0 is added at the end, and the address of the first character is used in place of the string. For example, in the following

```
printf("Enter a number:");
```

what is actually passed to printf is a character pointer whose value is the address of the first character of the string "Enter a number", stored somewhere in memory and terminated by \0.

Consider this declaration:

```
char *errorMessage;
```

It is permitted to write this:

```
errorMessage = "Cannot divide by 0\n";
```

The effect is that the characters of the string (properly terminated by \0) are stored somewhere in memory (starting at address 800, say), and the address of the first character (800) is assigned to errorMessage. This can be used as in

```
printf("%s", errorMessage);
```

or, simply,

```
printf(errorMessage);
```

Note that errorMessage is a pointer *variable* whose value can be changed, if desired. For example, the following sets errorMessage to point to the new string:

```
errorMessage = "Negative argument to square root\n";
```

Of course, the string previously pointed at by errorMessage now becomes inaccessible. If we wanted to save the old value of errorMessage, we could have done something like this:

```
char *oldMessage = errorMessage;
```

It is important to observe that this assignment simply stores the (pointer) value of errorMessage in oldMessage. No characters are copied. For example, suppose the following was stored starting at address 500:

```
"Cannot divide by 0\n"
```

After the assignment above, the value of oldMessage is 500 and, hence, points to the string. There is nothing wrong or invalid in having several variables point to the same location. It is the same as, for instance, several integer variables having the same value.

2.5 Pointer Arithmetic

We saw earlier that a pointer variable could be assigned to another pointer variable. C also permits us to increment and decrement pointer variables, but these operations have special meanings when applied to pointers.

Consider the following:

```
char *verse = "The day is done";
```

The string "The day is done" is stored somewhere in memory, and verse is assigned the address of the first character, T. In addition:

```
verse + 1   is the address of 'h';
verse + 2   is the address of 'e';
verse + 3   is the address of ' ';
  etc.
```

If required, we could change the value of verse with constructions such as these:

```
verse++;
verse += h;
```

As an example, the following will print the characters of the string pointed at by verse, one per line:

```
while (*verse != '\0')
    printf("%c\n", *verse++);
```

*verse refers to the character currently pointed at by verse. After this character has been printed, verse is incremented to point to the next character.

The previous discussion relates to character pointers. But suppose ptr is a pointer to integers. What is the meaning of the following?

```
ptr + 1 or ptr + k
```

To illustrate the ideas involved, consider an integer array num declared as follows:

```
int num[5];
```

We know by now that the name num refers to the address of num[0]. What is new is the following:

```
num + 1   is the address of   num[1];
num + 2   is the address of   num[2];
num + 3   is the address of   num[3];
num + 4   is the address of   num[4];
```

This holds true regardless of how many storage locations are occupied by an integer. For example, suppose an integer occupies 4 bytes and the address of num[0] is 800.

The value of the array name num is 800, and the value of, say, num + 1 (pointer arithmetic) is the address of num[1], that is, 800 + 4 = 804. Similarly:

```
the value of num + 2   is 808;
the value of num + 3   is 812;
the value of num + 4   is 816;
```

In general, suppose a pointer, p, is declared to point at a type of value that occupies k bytes of storage. Incrementing p by 1 has the effect of adding k to the current value of p so that p now points to the *next* item of the type that p is declared to point at.

Thus, using pointer arithmetic, "adding 1" means getting the address of the next item (no matter how many bytes away), and "adding i" means getting the address of the ith item beyond the current one. Thus, p + i is the address of the ith element beyond the one pointed to by p.

Since, for example, num + 2 is the address of num[2], i.e., &num[2], it follows that *(num + 2) is equivalent to *(&num[2]), that is, num[2]. (Think of * and & as cancelling each other.)

The following prints the values in the array num, one per line:

```
for (int h = 0 ; h < 5; h++)
    printf("%d\n", *(num + h));
```

*(num + h) could be replaced by num[h], and the effect would be the same.

You might wonder, in this example, about the meaning of num + 5. Theoretically, this is the address of element num[5], but this element does not exist. However, it is not invalid to attempt to use num + 5.

But if, for instance, we attempt to print *(num + 5), we will print whatever happens to be stored in memory at the address designated by num + 5 or, worse, get a memory access or address error. In either case, the moral is that you must not attempt to refer to array elements you have not declared and, hence, for which storage has not been allocated.

We will illustrate the intimate relationship between arrays and pointers by writing two versions of a function, length, which finds the length of a string.

Suppose word is declared as follows:

```
char word[MaxLength];   // MaxLength is a symbolic constant
```

In order to find the length of a string stored in word, you can make the call

```
length(word);
```

length assumes that word consists of characters terminated by \0. The value returned is the number of characters excluding \0. Since what is passed to the function is the address of the first character (in other words, &word[0]), the function can be written with the formal parameter declared either as an array or as a pointer. Which version is used has no effect on how the function is called. First we write the array version.

```
int length(char string[]) {
    int n = 0;
    while (string[n] != '\0') n++;
    return n;
}
```

Now we write the pointer version.

```
int length(char *sPtr) {   // string pointer
    int n = 0;
    while (*sPtr != '\0') {
        n++;
        sPtr++;
    }
    return n;
}
```

We could even increment sPtr as part of the while test, giving this version:

```
int length(char *sPtr) {
    int n = 0;
    while (*sPtr != '\0') {
        n++;
        sPtr++;
    }
    return n;
}
```

Which version is better? It depends on your point of view. Whereas the array version is more readable, the pointer version is more efficient. In the array version, it is clear that at each step we are looking at the nth element of the string. This is not so obvious in the pointer version. However, evaluating string[n] requires evaluation of the subscript n, which is then converted into the address of element n. The pointer version deals with the address directly.

We have mentioned that an array name is a constant and, hence, its value can't be changed. There may appear to be a conflict in that the function, when passed the array name, increments it (sPtr++) to move on to the next character.

But remember that the formal parameter in the function definition *is* a variable. When the function is called with length(word), say, the value of word (the address of the first character) is copied to a temporary location, and this location is passed to the function, where it is known as sPtr. The effect is that sPtr is simply initialized to the value of word. Incrementing sPtr in the function has no effect on the value of word in the calling function.

2.6 Pointers to Structures

Just as it is possible to take the address of an int or double variable, so too can we take the address of a structure variable. In Chapter 1, we mentioned that when we make the call fun6(text), where text is a structure variable of type Book, the fields of text are copied to the run-time heap and the copy is passed to fun6. That is, the structure is passed "by value". If a structure is complicated or contains arrays, the copying operation could be time-consuming. In addition, when the function returns, the values of the structure elements must be removed from the heap, and this adds to the overhead—the extra processing required to perform a function call.

To avoid this overhead, the address of the structure could be passed, as follows:

fun7(&text);

Of course, in fun7, the corresponding formal parameter must be declared appropriately, such as

void fun7(Book *bp)

Now, only a single value (the address) has to be copied to (and later removed from) the heap. And given the address, the function has access to the original argument text and can change it, if desired.

It is also possible to pass the address of an individual field to a function. For array fields, this happens automatically, as follows:

fun4(text.title);// address of text.title is passed

For simple variables, the structure name (*not* the field name) must be preceded by &, as in

```
fun3(&text.price);// address of text.price is passed
```

For example, we could read values for `price` and `quantity` with this:

```
scanf("%lf %d", &text.price, &text.quantity); //"lf" since price is double
```

Using this declaration:

```
typedef struct {
    char name[31];
    int age;
    char gender;
} Student;
```

consider the following:

```
Student child, *sp;
```

This declares `child` to be a structure variable of type `Student`. It also declares `sp` to be a pointer to a structure of the type `Student`. In other words, the values that `sp` can assume are addresses of variables of type `Student`. For example, the following statement is valid and assigns the *address* of the structure variable `child` to `sp`:

```
sp = &child;
```

If the fields of `child` are stored starting at memory location 6000, then the value 6000 is assigned to `sp`.

As with pointers to other types, `*sp` refers to the structure that `sp` is pointing at. In this example, `*sp` is a synonym for `child`. We can refer to the fields of the structure that `sp` is pointing at by using the dot operator (`.`):

```
(*sp).name, (*sp).age and (*sp).gender
```

The brackets around `*sp` are required since `.` has higher precedence than `*`. Without them, `*sp.age`, for instance, would be interpreted as `*(sp.age)`. This implies that `sp.age` is a pointer; since it is not, it will produce an error.

Pointers to structures occur so frequently in C that a special alternative notation is provided. If `sp` is pointing to a structure of type `Student`, then we can use `->` (a minus sign followed by a greater-than sign) to specify a field:

```
sp -> name      refers to the 'name' field,
sp -> age       refers to the 'age' field, and
sp -> gender    refers to the 'gender' field,
```

We will see many examples of the use of pointers to structures in the next chapter.

The following summarizes common operations on structures:

- A field can be accessed using the 'structure member' (`.`) operator, as in `text.author`.
- A structure variable can be assigned the value of another structure variable of the same type.
- The address-of operator & can be applied to a structure name to give the address of the structure, e.g. `&text`. & can also be applied to an element of a structure. However, & must

precede the structure name, not the field name. For example, &text.price is valid but text.&price and &price are not.

- If p is a pointer to a structure, then *p refers to the structure. For example, if p contains the address of the structure text, then

```
(*p).title //brackets required; . has higher precedence than *
```

refers to the title field. However, the *structure pointer* (arrow) operator -> (a minus sign immediately followed by >) is more commonly used to refer to a field, as in

```
p -> title
```

2.7 Pointers to Functions

In the same way that an array name is the address of its first element, so too a function name is the address of the function. Put another way, a function name is a *pointer* to the function in much the same way that an array name is a pointer to the array. In C, a pointer to a function can be manipulated in much the same way as other pointers; in particular, it can be passed to functions. This is especially handy for writing general-purpose routines.

Consider the problem of producing two-column tables such as tables of squares, reciprocals, square roots, weight conversions, temperature conversions, and so on. In each table, the first column consists of an ascending sequence of integers, and the second has the associated values.

We could write separate functions for each type of table we wanted to produce. But we could also write *one* function (called makeTable, say) that produced the various tables. Which specific table is produced depends on which function is passed to makeTable.

How do we specify a function as a parameter? Consider the following function definition:

```
void makeTable(int first, int last, double (*fp) (int)) {
    for (int h = first; h <= last; h++)
        printf("%2d %0.3f\n", h, (*fp)(h));
}
```

The heading says that makeTable takes three arguments; the first two are integers and the third, fp, is a pointer to a function that takes an int argument and returns a double value. The brackets around *fp in the following are necessary:

```
double (*fp) (int)
```

If they are omitted,

```
double *fp (int)
```

would mean that fp is a function returning a pointer to a double, which is quite different from what is intended.

In the printf statement, the function call (*fp)(h) is interpreted as follows:

- fp is a pointer to a function; *fp *is* the function.

- h is the actual argument to the function call; the brackets around h are the usual brackets around a function's argument(s).
- The value returned by the call should be a double, which would match the %f specification.
- The brackets around *fp are necessary since () has higher precedence than *. Without them, *fp(h) would be equivalent to *(fp(h)), which is meaningless in this context.

But how do we use makeTable to produce a table of reciprocals, say? Suppose we want to produce the table from 1 to 10. We would like to use a statement such as

makeTable(1, 10, reciprocal);

to get the required table, where reciprocal is a function that takes an int value and returns a double value—the reciprocal of the integer. It could be written as follows:

```
double reciprocal(int x) {
    return 1.0 / x;
}
```

Note that in the call

makeTable(1, 10, reciprocal);

the function name reciprocal is a pointer to a function, so it matches the third parameter of makeTable:

Program P2.4 shows all the pieces put together in one complete program.

Program P2.4

```
#include <stdio.h>
int main() {
    void makeTable(int, int, double (*fp) (int));
    double reciprocal(int);
    makeTable(1, 10, reciprocal);
} //end main

void makeTable(int first, int last, double (*fp) (int)) {
    for (int h = first; h <= last; h++)
        printf("%2d    %0.3f\n", h, (*fp)(h));
} //end makeTable

double reciprocal(int x) {
    return 1.0 / x;
} //end reciprocal
```

When run, Program P2.4 produces the following output:

```
1    1.000
2    0.500
3    0.333
4    0.250
5    0.200
```

```
 6       0.167
 7       0.143
 8       0.125
 9       0.111
10       0.100
```

If we now wish to create a table of squares, all we need are:

the function prototype:

```
double square(int);
```

the function call:

```
makeTable(1, 10, square);
```

and the function definition:

```
double square(int x) {
    return x * x;
}
```

Note that since the function argument (the last one) to makeTable is declared as double, we must declare the return type of square as double. Of course, if we wish, we could change all the declarations to int, as in Program P2.5.

Program P2.5

```
#include <stdio.h>
int main() {
    void makeTable(int, int, int (*fp) (int));
    int square(int);
    makeTable(1, 10, square);
} //end main

void makeTable(int first, int last, int (*fp) (int)) {
    for (int h = first; h <= last; h++)
        printf("%2d     %3d\n", h, (*fp)(h));
} //end makeTable

int square(int x) {
    return x * x;
}
```

When run, Program P2.5 produces the following output:

```
1       1
2       4
3       9
4       16
5       25
6       36
7       49
8       64
9       81
10      100
```

As another example, consider the problem of evaluating the definite integral

$$\int_a^b f(x)dx$$

using the Trapezoidal Rule with n strips. The rule states that an approximation to the above integral is given by the following, where $h = (b - a)/n$:

$$h\{(f(a) + f(b))/2 + f(a + h) + f(a + 2h) + ...+ f(a + (n-1)h)\}$$

We want to write a general function integral, which, given a, b, n, and a function, f, returns the value of the integral. To evaluate the integrals of different functions, we would need only to pass the appropriate function to integral. Consider the following version of integral:

```
double integral(double a, double b, int n, double (*fp) (double)) {
    double h, sum;
    h = (b - a) / n;
    sum = ((*fp)(a) + (*fp)(b)) / 2.0;
    for (int i = 1; i < n ; i++)
        sum += (*fp)(a + i * h);
    return h * sum;
} //end integral
```

The declaration

double (*fp) (double)

says that fp is a pointer to a function that takes a double argument and returns a double value.

*fp denotes the function, and (*fp)(a) is a call to the function with argument a.

To show how integral can be used, suppose we want to find an approximation to the following integral using 20 strips:

$$\int_0^2 (x^2 + 5x + 3)dx$$

We would need to write a function such as quadratic, like this:

```
double quadratic(double x) {
    return x * x + 5.0 * x + 3.0;
} //end quadratic
```

and the call

```
integral(0, 2, 20, quadratic)
```

would return the value of the integral. Putting it all together, we get Program P2.6 which finds the value of the above integral.

Program P2.6

```
#include <stdio.h>
int main() {
    double integral(double, double, int, double (*fp)(double));
    double quadratic(double);

    double answer = integral(0, 2, 20, quadratic);
    printf("The value of the integral is %3.2f\n", answer);
} //end main

double integral(double a, double b, int n, double (*fp) (double)) {
    double h, sum;
    h = (b - a) / n;
    sum = ((*fp)(a) + (*fp)(b)) / 2.0;
    for (int i = 1; i < n ; i++)
        sum += (*fp)(a + i * h);
    return h * sum;
} //end integral

double quadratic(double x) {
    return x * x + 5.0 * x + 3.0;
} //end quadratic
```

When run, the program prints the following:

```
The value of the integral is 18.67
```

Interestingly, the correct value of the integral is indeed 18.67—not bad for an "approximation".

2.8 Void Pointers

As we have emphasized, a pointer variable in C can point to only one type of value. However, C allows the declaration and use of void (also called *generic*) pointers—pointers that may point to any type of object. For example, the following declares pv as a void pointer:

```
void *pv;
```

And the following declares getNode as a function that returns a void pointer:

```
void *getNode(int size);
```

Any valid address can be assigned to a void pointer. In particular, a pointer to int (or double or float, and so on) can be assigned to a void pointer variable. Given the declaration

```
double d, *dp;
```

you can write the following:

```
dp = &d; //assign the address of d to dp
pv = dp; //assign a double pointer to a void pointer variable
```

Even though pv and dp have the same pointer value after the previous assignment, it is invalid to think of *pv as a double. In other words, we should not attempt to dereference a void pointer. However, if we *know* that pv contains a double pointer, we can tell this to C using a *cast*, and dereference it, like this:

```
* (double *) pv
```

Void pointers are useful for writing general-purpose functions where you do not want to restrict a function to returning a specific type of pointer. Also, declaring a function parameter as a void pointer allows the actual argument to be any type of pointer.

For example, suppose we want to write a function to accept an address and print the value stored at that address. If we know that the address will be a double pointer, say, we can write the function like this:

```
void dprint(double *p) {
    printf("%0.3f\n", *p); //print to 3 decimal places
} //end dprint
```

But what if we want the function to work no matter what type of pointer is passed? We can try to specify the parameter as a void pointer, as follows, but be warned that this won't work:

```
void vprint(void *p) { //this won't work
    printf("%0.3f\n", *p); //error: invalid use of void expression
} //end vprint
```

Why won't this work? Remember that an address is just a positive integer (8000, say). When this number is sent to the function, vprint will not know what type of value is stored at that address, so it will not know how to interpret *p in printf (is it a float, a double or something else?). In dprint, above, it *knows* that *p is a double value.

So, in addition to the pointer, we need to tell the function what type of value is stored so the pointer can be dereferenced correctly. We can do this via another argument (t, say). To illustrate, we write the following function assuming t = 1 means an int pointer is passed and t = 2 means a double pointer is passed.

```
void print(void *p, int t){
    if (t == 1) printf("%d\n", *(int *) p);
    else if (t == 2) printf("%0.3f\n", *(double *) p);
    else printf("error: unknown type\n");
} //end print
```

To illustrate its use, we write Program P2.7. We can extend print to handle other types.

Program P2.7

```c
#include <stdio.h>
int main() {
    void print(void *, int);
    int n = 375;
    double d = 2.71865;
    print(&n, 1); //int pointer passed
    print(&d, 2); //double pointer passed
}

void print(void *p, int t){
    if (t == 1) printf("%d\n", *(int *) p);
    else if (t == 2) printf("%0.3f\n", *(double *) p);
    else printf("error: unknown type\n");
} //end print
```

When run, this program prints the following:

```
375
2.719
```

C permits a `void` pointer to be assigned to any other type of pointer, as follows:

```c
float *fp =  pv;
```

However, it is up to you to ensure that the assignment makes sense. For instance, if pv contains an `int` pointer, it makes no sense to assign it to a `float` pointer variable. On the other hand, if you *know* that pv contains a `float` pointer, then the assignment is meaningful.

Programming note: if you use a C++ compiler to compile your C programs, you will get an error if you try to assign a `void` pointer to another pointer type. You will need to cast the `void` pointer to the appropriate type before assigning, as in the following example:

```c
fp = (float *) pv;
```

Even though assigning a `void` pointer without casting is permitted in C, good programming practice dictates you should use a cast anyway.

EXERCISES 2

1. What is meant by 'an argument is passed by value'?

2. Which type of argument in C is not passed by value? How is it passed?

3. How is it possible for a function to change the value of an actual argument?

4. In `main`, there are two `int` variables, a and b. Write a function which, when called, interchanges the values of a and b so that the change is known in `main`.

5. In `main`, there are three `int` variables, a, b and c. Write a function which, when called, stores the sum of a and b in c so that c is changed in `main`.

6. Explain the differences between a character pointer and a character array.

7. The character pointer `msgPtr` is pointing to a string of characters. What happens when `msgPtr` is assigned to another character pointer `oldPtr`?

8. How is a pointer similar to an integer?

9. How does pointer arithmetic differ from ordinary integer arithmetic?

10. What is the difference between `num[i]` and `*(num + i)`?

11. If `ps` is a pointer to a structure which contains an `int` field `score`, what is the difference between `(*ps).score` and `ps -> score`?

12. What is a `void` pointer? How are `void` pointers useful?

13. An `int` pointer is assigned to a void pointer variable, `vp`. How can we print the value pointed to by `vp`?

14. It is permitted to assign a void pointer to another type of pointer variable. What should you be mindful of in making such an assignment?

15. Apart from `void` pointers, where else can you use the word `void` in C?

16. If a function f is continuous in the interval $[a, b]$ and $f(a)f(b) < 0$ then, since f changes sign, there must exist some c in $[a, b]$ for which $f(c) = 0$. Assume there is one such c. It can be found as follows:
    - bisect the interval $[a, b]$;
    - determine in which half f changes sign;

    This is repeated giving a sequence of intervals, each smaller than the last and each containing c. The procedure can be terminated when the interval is arbitrarily small or f is 0 at one of the endpoints.

    Write a function which, given f, a and b, returns an approximation to c. Test your function using the function $5x^2 + 3x - 14$ with a solution in the interval $[2, 3]$.

17. Write a function to calculate the value of the definite integral

    $$\int_a^b f(x)dx$$

    using Simpson's rule (below) with n strips; n must be even. An approximation to the integral is given by

    $$\frac{h}{3}\{ (f(a) + 4f(a + h) + 2f(a + 2h) + ...+ 2f(a + (n-2)h) + 4f(a+ (n-1)h) + f(b) \}$$

    where $h = (b - a)/n$.

    Test your function on some simple integrals. What happens if the number of strips is increased?

CHAPTER 3

■ ■ ■

Linked Lists

In this chapter, we will explain the following:

- The notion of a linked list
- How to write declarations for working with a linked list
- How to count the nodes in a linked list
- How to search for an item in a linked list
- How to find the last node in a linked list
- The difference between static storage and dynamic storage allocation
- How to allocate and free storage in C using `malloc`, `calloc`, `sizeof`, and `free`
- How to build a linked list by adding a new item at the end of the list
- How to insert a node into a linked list
- How to build a linked list by adding a new item at the head of the list
- How to delete items from a linked list
- How to build a linked list by adding a new item in such a way that the list is always sorted
- How to use linked lists to determine whether a phrase is a palindrome
- How to save a linked list
- The differences between using linked lists and arrays for storing a list of items
- How to represent a linked list using arrays
- How to merge two sorted linked lists
- The concept of a circular list and a doubly linked list

3.1 Define Linked List

When values are stored in a one-dimensional array ($x[0]$ to $x[n]$), say), they can be thought of as being organized as a "linear list." Consider each item in the array as a *node*. A linear list means that the nodes are arranged in a linear order such that:

```
x[0] is the first node
x[n] is the last node
if 0 < k <= n, then x[k] is preceded by x[k - 1]
if 0 <= k < n then x[k ] is followed by x[k + 1]
```

Thus, given a node, the "next" node is assumed to be in the next location, if any, in the array. The order of the nodes is the order in which they appear in the array, starting from the first. Consider the problem of inserting a new node between two existing nodes, $x[k]$ and $x[k+1]$.

This can be done only if $x[k+1]$ and the nodes after it are moved to make room for the new node. Similarly, the deletion of $x[k]$ involves the movement of the nodes $x[k+1]$, $x[k+2]$, and so on. Accessing any given node is easy; all we have to do is provide the appropriate index (subscript).

In many situations, we use an array for representing a linear list. But we can also represent such a list by using an organization in which each node in the list points *explicitly* to the next node. This new organization is referred to as a *linked list*.

In a (singly) linked list, each node contains a pointer that points to the next node in the list. We can think of each node as a cell with two components, like this:

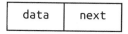

where `data` can actually be one or more fields (depending on what needs to be stored in a node), and `next` points to the next node of the list. (You can use any names you want instead of `data` and `next`.)

Since the `next` field of the last node does not point to anything, we must set it to a special value called the *null pointer*. In C, the null pointer value is denoted by the standard identifier `NULL`, defined in `<stdlib.h>` and `<stdio.h>`.

In addition to the cells of the list, we need a pointer variable (`top`, say) that points to the first item in the list. If the list is empty, the value of `top` is `NULL`.

Pictorially, we represent a linked list as follows:

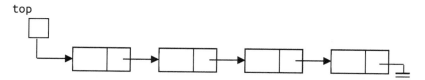

The electrical earth symbol is used to represent the null pointer:

Traversing a linked list is like going on a treasure hunt. You are told where the first item is. This is what `top` does. When you get to the first item, it directs you to where the second item is (this is the purpose of `next`). When you get to the second item, it tells you where the third item is (via `next`), and so on. When you get to the last item, its null pointer tells you that you are at the end of the hunt (the end of the list).

How can we represent a linked list in a C program? Since each node consists of at least two fields, we will need to use a `struct` to define the format of a node. The `data` component can consist of one or more fields (possibly including structures, perhaps nested). The type of these fields will depend on what kind of data needs to be stored.

But what is the type of the `next` field? We know it's a pointer, but a pointer to what? It's a pointer to a structure that is just like the one being defined! (This is usually called a *self-referencing structure*.) As an example, suppose the data at each node is an integer. We can define the node as follows (using `num` instead of `data`):

```
struct node {
    int num;
    struct node *next;
};
```

Or we can define it using `typedef`:

```
typedef struct node {
    int num;
    struct node *next;
} Node, *NodePtr; // we also declare a name for "struct node *"
```

The variable `top` can now be defined as a pointer to a `node`, like this:

```
Node *top;
or   NodePtr top;
```

As explained before, the `struct` declaration of `node`, as we have written it, does not allocate any storage for any variables. It simply specifies the form that such variables will take. However, the declaration of `top` does allocate storage, but only for a pointer to a `node`. The value of `top` can be the address of a node, but, so far, there are no nodes in the list. How can storage be allocated to nodes of the list? We will see how to do this in Section 3.3, but first we will look at some basic operations that may be performed on a linked list.

3.2 Basic Operations on a Linked List

For illustrative purposes, let's assume we have a linked list of integers. We ignore, for the moment, how the list might be built.

3.2.1 Count the Nodes in a Linked List

Perhaps the simplest operation is to count the number of nodes in a list. To illustrate, we write a function that, given a pointer to a linked list, returns the number of nodes in the list.

Before we write the function, let's see how we can traverse the items in the list, starting from the first one. Suppose `top` points to the head of the list. Consider the following code:

```
NodePtr curr = top;
while (curr != NULL) curr = curr -> next;
```

Initially, `curr` points to the first item, if any, in the list. If it is not `NULL`, the following statement is executed:

```
curr = curr -> next;
```

This sets `curr` to point to "whatever the current node is pointing to", in effect, the next node. For example, consider the following list:

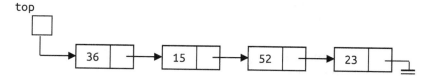

Initially, curr points to (the node containing) 36. Since curr is not NULL, it is set to point to whatever 36 is pointing to, that is, (the node containing) 15.

The while condition is tested again. Since curr is not NULL, curr = cur -> next is executed, setting curr to point to whatever 15 is pointing to, that is, 52.

The while condition is tested again. Since curr is not NULL, curr = cur -> next is executed, setting curr to point to whatever 52 is pointing to, that is, 23.

The while condition is tested again. Since curr is not NULL, curr = cur -> next is executed, setting curr to point to whatever 23 is pointing to, that is, NULL.

The while condition is tested again. Since curr is NULL, the while loop is no longer executed.

Note that each time curr is not NULL, we enter the while loop. But the number of times that curr is *not* NULL is the same as the number of items in the list. So, to count the number of items in the list, we just have to count how many times the while body is executed.

To do this, we use a counter initialized to 0 and increment it by 1 inside the while loop. We can now write the function as follows (we call it length):

```
int length(NodePtr top) {
    int n = 0;
    NodePtr curr = top;
    while (curr != NULL) {
        n++;
        curr = curr -> next;
    }
    return n;
} //end length
```

Note that if the list is empty, curr will be NULL the first time, and the while loop will not be executed. The function will return 0, the correct result.

Strictly speaking, the variable curr is not necessary. The function will work fine if we omit curr and replace curr by top in the function. At the end of the execution of the function, top will be NULL.

You may be worried that you have lost access to the list, but do not be. Remember that top in length is a *copy* of whatever variable (head, say) is pointing to the list in the calling function. Changing top has no effect whatsoever on head. When length returns, head is still pointing to the first item in the list.

3.2.2 Search a Linked List

Another common operation is to search a linked list for a given item. For example, given the following list, we may want to search for the number 52:

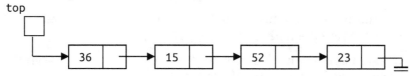

Our search should be able to tell us that 52 is in the list. On the other hand, if we searched for 25, our search should report that 25 is not in the list.

Suppose the number we are searching for is stored in the variable key. The search proceeds by comparing key with each number in the list, starting from the first one. If key matches with any item, we have found it. If we get to the end of the list and key does not match any item, we can conclude that key is not in the list.

We must write the logic so that the search ends if we find a match *or* we reach the end of the list. Put another way, the search continues if we have not reached the end of the list *and* we do not have a match. If curr points to some item in the list, we can express this logic as follows:

```
while (curr != NULL && key != curr -> num) curr = curr -> next;
```

C guarantees that the operands of && are evaluated from left to right and evaluation ceases as soon as the truth value of the expression is known, in this case, as soon as one operand evaluates to false or the entire expression has been evaluated. We take advantage of this by writing the condition curr != NULL first.

If curr *is* NULL, the && is false, and the second condition key != curr -> num is not evaluated.

If we wrote this:

```
while (key != curr -> num && curr != NULL) curr = curr -> next; //wrong
```

and curr happens to be NULL, our program will crash when it tries to retrieve

```
curr -> num
```

In effect, this asks for the number pointed to by curr, but if curr is NULL, it does not point to anything. We say we are trying to *dereference a NULL pointer*, and that is an error.

Let us write the search as a function that, given a pointer to the list and key, returns the node containing key if it is found. If it's not found, the function returns NULL.

We assume the node declaration from the previous section. Our function will return a value of type NodePtr. Here it is:

```
NodePtr search(NodePtr top, int key) {
    while (top != NULL && key != top -> num)
        top = top -> next;
    return top;
} //end search
```

If key is not in the list, top will become NULL, and NULL will be returned. If key is in the list, the while loop is exited when key = top -> num; at this stage, top is pointing to the node containing key, and *this* value of top is returned.

3.2.3 Find the Last Node in a Linked List

Sometimes we need to find the pointer to the last node in a list. Recall that the last node in the list is distinguished by its next pointer being NULL. Here is a function that returns a pointer to the last node in a given list. If the list is empty, the function returns NULL.

```
NodePtr getLast(NodePtr top) {
    if (top == NULL) return NULL;
    while (top -> next != NULL)
        top = top -> next;
    return top;
} //end getLast
```

If the list is empty, we return NULL. If not, we get to the while statement and top is not NULL. It therefore makes sense to ask about top -> next. If this is not NULL, the loop is entered, and top is set to this non-NULL value. This ensures that the while condition is defined the next time it is executed. When top -> next *is* NULL, top is pointing at the last node, and *this* value of top is returned.

3.3 malloc, calloc, sizeof, free

Consider the problem of reading positive integers (terminated by 0) and building a linked list that contains the numbers in the order in which they were read. For example, consider the following data:

36 15 52 23 0

Suppose we want to build the following linked list:

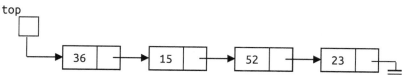

One question that arises is, how many nodes will there be in the list? This, of course, depends on how many numbers are supplied. One disadvantage of using an array for storing a linear list is that the size of the array must be specified beforehand. If, when the program is run, it finds that it needs to store more items than this size allows, it may have to be aborted.

With the linked list approach, whenever a new node must be added to the list, storage is allocated for the node, and the appropriate pointers are set. Thus, we allocate just the right amount of storage for the list—no more, no less.

We do use extra storage for the pointers, but this is more than compensated for by more efficient use of storage as well as easy insertions and deletions. Allocating storage "as needed" is usually referred to as *dynamic storage allocation*. (On the other hand, array storage is referred to as *static* storage.)

In C, storage can be allocated dynamically by using the standard functions `malloc` and `calloc`. In order to use these functions (and `free`, later), your program must be preceded by the following header line:

```
#include <stdlib.h>
```

This line is also needed to use NULL, the null pointer definition in C.

3.3.1 `malloc`

The prototype for `malloc` is as follows, where `size_t` is an implementation-defined unsigned integer type defined in the standard header `<stddef.h>`:

```
void *malloc(size_t size);
```

Typically, `size_t` is an `unsigned int` or `unsigned long int`. For all intents and purposes, we can think of `size` as a positive integer.

`malloc` allocates `size` bytes of memory and returns a pointer to the first byte. The storage is *not* initialized. If `malloc` is unable to find the requested amount of storage, it returns NULL.

When your program calls `malloc`, it is important to verify that the requested storage has been successfully allocated. To use the storage allocated, the pointer returned must be assigned to a pointer variable of the appropriate type. For example, assuming that `cp` is a character pointer, the following statement allocates 20 bytes of storage and stores the address of the first byte in `cp`:

```
cp = malloc(20);
```

To be safe, your program should check that `cp` is not NULL before continuing.

In general, a pointer to one type may not be *directly* assigned to a pointer of another type; however, assignment is possible if an explicit cast is used. For example, given these declarations:

```
int *ip;
double *dp;
```

the following assignment is invalid:

```
ip = dp;        // wrong
```

But it is valid to write this:

```
ip = (int *) dp;      // right
```

However, it is up to the programmer to ensure that this assignment is meaningful.

On the other hand, values of type void * may be assigned to pointers of other types without using a cast. In the previous example, no cast is required to assign the void * returned by `malloc` to the character pointer `cp`. However, even though assigning a void pointer without casting is permitted in C, good programming practice dictates that you should use a cast anyway. In the above example, it is better to use this:

```
char *cp = (char *) malloc(20);
```

3.3.2 calloc

The prototype for calloc is as follows:

```
void *calloc(size_t num, size_t size);
```

calloc allocates num * size bytes of memory and returns a pointer to the first byte. (Another way of looking at it is that calloc allocates enough memory for an array of num objects each of size size.) All bytes returned are initialized to 0. If calloc is unable to find the requested amount of storage, it returns NULL.

When your program calls calloc, it is important to verify that the requested storage has been successfully allocated. To use the storage allocated, the pointer returned must be assigned to a pointer variable of the appropriate type. As an example, assuming that cp is a character pointer, the following statement allocates $10 \times 20 = 200$ bytes of storage and stores the address of the first byte in cp:

```
char *cp = calloc(10, 20);
```

To be safe, the program should check that cp is not NULL before continuing. As mentioned, it is good programming practice to use an explicit cast, as in

```
char *cp = (char *) calloc(10, 20);
```

calloc is useful for allocating storage for arrays. For example, if we know that a double variable occupies 8 bytes and we want to allocate space for 25 elements, we could use this:

```
double *dp = (double *) calloc(25, 8);
```

When executed, dp will point to the first element of the array, dp + 1 will point to the second, and, in general, dp + i - 1 will point to the ith element.

If we do not know the size of a type, and even if we do, we should use sizeof (see the next section).

3.3.3 sizeof

sizeof is a standard unary operator that returns the number of bytes needed for storing its argument. For example, the following returns the number of bytes needed for storing an int variable:

```
sizeof (int)
```

The argument to sizeof is either a type or a variable. If it is a type (like int or float or double), it must be enclosed in parentheses. If it is a variable or a type defined using typedef, the parentheses are optional. For example, if root is a variable of type double, then both sizeof root and sizeof (root) are valid and return the number of bytes needed for storing root. Similarly, sizeof Book and sizeof (Book) are both valid and return the number of bytes needed for storing a Book structure (see Section 2.10).

sizeof is used mainly for writing portable code, where the code depends on the number of bytes needed for storing various data types. For example, an integer may occupy 2 bytes on one machine but 4 bytes on another. Using sizeof (int) (instead of 2 or 4) in your program ensures that the program will work on either machine.

sizeof is used quite often with the functions malloc and calloc. For example, the following statement allocates enough storage for storing a double variable and assigns the address of the first byte to dp:

```
double *dp = (double *) malloc(sizeof (double));
```

Here's another example:

```
float *fp = (float *) calloc(10, sizeof (float));
```

Storage is allocated for 10 floats, and the address of the first is stored in fp.

You can also use type names defined with typedef as the argument to sizeof. Using the declarations above, the following allocates enough storage for one Node structure and assigns the address of the first byte to np:

```
Node *np = malloc(sizeof (Node));
```

3.3.4 free

The function free is related to malloc and calloc. It is used to free storage acquired by calls to malloc and calloc. Here is its prototype:

```
void free(void *ptr);
```

It releases the storage pointed to by ptr. For example, to free the storage pointed to by np, above, you could use this:

```
free(np);
```

Observe that even though free expects a void pointer, it is not necessary to explicitly cast np (a Node pointer) into a void pointer. Of course, it is perfectly acceptable, but a bit cumbersome, to use this:

```
free((void *) np);
```

It is a *fatal error* to attempt any of the following:

- Free storage not obtained by a call to malloc or calloc.
- Use a pointer to memory that has been freed.
- Free pointers twice.

Note: Alert readers may wonder how C knows how much memory to free. Easy. For each block allocated (using malloc, say), C keeps track of its size, usually by storing the size adjacent to the block.

3.4 Build Linked List: Add Item at Tail

Consider again the problem of building a linked list of positive integers in the order in which they are given. Suppose the incoming numbers are as follows (0 terminates the data):

```
36 15 52 23 0
```

We want to build the following linked list:

top
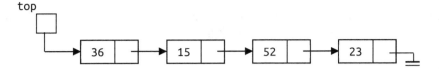

In our solution, we start with an empty list. Our program will reflect this with the statement

```
top = NULL;
```

The symbolic constant NULL, denoting the null pointer value, is defined in <stdio.h> and <stdlib.h>.

When we read a new number, we must do the following:

1. Allocate storage for a node.
2. Put the number in the new node.
3. Make the new node the last one in the list.

We assume the following declaration for defining a node:

```
typedef struct node {
    int num;
    struct node *next;
} Node, *NodePtr;
```

Let's write a function called makeNode that, given an integer argument, allocates storage for the node, stores the integer in it, and returns a pointer to the new node. It will also set the next field to NULL. Here is makeNode:

```
NodePtr makeNode(int n) {
    NodePtr np = (NodePtr) malloc(sizeof (Node));
    np -> num = n;
    np -> next = NULL;
    return np;
} //end makeNode
```

Consider the following call:

```
makeNode(36);
```

First, storage for a new node is allocated. Assuming an int occupies 4 bytes and a pointer occupies 4 bytes, the size of Node is 8 bytes. So, 8 bytes are allocated starting at address 4000, say. This is illustrated by the following:

4000

makeNode then stores 36 in the num field and NULL in the next field, giving us this:

4000
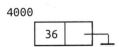

The value 4000 is then returned by makeNode.

When we read the first number, we must create a node for it and set top to point to the new node. In our example, when we read 36, we must create the following:

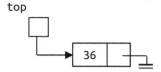

If n contains the new number, this can be accomplished with a statement such as this:

```
if (top == NULL) top = makeNode(n);
```

From the previous example, makeNode returns 4000, which is stored in top. Effectively, top now "points to" the node containing 36. There are no arrows inside the computer, but the effect is achieved with the following:

For each subsequent number, we must set the next field of the current last node to point to the new node. The new node becomes the last node. Suppose the new number is 15. We must create this:

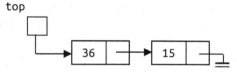

But how do we find the last node of the existing list? One method is to start at the top of the list and follow the next pointers until we encounter NULL. This is time-consuming if we have to do it for each new number and the list is long. A better approach is to keep a pointer (last, say) to the last node of the list. This pointer is updated as new nodes are added. The code for this could be written like this:

```
np = makeNode(n);//create a new node
if (top == NULL) top = np; //set top if first node
else last -> next = np;     //set last -> next for other nodes
last = np;  //update last to  new node
```

Suppose there is just one node in the list; this is also the last node. In our example, the value of last will be 4000. Suppose the node containing 15 is stored at location 2000. We have the following situation:

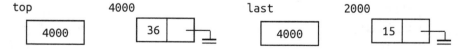

The code above will set the next field at location 4000 to 2000 and set last to 2000. The following is the result:

Now top (4000) points to the node containing 36; this node's next field is 2000 and, hence, points to the node containing 15. This node's next field is NULL, indicating the end of the list. The value of last is 2000, which is the address of the last node in the list.

Program P3.1 reads the numbers and creates the linked list as discussed. To verify that the list has been built correctly, we should print its contents. The function printList traverses the list from the first node to the last, printing the number at each node.

Program P3.1

```c
#include <stdio.h>
#include <stdlib.h>
typedef struct node {
    int num;
    struct node *next;
} Node, *NodePtr;

int main() {
    void printList(NodePtr);
    NodePtr makeNode(int);
    int n;
    NodePtr top, np, last;

    top = NULL;
    if (scanf("%d", &n) != 1) n = 0;
    while (n != 0) {
        np = makeNode(n); //create a new node containing n
        if (top == NULL) top = np; //set top if first node
        else last -> next = np; //set last -> next for other nodes
        last = np; //update last to new node
        if (scanf("%d", &n) != 1) n = 0;
    }
    printList(top);
} //end main

NodePtr makeNode(int n) {
    NodePtr np = (NodePtr) malloc(sizeof (Node));
    np -> num = n;
    np -> next = NULL;
    return np;
} //end makeNode

void printList(NodePtr np) {
    while (np != NULL) { // as long as there's a node
        printf("%d\n", np -> num);
        np = np -> next; // go on to the next node
    }
} //end printList
```

Point to note: The following statement deserves special mention:

```c
if (scanf("%d", &n) != 1) n = 0;
```

Normally, we would have written just this:

```
scanf("%d", &n);
```

But, here, we take advantage of the value returned by scanf to do some error checking.

When scanf is called, it stores data in the requested variable(s) and returns the number of values successfully stored. So, if we ask it to read one value, it should return 1 unless some error occurred (like end-of-file being reached or non-numeric data found when a number was expected). If we ask it to read two values and only one is assigned, it will return 1.

In this program, if a value was not successfully read into n, scanf will return 0. In this case, n is set to 0, forcing an exit from the while loop.

3.5 Insertion into a Linked List

A list with one pointer in each node is called a *one-way*, or *singly linked*, list. One important characteristic of such a list is that access to the nodes is via the "top of list" pointer and the pointer field in each node. (However, other explicit pointers may point to specific nodes in the list, for example, the pointer last, shown earlier, which pointed to the last node in the list.) This means that access is restricted to being sequential. The only way to get to node 4, say, is via nodes 1, 2, and 3. Since we can't access the *k*th node directly, we will not be able, for instance, to perform a binary search on a linked list. The great advantage of a linked list is that it allows for easy insertions and deletions anywhere in the list.

Suppose we want to insert a new node between the second and third nodes. We can view this simply as insertion after the second node. For example, suppose prev points to the second node and np points to the new node.

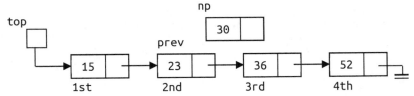

We can insert the new node by setting its next field to point to the third node and the next field of the second node to point to the new node. Note that the second node is all we need to do the insertion; *its* next field will give us the third node. The insertion can be done with this:

```
np -> next = prev -> next;
prev -> next = np;
```

The first statement says, "Let the new node point to whatever the second node is pointing at, in other words, the third node." The second statement says, "Let the second node point to the new node." The net effect is that the new node is inserted between the second and the third. The new node becomes the third node, and the original third node becomes the fourth node. This changes the above list into this:

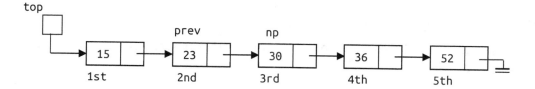

Does this code work if prev were pointing at the last node so that we are, in fact, inserting after the last node? Yes. If prev is the last node, then prev -> next is NULL. Therefore, the following statement sets np -> next to NULL so that the new node becomes the last node:

```
np -> next = prev -> next;
```

As before, prev -> next is set to point to the new node. This is illustrated by changing this:

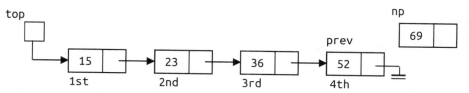

to this:

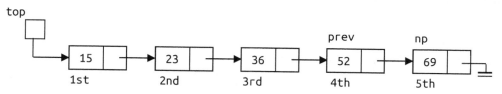

In many situations, it is required to insert a new node at the head of the list. That is, we want to make the new node the first node. Assuming that np points to the new node, we want to convert this:

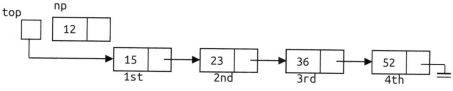

to this:

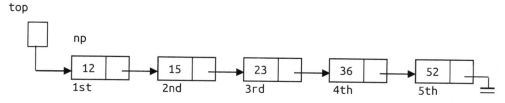

We can do that with the following:

```
np -> next = top;
top = np;
```

The first statement sets the new node to point to whatever top is pointing at (that is, the first node), and the second statement updates top to point to the new node.

You should observe that the code works even if the list is initially empty (that is, if top is NULL). In that case, it converts this:

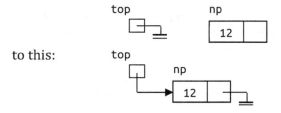

to this:

3.6 Build Linked List: Add Item at Head

Consider again the problem of building a linked list of positive integers but, this time, we insert each new number at the head of the list rather than at the end. The resulting list will have the numbers in reverse order to how they are given. Suppose the incoming numbers are as follows (0 terminates the data):

36 15 52 23 0

We want to build the following list:

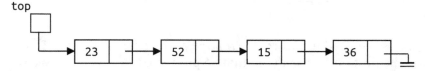

The program to build the list in reverse order is actually simpler than the previous one. We show it as Program P3.2.

The only changes are in the while loop. As each new number is read, we set its link to point to the first node, and we set top to point to the new node, making it the (new) first node.

Program P3.2

```
#include <stdio.h>
#include <stdlib.h>
typedef struct node {
    int num;
    struct node *next;
} Node, *NodePtr;

int main() {
    void printList(NodePtr);
    NodePtr makeNode(int);
    int n;
    NodePtr top, np;
    top = NULL;
    if (scanf("%d", &n) != 1) n = 0;
```

```
    while (n != 0) {
        np = makeNode(n);      //create a new node containing n
        np -> next = top;      //set link of new node to first node
        top = np;              //set top to point to new node
        if (scanf("%d", &n) != 1) n = 0;
    }
    printList(top);
} //end main

NodePtr makeNode(int n) {
    NodePtr np = (NodePtr) malloc(sizeof (Node));
    np -> num = n;
    np -> next = NULL;
    return np;
} //end makeNode

void printList(NodePtr np) {
    while (np != NULL) {                // as long as there's a node
        printf("%d\n", np -> num);
        np = np -> next;                // go on to the next node
    }
} //end printList
```

Program P3.1 inserts incoming numbers at the tail of the list. This is an example of adding an item to a queue. A *queue* is a linear list in which insertions occur at one end and deletions (see the next section) occur at the other end.

Program P3.2 inserts incoming numbers at the head of the list. This is an example of adding an item to a stack. A *stack* is a linear list in which insertions and deletions occur at the same end. In stack terminology, when we add an item, we say the item is *pushed* onto the stack. Deleting an item from a stack is referred to as *popping* the stack.

3.7 Deletion from a Linked List

Deleting a node from the top of a linked list is accomplished by doing this:

```
top = top -> next;
```

This says let top point to whatever the first node was pointing at (that is, the second node, if any). Since top is now pointing at the second node, effectively the first node has been deleted from the list. This statement changes the list from this:

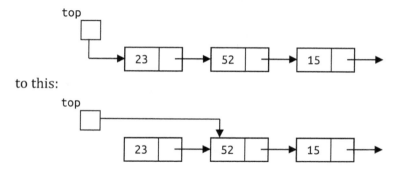

to this:

59

Of course, before we delete, we should check that there *is* something to delete, in other words, that top is not NULL.

If there is only one node in the list, deleting it will result in the empty list; top will become NULL.

Deleting an arbitrary node from a linked list requires more information. Suppose curr (for "current node") points to the node to be deleted. Deleting this node requires that we change the next field of the *previous* node. This means we must know the pointer to the previous node; suppose it is prev (for "previous node"). Then deletion of node curr can be done with this statement:

```
prev -> next = curr -> next;
```

This changes the list from this:

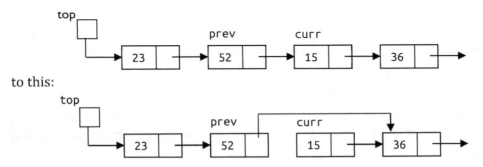

to this:

Effectively, the node pointed to by curr is no longer in the list—it has been deleted.

You may wonder what happens to nodes that have been deleted. In our discussion so far, *deletion* has meant "logical deletion". That is, as far as *processing* the list is concerned, the deleted nodes are not present. But the nodes are still in memory, occupying storage, even though we may have lost the pointers to them.

If we have a large list in which many deletions have occurred, then there will be a lot of "deleted" nodes scattered all over memory. These nodes occupy storage even though they will never, and cannot, be processed. We may need to delete them physically from memory.

As discussed in Section 3.3, C provides us with a function, free, to free the storage space occupied by nodes that we need to delete. The space to be freed should have been obtained by a call to malloc or calloc. The function call free(p) frees the space pointed to by p.

To illustrate its use, deleting the first node of the list can be accomplished by doing the following, where old is the same kind of pointer as top:

```
old = top; // save the pointer to the node to be deleted
top = top -> next; // set top to point to the 2nd node, if any
free(old); // free the space occupied by the first node
```

To delete a node from elsewhere in the list where curr points to the node to be deleted and prev points to the previous node, we can use this:

```
prev -> next = curr -> next; // logical deletion
free(curr); // free the space occupied by the deleted node
```

The free statement will change this:

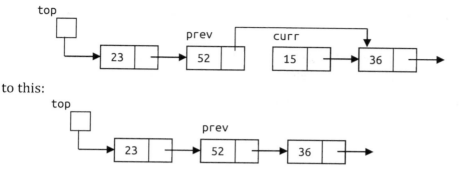

to this:

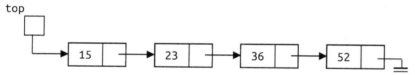

The storage occupied by curr no longer exists as far as our program is concerned.

3.8 Build a Sorted Linked List

As a third possibility, suppose we want to build the list of numbers so that it is always sorted in ascending order. Assume the incoming numbers are as follows (0 terminates the data):

36 15 52 23 0

We want to build the following list:

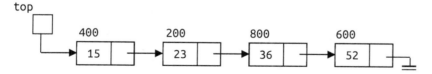

When a new number is read, it is inserted in the existing list (which is initially empty) in its proper place. The first number is simply added to the empty list, making a list with one item.

Each subsequent number is compared with the numbers in the existing list. As long as the new number is greater than a number in the list, we move down the list until the new number is smaller than, or equal to, an existing number or we come to the end of the list.

To facilitate the insertion of the new number, before we leave a node and move on to the next one, we must save the pointer to it in case the new number must be inserted after this node. However, we can know this only when we compare the new number with the number in the next node.

To illustrate these ideas, consider the following sorted list and suppose we want to add a new number (30, say) to the list so that it remains sorted:

Assume the number labelling a node is the address of the node. Thus, the value of top is 400 and the value of top -> next is 200.

First, we compare 30 with 15. It is bigger, so we move on to the next number, 23, remembering the address (400) of 15.

Next, we compare 30 with 23. It is bigger, so we move on to the next number, 36, remembering the address (200) of 23. We no longer need to remember the address (400) of 15.

Next, we compare 30 with 36. It is smaller, so we have found the number *before* which we must insert 30. This is the same as inserting 30 *after* 23. Since we have remembered the address of 23, we can now perform the insertion.

We will use the following code to process the new number, n:

```
prev = NULL;
curr = top;
while (curr != NULL && n > curr -> num) {
    prev = curr;
    curr = curr -> next;
}
```

Initially, prev is NULL and curr is 400. The insertion of 30 proceeds as follows:

- 30 is compared with curr -> num, 15. It is bigger, so we set prev to curr (400) and set curr to curr -> next, 200; curr is not NULL.
- 30 is compared with curr -> num, 23. It is bigger, so we set prev to curr (200) and set curr to curr -> next, 800; curr is not NULL.
- 30 is compared with curr -> num, 36. It is smaller, so we exit the while loop with prev being 200 and curr being 800.

We have the following situation:

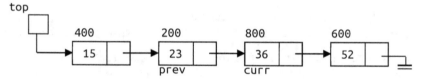

If the new number is stored in a node pointed to by np, we can now add it to the list (except at the head, see next), with the following code:

```
np -> next = curr;   //we could also use prev -> next instead of curr
prev -> next = np;
```

This will change this:

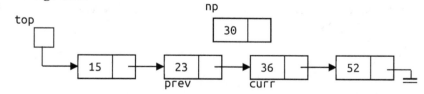

to this:

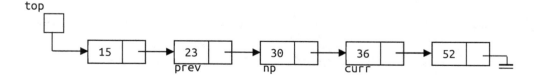

As an exercise, verify that this code will work if the number to be added is bigger than all the numbers in the list. Hint: when will the `while` loop exit?

If the number to be added is *smaller* than all the numbers in the list, it must be added at the head of the list and becomes the new first node in the list. This means the value of `top` has to be changed to the new node.

The `while` loop shown above, and reproduced here, will work in this case as well.

```
while (curr != NULL && n > curr -> num) {
    prev = curr;
    curr = curr -> next;
}
```

The `while` condition will be `false` on the very first test (since n is smaller than `curr -> num`). On exit, we simply test whether `prev` is still `NULL`; if it is, the new node must be inserted at the top of the list.

If the list were initially empty, the `while` loop will exit immediately (since `curr` will be `NULL`). In this case also, the new node must be inserted at the top of the list, becoming the only node in the list.

Program P3.3 contains all the details. The insertion of a new node in its proper position in the list is delegated to the function `addInPlace`. This function returns a pointer to the top of the modified list.

Program P3.3

```
#include <stdio.h>
#include <stdlib.h>

typedef struct node {
    int num;
    struct node *next;
} Node, *NodePtr;

int main() {
    void printList(NodePtr);
    NodePtr addInPlace(NodePtr, int);
    int n;
    NodePtr top = NULL;
    if (scanf("%d", &n) != 1) n = 0;
    while (n != 0) {
        top = addInPlace(top, n);
        if (scanf("%d", &n) != 1) n = 0;
    }
    printList(top);
} //end main

NodePtr addInPlace(NodePtr top, int n) {
// This functions inserts n in its ordered position in a (possibly empty)
// list pointed to by top, and returns a pointer to the new list
    NodePtr np, curr, prev, makeNode(int);

    np = makeNode(n);
    prev = NULL;
    curr = top;
```

```
    while (curr != NULL && n > curr -> num) {
        prev = curr;
        curr = curr -> next;
    }
    if (prev == NULL) { //new number must be added at the top
        np -> next = top;
        return np; //the top of the list has changed to the new node
    }
    np -> next = curr;
    prev -> next = np;
    return top; //the top of the list has not changed
} //end addInPlace

NodePtr makeNode(int n) {
    NodePtr np = (NodePtr) malloc(sizeof (Node));
    np -> num = n;
    np -> next = NULL;
    return np;
} // end makeNode

void printList(NodePtr np) {
    while (np != NULL) {   // as long as there's a node
        printf("%d\n", np -> num);
        np = np -> next;   // go on to the next node
    }
} //end printList
```

3.9 Example: Palindrome

Consider the problem of determining whether a given string is a *palindrome* (the same when spelled forward or backward). The following are examples of palindromes (ignoring case, punctuation, and spaces):

```
civic
Racecar
Madam, I'm Adam.
A man, a plan, a canal, Panama.
```

If all the letters were of the same case (upper or lower) and the string (word, say) contained no spaces or punctuation marks, we *could* solve the problem as follows:

```
compare the first and last letters
if they are different, the string is not a palindrome
if they are the same, compare the second and second to last letters
if they are different, the string is not a palindrome
if they are the same, compare the third and third to last letters
```

We continue until we find a non-matching pair (and it's not a palindrome) or there are no more pairs to compare (and it is a palindrome).

This method is efficient, but it requires us to be able to access any letter in the word directly. This is possible if the word is stored in an array and we use a subscript to access any letter. However, if the letters of the word are stored in a linked list, we cannot use this method since we can access the letters only sequentially.

To illustrate how linked lists may be manipulated, we will use linked lists to solve the problem using the following idea:

1. Store the original phrase in a linked list, one character per node.
2. Create another list containing the letters only of the phrase, all converted to lowercase and stored in reverse order; call this `list1`.
3. Reverse `list1` to get `list2`.
4. Compare `list1` with `list2`, letter by letter, until we get a mismatch (the phrase is not a palindrome) or we come to the end of the lists (the phrase is a palindrome).

Consider the phrase `Damn Mad!`; this will be stored as follows:

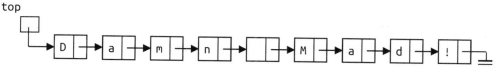

Step 2 will convert it to this:

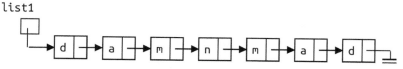

Step 3 will reverse this list to give `list2`:

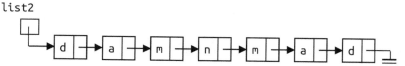

Comparing `list1` and `list2` will reveal that `Damn Mad!` is a palindrome.

We will write a program that prompts the user to type a phrase and tells her if it is a palindrome. It then prompts for another phrase. To stop, the user must press `Enter`.

We will write a function, `getPhrase`, that will read the data and store the characters of the phrase in a linked list, one character per node. The function will return a pointer to the list. This function must build the linked list in the order in which the characters are read—each new character is added at the end of the list.

We will write another function, `reverseLetters`, which, given a pointer to a list of characters, creates another list containing the letters only, all converted to lowercase and stored in reverse order. As each letter is encountered, it is converted to lowercase and added to the *front* of the new list.

To complete the job, we will write a function called `compare` that implements step 4 above. These functions are shown in Program P3.4, which solves the palindrome problem.

Program P3.4

```
#include <stdio.h>
#include <stdlib.h>
#include <ctype.h>
```

```
typedef struct node {
    char ch;
    struct node * next;
} Node, *NodePtr;

int main() {
    NodePtr getPhrase();
    NodePtr reverseLetters(NodePtr);
    int compare(NodePtr, NodePtr);
    NodePtr phrase, s1, s2;

    printf("Type a phrase. (To stop, press 'Enter' only): ");
    phrase = getPhrase();
    while (phrase != NULL) {
        s1 = reverseLetters(phrase);
        s2 = reverseLetters(s1);
        if (compare(s1, s2) == 0) printf("is a palindrome\n");
        else printf("is not a palindrome\n");
        printf("Type a word. (To stop, press 'Enter' only): ");
        phrase = getPhrase();
    }
} //end main

NodePtr getPhrase() {
    NodePtr top = NULL, last, np;
    char c = getchar();
    while (c != '\n') {
        np = (NodePtr) malloc(sizeof(Node));
        np -> ch = c;
        np -> next = NULL;
        if (top == NULL) top = np;
        else last -> next = np;
        last = np;
        c = getchar();
    }
    return top;
} //end getPhrase

NodePtr reverseLetters(NodePtr top) {
    NodePtr rev = NULL, np;
    char c;
    while (top != NULL) {
        c = top -> ch;
        if (isalpha(c)) { // add to new list
            np = (NodePtr) malloc(sizeof(Node));
            np -> ch = tolower(c);
            np -> next = rev;
            rev = np;
        }
        top = top -> next; //go to next character of phrase
    }
    return rev;
} //end reverseLetter

int compare(NodePtr s1, NodePtr s2) {
//return -1 if s1 < s2, +1 if s1 > s2 and 0 if s1 = s2
    while (s1 != NULL) {
        if (s1 -> ch < s2 -> ch) return -1;
        else if (s1 -> ch > s2 -> ch) return 1;
```

```
        s1 = s1 -> next;
        s2 = s2 -> next;
    }
    return 0;
} //end compare
```

Here is a sample run of the program:

```
Type a phrase. (To stop, press "Enter" only): Damn Mad!
is a palindrome
Type a phrase. (To stop, press "Enter" only): So Many Dynamos!
is a palindrome
Type a phrase. (To stop, press "Enter" only): Rise to vote, sir.
is a palindrome
Type a phrase. (To stop, press "Enter" only): Thermostat
is not a palindrome
Type a phrase. (To stop, press "Enter" only): A Toyota's a Toyota.
is a palindrome
Type a phrase. (To stop, press "Enter" only):
```

Note The solution presented was used mainly to show how linked lists can be manipulated. The problem can be solved more efficiently using arrays, where we would have direct access to any character of the given phrase. For instance, we would be able to compare the first and last letters directly. Even in the solution presented here, we could clean up the phrase as it is being input by retaining letters only and converting them to lowercase. As an exercise, write a program to solve the problem using arrays.

3.10 Save a Linked List

When we create a linked list, the actual "pointer" value in a node is determined at runtime depending on where in memory storage for the node is allocated. Each time the program is run, the pointer values will change. So, what do we do if, having created a linked list, we need to save it for later use?

Since it would be useless to save the pointer values, we must save the contents of the nodes in such a way that we would be able to re-create the list when needed. The simplest way to do this is to write the items to a file in the order that they appear in the linked list. Later, we can read the file and re-create the list as each item is read.

Sometimes we may want to compact a linked list into an array. One reason might be that the linked list is sorted and we want to search it quickly. Since we are restricted to a sequential search on a linked list, we can transfer the items to an array where we can use a binary search.

For example, suppose we have a linked list of at most 50 integers pointed to by top. If num and next are the fields of a node, we can store the integers in an array called saveLL with the following code:

```
int saveLL[50], n = 0;
while (top != NULL & n < 50) {
    saveLL[n++] = top -> num;
    top = top -> next;
}
```

On completion, the value of n will indicate how many numbers were saved. They will be stored in saveLL[0..n-1].

3.11 Arrays vs. Linked Lists

Arrays and linked lists are the two common ways to store a linear list, and each has its advantages and disadvantages.

The big difference between the two is that we have direct access to any element of an array by using a subscript, whereas to get to any element of a linked list, we have to traverse the list starting from the top.

If the list of items is unsorted, we must search the list using a sequential search whether the items are stored in an array or a linked list. If the list is sorted, it is possible to search the array using a binary search. Since binary search requires direct access to an element, we cannot perform a binary search on a linked list. The only way to search a linked list is sequential.

Inserting an item at the tail of a list stored in an array is easy (assuming there is room), but inserting an item at the head requires that all the other items be moved to make room for the new one. Inserting an item in the middle would require about half of the items to be moved to make room for the new one. Inserting an item anywhere in a linked list is easy since it requires setting/changing just a couple links.

Similarly, deleting an item from a linked list is easy regardless of where the item is located (head, tail, middle). Deleting an item from an array is easy only if it is the last one; deleting any other item would require other items to be moved to "close the space" previously occupied by the deleted item.

Maintaining an array in sorted order (when new items are added) is cumbersome since each new item has to be inserted "in place," and, as we've seen, this would normally require that other items be moved. However, finding the *location* in which to insert the item can be done quickly using a binary search.

Finding the *position* at which to insert a new item in a sorted linked list must be done using a sequential search. However, once the position is found, the item can be quickly inserted by setting/changing a couple links.

Table 3-1 summarizes the strengths and weaknesses of storing a list of items in an array versus storing them in a linked list.

Table 3-1. Array vs. Linked List for Storing List of Items

Array	Linked List
Direct access to any element	Must traverse list to get to element
If unsorted, sequential search	If unsorted, sequential search
If sorted, binary search	If sorted, sequential search
Easy-to-insert item at the tail of the list	Easy to insert item anywhere in the list
Must move items to insert anywhere but the tail	Easy to insert item anywhere in the list
Deletion (except the last one) requires items to be moved	Deletion of any item is easy
Need to move items when adding a new item to a sorted list	Adding a new item to a sorted linked list is easy
Can use binary search on a sorted list to find the position at which to insert new item	Must use sequential search to find the position at which to insert new item in a sorted linked list

3.12 Store a Linked List Using Arrays

We have seen how to create a linked list using dynamic storage allocation. When we need to add another node to a linked list, we request the storage for that node. If we need to delete a node from a linked list, we first delete it logically by changing pointers and then physically by freeing the storage occupied by the node.

It is also possible to represent a linked list using arrays. Consider, once again, the following linked list:

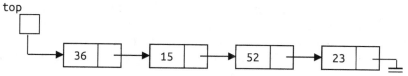

We can store this as follows:

```
              data  next
          0
top   5   1   15    7
          2
          3   23   -1
          4
          5   36    1
          6
          7   52    3
          8
          9
```

Here, the links (pointers) are merely array subscripts. Since an array subscript is just an integer, top is an int variable, and next is an int array. In this example, the data happens to be integers (so data is an int array), but it could be of any other type, even a structure. (Typically, you would use a struct array, with next being one of the fields and the other fields holding the data.)

The value of top is 5, so this says that the first item in the list is found at array index 5; data[5] holds the data (36, in this case), and next[5] (1, in this case) tells us where to find the next (second) item in the list.

So, the second item is found at array index 1; data[1] holds the data (15), and next[1] (7) tells us where to find the next (third) item in the list.

The third item is found at array index 7; data[7] holds the data (52), and next[7] (3) tells us where to find the next (fourth) item in the list.

The fourth item is found at array index 3; data[3] holds the data (23), and next[3] (-1) tells us where to find the next item in the list. Here, we use -1 as the null pointer, so we've come to the end of the list. Any value that cannot be confused with a valid array subscript can be used to denote the null pointer, but it is common to use -1.

All the operations described in this chapter for working with linked lists (for example, adding, deleting, and traversing) can be performed in a similar manner on linked lists stored using arrays. The main difference is that, previously, if curr points to the current node, curr -> next points to the next node. Now, if curr points to the current node, next[curr] points to the next node.

One disadvantage of using arrays to store a linked list is that you must have some idea of how big the list is expected to be in order to declare the arrays. Another is that storage for deleted items cannot be freed. However, the storage can be reused to store new items.

3.13 Merge Two Sorted Linked Lists

In this section, we show how to merge two sorted linked lists into one sorted list.

Suppose the given lists are as follows:

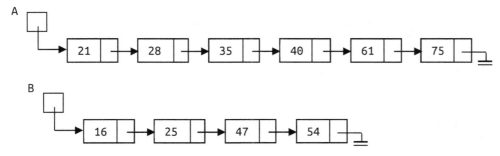

We want to create one linked list with all the numbers in ascending order, like this:

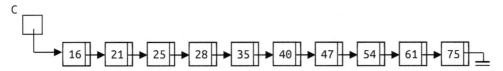

We *could* create the merged list by creating a new node for each number that we add to the list C. In other words, we leave the lists A and B untouched. However, we will perform the merge by *not* creating any new nodes. All numbers will remain in their original nodes. We will simply adjust pointers to create the merged list. At the end, the lists A and B will no longer exist.

We will use the following algorithm:

```
while (at least one number remains in A and B) {
    if (smallest in A < smallest in B)
        add smallest in A to C
        move on to next number in A
    else
        add smallest in B to C
        move on to next number in B
    endif
}
if (A has ended) add remaining numbers in B to C
else add remaining numbers in A to C
```

We assume that the nodes of the lists are defined using this declaration:

```
typedef struct node {
    int num;
    struct node *next;
} Node, *NodePtr;
```

And we assume A, B, and C are declared with

```
NodePtr A, B, C = NULL;
```

A and B point to the given lists, and C will point to the merged list. Initially, C is NULL. Each new number must be added at the tail of C. To make this easy to do, we will keep a pointer to the current last node in C (we call it last).

The algorithm above translates into the code shown here. To keep the presentation simple for now, this code assumes that both A and B are nonempty. We will deal with an empty A or B later.

71

```
NodePtr C = NULL, last == NULL;
while (A != NULL && B != NULL) {
    if (A -> num < B -> num) {
        //add node pointed to by A to the tail of C;
        A = A -> next ;
    }
    else {
        //add node pointed to by B to the tail of C;
        B = B -> next ;
    }
}
if (A == NULL) last -> next = B;
else last -> next = A;
```

Note the last if statement and how easy it is to "add the remaining elements" of a list to C. All we have to do is set the current last node of C to point to the non-empty list (A or B).

To complete the translation of the algorithm, we must show how to add a node (pointed to by N, say) to the tail of C. If C is empty, N becomes the only node in the list. If C is not empty, the current last node of C is set to point to N. In either case, N becomes the current last node of C. Thus, the following:

```
//add node pointed to by A to the tail of C;
```

is translated into this:

```
if (C == NULL) C = A; else last -> next = A;
last = A;
```

The case for adding the node pointed to by B is handled by replacing A with B.

In Program P3.5, we write a function called merge that, given the sorted lists A and B, performs the merge and returns a pointer to the merged list. This function also deals with the case when either A or B is empty. We test merge by using the code from Program P3.1 to create two sorted lists, merge them, and print the merged list.

Recall that Program P3.1 builds a list in the order in which the numbers are supplied. Thus, you must enter the numbers for a list in ascending order. As an exercise, you can use code from Program P3.3 to build the lists in ascending order regardless of the order in which the numbers are supplied.

A sample run of Program P3.5 is shown here:

```
Enter sorted numbers for the first list (0 to end)
2 4 6 8 10 12 0
Enter sorted numbers for the second list (0 to end)
1 3 5 7 0

The merged list is
1 2 3 4 5 6 7 8 10 12
```

Program P3.5

```
#include <stdio.h>
#include <stdlib.h>
```

```
typedef struct node {
    int num;
    struct node *next;
} Node, *NodePtr;

int main() {
    void printList(NodePtr);
    NodePtr makeList(void);
    NodePtr merge(NodePtr, NodePtr);
    NodePtr A, B;

    printf("Enter sorted numbers for the first list (0 to end)\n");
    A = makeList();
    printf("Enter sorted numbers for the second list (0 to end)\n");
    B = makeList();
    printf("\nThe merged list is\n");
    printList(merge(A, B));
} //end main

NodePtr makeList() {
    NodePtr makeNode(int), np, top, last;
    int n;
    top = NULL;
    if (scanf("%d", &n) != 1) n = 0;
    while (n != 0) {
        np = makeNode(n);    //create a new node containing n
        if (top == NULL) top = np;   //set top if first node
        else last -> next = np;   //set last -> next for other nodes
        last = np;    //update last to  new node
        if (scanf("%d", &n) != 1) n = 0;
    }
    return top;
} //end makeList

NodePtr makeNode(int n) {
    NodePtr np = (NodePtr) malloc(sizeof (Node));
    np -> num = n;
    np -> next = NULL;
    return np;
} //end makeNode

void printList(NodePtr np) {
    while (np != NULL) {   // as long as there's a node
        printf("%d ", np -> num);
        np = np -> next;  // go on to the next node
    }
    printf("\n\n");
} //end printList

NodePtr merge(NodePtr A, NodePtr B) {
    NodePtr C = NULL, last = NULL;
    // check if either A or B is empty
    if (A == NULL) return B;
    if (B == NULL) return A;
    //both lists are non-empty
    while (A != NULL && B != NULL) {
        if (A -> num < B -> num) {
            if (C == NULL) C = A; else last -> next = A;
            last = A;
            A = A -> next;
        }
```

```
        else {
            if (C == NULL) C = B; else last -> next = B;
            last = B;
            B = B -> next;
        }
    } //end while
    if (A == NULL) last -> next = B;
    else last -> next = A;
    return C;
} //end merge
```

3.14 Circular and Two-Way Linked Lists

So far, our discussion has been primarily about one-way (singly linked) lists. Each node contains one pointer that tells us the location of the next item. The last node has a null pointer, indicating the end of the list. While this is the most commonly used type of list, two common variations are the *circular* list and the *two-way* (or doubly linked) list.

3.14.1 Circular Lists

In a circular list, we let the last item point back to the first, as follows:

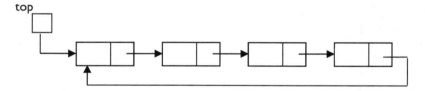

Now, there is no null pointer to tell us when we have reached the end of the list, so we must be careful in traversing that we do not end up in an infinite loop. In other words, say we were to write something like this:

```
NodePtr curr = top;
while (curr != NULL) {
    //do something with node pointed to by curr
    curr = curr -> next;
}
```

This loop will *never* terminate since curr never becomes NULL. To avoid this problem, we can save the pointer of our starting node and recognize when we have returned to this node. Here's an example:

```
NodePtr curr = top;
do {
    //do something with node pointed to by curr
    curr = curr -> next;
} while (curr != top);
```

Alert readers will observe that since the body of a do...while loop is executed at least once, we should ensure that the list is not empty before going into the loop and trying to dereference a null pointer.

Circular lists are useful for representing situations that are, well, circular. For example, in a card or board game in which players take turns, we can represent the order of play using a circular list. If there are four players, they will play in the order 1, 2, 3, 4, 1, 2, 3, 4, 1, 2, and so on. After the last person plays, it's the turn of the first.

In the children's game *count-out*, the children are arranged in a circle and some variation of "eenie, meenie, mynie, mo; sorry, child, you've got to go" is used to eliminate one child at a time. The last remaining child wins the game.

We will write a program that uses a circular list to find the winner of the game described next.

The count-out game: *n children (numbered 1 to n) are arranged in a circle. A sentence consisting of m words is used to eliminate one child at a time until one child is left. Starting at child 1, the children are counted from 1 to m and the mth child is eliminated. Starting with the child after the one just eliminated, the children are again counted from 1 to m and the mth child eliminated. This is repeated until one child is left. Counting is done circularly, and eliminated children are not counted. Write a program to read values for n and m (> 0), play the game as described, and print the number of the last remaining child.*

It is possible to use an array (child, say) to solve this problem. To declare the array, we would need to know the maximum number (max, say) of children to cater for. We could set child[1] to child[n] to 1 to indicate that all *n* children are initially in the game. When a child (h, say) is eliminated, we would set child[h] to 0 and start counting out from the next child still in the game.

As the game progresses, several entries in child will be set to 0, and when we count, we must ensure that 0s are not counted. In other words, even when a child has been eliminated, we must still inspect the array item and skip it if 0. As more children are eliminated, we will need to inspect and skip more zero entries. This is the main disadvantage of using an array to solve this problem.

We can write a more efficient solution using a circular linked list. First, we create the list with n nodes. The value at each node is the child's number. For *n* = 4, the list will look like the following, assuming curr points to the first child:

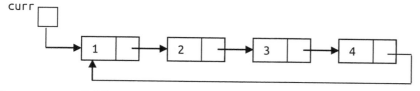

Suppose *m* = 5. We start counting from 1; when we reach 4, the count of 5 takes us back to child 1, which is eliminated. The list will look like this:

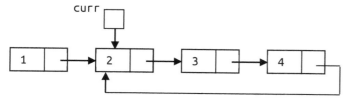

As shown, child 1 is no longer in the list; the storage for this node would be freed. We count to 5 again, starting from child 2. The count ends at child 3, which is eliminated by setting child 2's pointer to point to child 4. The list will look like this:

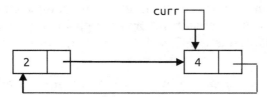

Finally, we count to 5 starting at child 4. The count ends at child 4, which is eliminated. Child 2 is the winner.

Note that this solution (as opposed to the array version) really does eliminate a child from the game by deleting its node. Eliminated children are neither inspected nor counted since they are gone! This is more in keeping with the way the game is played.

Program P3.6 plays the game and finds the winner as described.

Program P3.6

```c
#include <stdio.h>
#include <stdlib.h>

typedef struct node {
    int num;
    struct node *next;
} Node, *NodePtr;

int main() {
    NodePtr curr, linkCircular(int), playGame(NodePtr, int, int);
    int n, m;

    do {
        printf("Enter number of children and length of count-out: ");
        scanf("%d %d", &n, &m);
    } while (n < 1 || m < 1);

    curr = linkCircular(n); //link children in a circular list
    curr = playGame(curr, n-1, m); //eliminate n-1 children
    printf("The winning child: %d\n", curr -> num);
} //end main

NodePtr makeNode(int n) {
    NodePtr np = (NodePtr) malloc(sizeof (Node));
    np -> num = n;
    np -> next = NULL;
    return np;
} //end makeNode

NodePtr linkCircular(int n) {
    //link n children in a circular list; return pointer to first child
    NodePtr first, np, makeNode(int);

    first = np = makeNode(1);   //first child
    for (int h = 2; h <= n; h++) { //link the others
        np -> next = makeNode(h);
        np = np -> next;
    }
    np -> next = first; //set last child to point to first
    return first;
} //end linkCircular
```

```
NodePtr playGame(NodePtr first, int x, int m) {
    NodePtr prev, curr = first;
    //eliminate x children
    for (int h = 1; h <= x; h++) {
        //curr is pointing at the first child to be counted;
        //count m-1 more to get to the mth child
        for (int c = 1; c < m; c++) {
            prev = curr;
            curr = curr -> next;
        }
        //delete the mth child
        prev -> next = curr -> next;
        free(curr);
        curr = prev -> next; //set curr = child after the one eliminated
    }
    return curr;
} //end playGame
```

The following is a sample run:

```
Enter number of children and length of count-out: 4 5
The winning child: 2
```

As a final note to this problem, probably the best solution is obtained by using arrays (as in Section 3.12) or a struct array to link the children in a circle. This is left as an interesting exercise for the reader.

3.14.2 Two-Way (Doubly Linked) Lists

As the name implies, each node will contain two pointers—one points to the next node, and the other points to the previous node. While this requires more work to implement and maintain, there are some advantages.

The obvious one is that it is now possible to traverse the list in both directions, starting from either end. If required, reversing the list is now a simple operation.

If we land at a node (the current node) in a singly linked list, there is no way to get to (or know) the previous node unless that information was kept as the list was traversed. With a doubly linked list, we have a direct pointer to the previous node so we can move in either direction.

One possible disadvantage is that more storage is required for the extra link. Another is that adding and deleting nodes is more complicated since more pointers have to be set.

EXERCISES 3

1. Write a function that, given a pointer to a linked list of integers, returns 1 if the list is sorted in ascending order and returns 0 otherwise.

2. Write code to reverse the nodes of a linked list by manipulating pointer fields only. No new nodes must be created.

3. Write a function to sort a linked list of integers as follows:

   (a) Find the largest value in the list.

   (b) Delete it from its position and insert it at the head of the list.

   (c) Starting from what is now the second element, repeat (a) and (b).

   (d) Starting from what is now the third element, repeat (a) and (b).

   Continue until the list is sorted.

4. Write a function to free all the nodes of a given linked list.

5. Write a function that takes three arguments—a pointer to a linked list of integers and two integers, n and i—and inserts n after the ith element of the list. If i is 0, n is inserted at the head of the list. If i is greater than the number of elements in the list, n is inserted after the last one.

6. The characters of a string are held on a linked list, one character per node.

   (a) Write a function that, given a pointer to a string and two characters, c1 and c2, replaces all occurrences of c1 with c2.

   (b) Write a function that, given a pointer to a string and a character, c, deletes all occurrences of c from the string. Return a pointer to the modified string.

   (c) Write a function that, given a pointer to a string, converts all lowercase letters to uppercase, leaving all the other characters unchanged.

   (d) Write a function that creates a new list consisting of the letters only in the given list, all converted to lowercase and stored in alphabetical order. Return a pointer to the new list.

   (e) Write a function that, given pointers to two strings, determines whether the first is a substring of the other.

7. Write a function that, given an integer n, converts n to binary and stores each bit in one node of a linked list with the *least* significant bit at the head of the list and the *most* significant bit at the tail. For example, given 13, the bits are stored in the order 1 0 1 1, from head to tail. Return a pointer to the head of the list.

8, Write a function that, given a pointer to a linked list of bits stored as in 7, *traverses the list once* and returns the decimal equivalent of the binary number.

9. You are given two pointers, b1 and b2, each pointing to a binary number stored as in 7. You must return a pointer to a newly created linked list representing the binary sum of the given numbers with the *least* significant bit at the head of the list and the *most* significant bit at the tail of the list. Write functions to do this in two ways:

   (i) Using the functions from 7 and 8

   (ii) Performing a "bit-by-bit" addition

10. Repeat exercises 7, 8, and 9, but this time, store the bits with the *most* significant bit at the head of the list and the *least* significant bit at the tail.

11. Two words are anagrams if one word can be formed by rearranging all the letters of the other word, for example *treason*, *senator*. A word is represented as a linked list with one letter per node of the list.

    Write a function that, given w1 and w2 each pointing to a word of lowercase letters, returns 1 if the words are anagrams and 0 if they are not. Base your algorithm on the following: for each letter in w1, search w2 for it; if found, delete it and continue. Otherwise, return 0.

12. The digits of an integer are held on a linked list in reverse order, one digit per node. For example, the number 345 is stored in the list as 5 4 3.Write a function that, given pointers to two such integers, performs a digit-by-digit addition and returns a pointer to the digits of the sum stored in reverse order. Note: This idea can be used to add arbitrarily large integers.

13. Write a program to read an integer, n, and determine whether it's binary equivalent is a palindrome. For example, 51 = 110011 is a palindrome but 35 = 100011 is not.

14. Write a program to solve the *count-out* problem using arrays or an array of struct.

CHAPTER 4

■ ■ ■

Stacks and Queues

In this chapter, we will explain the following:

- The notion of an abstract data type
- What a stack is
- How to implement a stack using an array
- How to implement a stack using a linked list
- How to create a header file for use by other programs
- How to implement a stack for a general data type
- How to convert an expression from infix to postfix
- How to evaluate an arithmetic expression
- What a queue is
- How to implement a queue using an array
- How to implement a queue using a linked list

4.1 Abstract Data Types

We are familiar with the notion of declaring variables of a given type (double, say) and then performing operations on those variables (for example, add, multiply, and assign) without needing to know *how* those variables are stored in the computer. In this scenario, the compiler designer can change the way a double variable is stored, and the programmer would not have to change any programs that use double variables. This is an example of an abstract data type.

An *abstract data type* is one that allows a user to manipulate the data type without any knowledge of how the data type is represented in the computer. In other words, as far as the user is concerned, all he needs to know are the operations that can be performed on the data type. The person who is implementing the data type is free to change its implementation without affecting the users.

In this chapter, we will show how to implement stacks and queues as abstract data types.

4.2 Stacks

A *stack* as a linear list in which items are added at one end and deleted from the same end. The idea is illustrated by a "stack of plates" placed on a table, one on top the other. When a plate is needed, it is taken from the top of the stack. When a plate is washed, it is added at the top of the stack. Note that if a plate is now needed, this "newest" plate is the one that is taken. A stack exhibits the "last in, first out" property.

To illustrate the stack idea, we will use a stack of integers. Our goal is to define a data type called Stack so that a user can declare variables of this type and manipulate it in various ways. What are some of these ways?

As indicated above, we will need to add an item to the stack; the term commonly used is *push*. We will also need to take an item off the stack; the term commonly used is *pop*.

Before we attempt to take something off the stack, it is a good idea to ensure that the stack has something on it, in other words, that it is not *empty*. We will need an operation that tests whether a stack is empty.

Given these three operations—*push*, *pop*, and *empty*—let's illustrate how they can be used to read some numbers and print them in reverse order. For example, say we have these numbers:

```
36 15 52 23
```

We want to print the following:

```
23 52 15 36
```

We can solve this problem by adding each new number to the top of a stack, S. After all the numbers have been placed on the stack, we can picture the stack as follows:

```
23(top of stack)
52
15
36(bottom of stack)
```

Next, we remove the numbers, one at a time, printing each as it is removed.

We will need a way of telling when all the numbers have been read. We will use 0 to end the data. The logic for solving this problem can be expressed as follows:

```
create an empty stack, S
read(num)
while (num != 0) {
    push num onto S
    read(num)
}

while (S is not empty) {
    pop S into num //store the number at the top of S in num
    print num
}
```

We now show how we can implement a stack of integers and its operations.

4.2.1 Implement Stack Using an Array

In the array implementation of a stack (of integers), we use an integer array (ST, say) for storing the numbers and an integer variable (top, say) that contains the index (subscript) of the item at the top of the stack.

Since we are using an array, we will need to know its size in order to declare it. We will need to have some information about the problem to determine a reasonable size for the array. We will use the symbolic constant MaxStack. If an attempt is made to push more than MaxStack elements onto the stack, we will report a *stack overflow* error.

We can use the following to define the data type Stack:

```
typedef struct {
    int top;
    int ST[MaxStack];
} StackType, *Stack;
```

Valid values for top will range from 0 to MaxStack - 1. When we initialize a stack, we will set top to the invalid subscript -1.

We can now declare a stack variable, S, with

```
Stack S;
```

Observe that Stack is declared as a pointer to the structure we call StackType. So, for instance, S is a pointer to a structure consisting of the variable top and the array ST. This is necessary since top and ST would need to be changed by the *push* and *pop* routines and the changes known to the calling function (main, say). This can be achieved by passing a pointer to them, in effect, the Stack variable.

To work with a stack, the first task is to create an empty stack. This is done by allocating storage for a StackType, assigning its address to a Stack variable, and setting top to -1. We can use the following:

```
Stack initStack() {
    Stack sp = (Stack) malloc(sizeof(StackType));
    sp -> top = -1;
    return sp;
}
```

In main, say, we can declare and initialize a stack, S, with this:

```
Stack S = initStack();
```

When this statement is executed, the situation in memory can be represented by that shown in Figure 4-1.

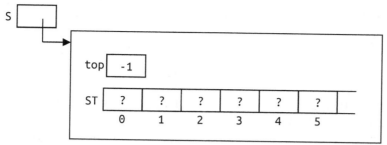

Figure 4-1. Array representation of stack in memory

This represents the empty stack. In working with stacks, we will need a function that tells us whether a stack is empty. We can use this:

```
int empty(Stack S) {
    return (S -> top == -1);
}
```

This simply checks whether top has the value -1.

The major operations on a stack are *push* and *pop*. To push an item, n, onto a stack, we must store it in ST and update top to point to it. The basic idea is as follows:

```
add 1 to top
set ST[top] to n
```

However, we must guard against trying to add something to the stack when it is already full. The stack is full when top has the value MaxStack - 1, the subscript of the last element. In this case, we will report that the stack is full and halt the program. Here is push:

```
void push(Stack S, int n) {
    if (S -> top == MaxStack - 1) {
        printf("\nStack Overflow\n");
        exit(1);
    }
    ++(S -> top);
    S -> ST[S -> top] = n;
}
```

After 36, 15, 52, and 23 have been pushed onto S, memory looks like Figure 4-2.

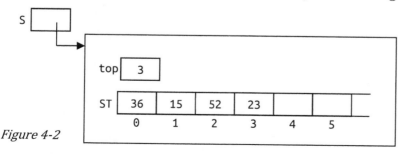

Figure 4-2

Finally, to pop an item off the stack, we return the value in location top and decrease top by 1. The basic idea is as follows:

```
set hold to ST[top]
subtract 1 from top
return hold
```

Again, we must guard against trying to take something off an empty stack. What should we do if the stack is empty and pop is called? We could simply report an error and halt the program. However, it might be better to return some "rogue" value, indicating that the stack is empty. We take the latter approach in our function, pop.:

```c
int pop(Stack S) {
    if (empty(S)) return RogueValue; //a symbolic constant
    int hold = S -> ST[S -> top];
    --(S -> top);
    return hold;
}
```

Note that even though we have written pop to do something reasonable if it is called and the stack is empty, it is better if the programmer establishes that the stack is *not* empty (using the empty function) before calling pop.

We now write Program P4.1, which reads some numbers, terminated by 0, and prints them in reverse order.

Program P4.1

```c
#include <stdio.h>
#include <stdlib.h>
#define RogueValue -9999
#define MaxStack 10

typedef struct {
    int top;
    int ST[MaxStack];
} StackType, *Stack;

int main() {
    Stack initStack();
    int empty(Stack);
    void push(Stack, int);
    int pop(Stack);
    int n;
    Stack S = initStack();
    printf("Enter some integers, ending with 0\n");
    scanf("%d", &n);
    while (n != 0) {
        push(S, n);
        scanf("%d", &n);
    }
    printf("Numbers in reverse order\n");
    while (!empty(S))
        printf("%d ", pop(S));
    printf("\n");
} //end main
```

```
Stack initStack() {
    Stack sp = (Stack) malloc(sizeof(StackType));
    sp -> top = -1;
    return sp;
} //end initStack

int empty(Stack S) {
    return (S -> top == -1);
} //end empty

void push(Stack S, int n) {
    if (S -> top == MaxStack - 1) {
        printf("\nStack Overflow\n");
        exit(1);
    }
    ++(S -> top);
    S -> ST[S -> top]= n;
} //end push

int pop(Stack S) {
    if (empty(S)) return RogueValue;
    int hold = S -> ST[S -> top];
    --(S -> top);
    return hold;
} //end pop
```

The following shows a sample run of the program:

```
Enter some integers, ending with 0
1 2 3 4 5 6 7 8 9 0

Numbers in reverse order
9 8 7 6 5 4 3 2 1
```

It is important to observe that the code in main that uses the stack does so via the functions initStack, push, pop, and empty and makes no assumption about how the stack elements are stored. This is the hallmark of an abstract data type—it can be used without the user needing to know how it is implemented.

Next, we will implement the stack using a linked list, but main will remain the same for solving the problem of printing the numbers in reverse order.

4.2.2 Implement Stack Using a Linked List

The array implementation of a stack has the advantages of simplicity and efficiency. However, one major disadvantage is the need to know what size to declare the array. Some reasonable guess has to be made, but this may turn out to be too small (and the program has to halt) or too big (and storage is wasted).

To overcome this disadvantage, a linked list can be used. Now, we will allocate storage for an element only when it is needed.

The stack is implemented as a linked list with new items added at the head of the list. When we need to pop the stack, the item at the head is removed.

We will define a `Stack` data type as a pointer to the linked list, defined by its "top" variable. So, a `Stack` variable points to the variable that points to the first item in the linked list. As in the case of the array implementation, this is necessary so that changes made in the push and pop routines will be known in the calling function. We will use the following declarations:

```
typedef struct node {
    int num;
    struct node *next;
} Node, *NodePtr;

typedef struct {
    NodePtr top;
} StackType, *Stack;
```

After 36, 15, 52, and 23 (in that order) have been pushed onto a stack, S, we can picture it as shown in Figure 4-3. S is a pointer to `top`, which is a pointer to the linked list of stack elements.

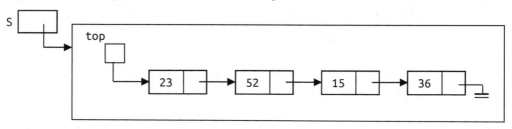

Figure 4-3. Stack view after pushing 36, 15, 52, and 23

The empty stack is represented as shown in Figure 4-4.

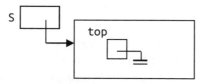

Figure 4-4. Empty stack

Creating an empty stack involves allocating storage for a `StackType` structure that consists of the single pointer variable, `top`, and setting `top` to NULL. Here is the function, `initStack`:

```
Stack initStack() {
    Stack sp = (Stack) malloc(sizeof(StackType));
    sp -> top = NULL;
    return sp;
} //end initStack
```

We can test for an empty stack with this:

```
int empty(Stack S) {
    return (S -> top == NULL);
} //end empty
```

This simply checks whether top is NULL.

To push an item onto a stack, we need to allocate storage for a node and add it to the head of the list. Here is push:

```
void push(Stack S, int n) {
    NodePtr np = (NodePtr) malloc(sizeof(Node));
    np -> num = n;
    np -> next = S -> top;
    S -> top = np;
} //end push
```

To pop an item from the stack, we first check whether the stack is empty. If it is, a rogue value is returned. If not, the item at the head of the list is returned and the node containing the item is deleted. Here is pop:

```
int pop(Stack S) {
    if (empty(S)) return RogueValue;
    int hold = S -> top -> num;
    NodePtr temp = S -> top;
    S -> top = S -> top -> next;
    free(temp);
    return hold;
} //end pop
```

Putting these functions together with main from Program P4.1 gives us Program P4.2, which reads a set of numbers, terminated by 0, and prints them in reverse order.

Program P4.2

```
#include <stdio.h>
#include <stdlib.h>
#define RogueValue -9999

typedef struct node {
    int num;
    struct node *next;
} Node, *NodePtr;

typedef struct stackType {
    NodePtr top;
} StackType, *Stack;

int main() {
    Stack initStack();
    int empty(Stack);
    void push(Stack, int);
    int pop(Stack);
```

```
    int n;

    Stack S = initStack();
    printf("Enter some integers, ending with 0\n");
    scanf("%d", &n);
    while (n != 0) {
        push(S, n);
        scanf("%d", &n);
    }
    printf("Numbers in reverse order\n");
    while (!empty(S))
        printf("%d ", pop(S));
    printf("\n");
} //end main

Stack initStack() {
    Stack sp = (Stack) malloc(sizeof(StackType));
    sp -> top = NULL;
    return sp;
}

int empty(Stack S) {
    return (S -> top == NULL);
} //end empty

void push(Stack S, int n) {
    NodePtr np = (NodePtr) malloc(sizeof(Node));
    np -> num = n;
    np -> next = S -> top;
    S -> top = np;
} //end push

int pop(Stack S) {
    if (empty(S)) return RogueValue;
    int hold = S -> top -> num;
    NodePtr temp = S -> top;
    S -> top = S -> top -> next;
    free(temp);
    return hold;
} //end pop
```

4.3 Create Stack Header File

Now that we have created a set of declarations/functions for manipulating an integer stack, we can put them together in one file so that *any* user can have access to them without having to repeat the code in their program. To illustrate, we create a file called stack.h, say, and put the following in it:

```
#include <stdlib.h>
#define RogueValue -9999

typedef struct node {
    int num;
    struct node *next;
} Node, *NodePtr;
```

```
typedef struct stackType {
    NodePtr top;
} StackType, *Stack;

Stack initStack() {
    Stack sp = (Stack) malloc(sizeof(StackType));
    sp -> top = NULL;
    return sp;
} //end initStack

int empty(Stack S) {
    return (S -> top == NULL);
} //end empty

void push(Stack S, int n) {
    NodePtr np = (NodePtr) malloc(sizeof(Node));
    np -> num = n;
    np -> next = S -> top;
    S -> top = np;
} //end push

int pop(Stack S) {
    if (empty(S)) return RogueValue;
    int hold = S -> top -> num;
    NodePtr temp = S -> top;
    S -> top = S -> top -> next;
    free(temp);
    return hold;
} //end pop
```

Next, we put stack.h in the "include library" of C functions. Typically, most C compilers will have a folder called include. This is the same folder that contains files such as stdio.h, string.h, and so on. Simply put stack.h in this folder. (Note that some compilers may already have a file called stack.h. In this case, you can add your declarations to this file or just use another name for your file.) Now, any program that wants to use the stack functions must contain this declaration:

```
#include <stack.h>
```

For example, Program P4.2 can now be written as Program P4.3.

Program P4.3

```
#include <stdio.h>
#include <stack.h>

int main() {
    int n;
    Stack S = initStack();
    printf("Enter some integers, ending with 0\n");
    scanf("%d", &n);
    while (n != 0) {
        push(S, n);
        scanf("%d", &n);
    }
    printf("\nNumbers in reverse order\n");
    while (!empty(S))
        printf("%d ", pop(S));
```

```
    printf("\n");
} //end main
```

Note how much shorter this program is, now that the stack declarations/functions are hidden away in stack.h.

4.4 A General Stack Type

To simplify our presentation, we have worked with a stack of integers. We remind you of those places in the program that are tied to the decision to use integers.

- In the declaration of Node, we declare an int called num.
- In push, we pass an int argument.
- In pop, we return an int result.

No changes are needed in initStack and empty.

This means that if we need a stack of characters, for example, we will have to change int to char in all of the above mentioned places. Similar changes will have to be made for stacks of other types.

It would be nice if we could minimize the changes needed when a different type of stack is required. We now show how this could be done.

Our first generalization lets us have a stack of *any* type, including structures. So, for instance, if we have a structure representing a fraction (see Section 1.8), we can have a stack of fractions. We can also have stacks of primitive types such as int, char, and double. To this end, we declare a structure called StackData; this structure will contain the field or fields that will comprise a stack element.

Consider the following:

```
typedef struct {
    //declare all the data fields here
    char ch; //for example
} StackData;
```

Whichever kind of stack we want, we declare the data fields within the structure. In this example, if we want a stack of characters, we declare one field of type char.

Now, a linked list node will consist of two fields: a data field of type StackData and a field that points to the next node. Here is its declaration:

```
typedef struct node {
    StackData data;
    struct node *next;
} Node, *NodePtr;
```

The only change from before is that we use StackData instead of int.

The major change in push is in the function heading. We change

```
void push(Stack S, int n)
```

to

```
void push(Stack S, StackData d)
```

In the function body, we change

```
np -> num = n;
```

to

```
np -> data = d;
```

The major change in pop is also in the function heading. We change

```
int pop(Stack S)
```

to

```
StackData pop(Stack S)
```

In the function body, we change

```
int hold = S -> top -> num;
```

to

```
StackData hold = S -> top -> data;
```

For variation, we will write pop such that if it is called and the stack is empty, a message is printed and the program halts.

With these changes, it is now easy to change the kind of stack we want to work with. We need to change only the declaration of StackData, including the field or fields we want for our stack elements.

To illustrate, suppose we want to read a line of data and print it reversed. We need a stack of characters. We declare StackData as follows:

```
typedef struct {
    char ch;
} StackData;
```

Suppose the following statements are stored in an include file, stack.h:

```
#include <stdlib.h>

typedef struct node {
    StackData data;
    struct node *next;
} Node, *NodePtr;

typedef struct stackType {
    NodePtr top;
} StackType, *Stack;

Stack initStack() {
    Stack sp = (Stack) malloc(sizeof(StackType));
    sp -> top = NULL;
    return sp;
} //end initStack
```

```
int empty(Stack S) {
    return (S -> top == NULL);
} //end empty

void push(Stack S, StackData d) {
    NodePtr np = (NodePtr) malloc(sizeof(Node));
    np -> data = d;
    np -> next = S -> top;
    S -> top = np;
} //end push

StackData pop(Stack S) {
    if (empty(S)) {
        printf("\nAttempt to pop an empty stack\n");
        exit(1);
    }
    StackData hold = S -> top -> data;
    NodePtr temp = S -> top;
    S -> top = S -> top -> next;
    free(temp);
    return hold;
} //end pop
```

The StackData declaration is *not* included here. This is desirable since each user may need a different type of stack and must be given the opportunity to declare whatever she wants StackData to be. She can do this in her own program as illustrated in Program P4.4, which reads a line of input and prints it reversed.

Program P4.4

```
#include <stdio.h>

typedef struct {
    char ch;
} StackData;

#include <stack.h>

int main() {
    StackData temp;
    char c;
    Stack S = initStack();
    printf("Type some data and press Enter\n");
    while ((c = getchar()) != '\n') {
        temp.ch = c;
        push(S, temp);
    }
    printf("\nData in reverse order\n");
    while (!empty(S))
        putchar(pop(S).ch);
    putchar('\n');
} //end main
```

Note the placement of #include <stack.h>—it comes *after* the declaration of StackData. This is necessary since there are functions/declarations in stack.h that make reference to StackData.

Note also that the stack functions work with the data type StackData. Even though we want a "stack of characters", a character must be stored in a StackData variable (temp is used) before it can be pushed onto the stack. Similarly, pop returns a StackData value; we must retrieve the ch field of the value returned to get at the character.

The following is a sample run of Program P4.4:

```
Type some data and press Enter
Was it a rat I saw?

Data in reverse order
?was I tar a ti saW
```

As another example, if a programmer needs to work with a stack of fractions, she can use this:

```
typedef struct {
    int num; //numerator
    int den; //denominator
} StackData;
```

4.4.1 Example: Convert from Decimal to Binary

Consider the problem of converting a positive integer from decimal to binary. We can use an integer stack, S, to do this using repeated division by 2 and saving the remainders. Here is the algorithm:

```
initialize S to empty
read the number, n
while (n > 0) {
    push n % 2 onto S
    n = n / 2
}
while (S is not empty) print pop(S)
```

This algorithm is implemented as Program P4.5.

Note, again, that each bit must be stored in a StackData variable (temp is used).

Program P4.5

```
#include <stdio.h>

typedef struct {
    int bit;
} StackData;

#include <stack.h>

int main() {
    StackData temp;
    int n;
    Stack S = initStack();
```

```
    printf("Enter a positive integer: ");
    scanf("%d", &n);
    while (n > 0) {
        temp.bit = n % 2;
        push(S, temp);
        n = n / 2;
    }
    printf("\nIts binary equivalent is ");
    while (!empty(S))
        printf("%d", pop(S).bit);
    printf("\n");
} //end main
```

A sample run of Program P4.5 is shown here:

```
Enter a positive integer: 97

Its binary equivalent is 1100001
```

4.5 Convert Infix to Postfix

Consider the expression 7 + 3 * 4. What is its value? Without any knowledge about which operation should be performed first, we would probably work out the value from left to right as (7 + 3 = 10) * 4 = 40. However, normal rules of arithmetic state that multiplication *has higher precedence* than addition. This means that, in an expression like the one shown here, multiplication (*) is performed before addition (+). Knowing this, the value is 7 + 12 = 19.

We can, of course, force the addition to be performed first by using brackets, as in (7 + 3) * 4. Here, the brackets mean that + is done first.

These are examples of *infix* expressions; the operator (+, *) is placed *between* its operands. One disadvantage of infix expressions is the need to use brackets to override the normal *precedence rules.*

Another way of representing expressions is to use *postfix* notation. Here, the operator comes *after* its operands and there is no need to use brackets to specify which operations to perform first. For example, the postfix form of

7 + 3 * 4

is

7 3 4 * +

and the postfix form of

(7 + 3) * 4

is

7 3 + 4 *

One useful observation is that the operands appear in the same order in both the infix and postfix forms but operators differ in order and placement.

Why is postfix notation useful? As mentioned, we do not need brackets to specify the precedence of operators. More importantly, though, it is a convenient form for evaluating the expression.

Given the postfix form of an expression, it can be evaluated as follows:

```
initialize a stack, S, to empty
while we have not reached the end of the expression
    get the next item, x, from the expression
    if x is an operand, push it onto S
    if x is an operator, pop its operands from S, apply the operator,
        and push the result onto S
endwhile
pop S; // this is the value of the expression
```

Consider the expression (7 + 3) * 4 whose postfix form is 7 3 + 4 *. It is evaluated by traversing from left to right.

1. The next item is 7; push 7 onto S; S contains 7.
2. The next item is 3; push 3 onto S; S contains 7 3 (the top is on the right).
3. The next item is +; pop 3 and 7 from S; apply + to 7 and 3, giving 10; push 10 onto S; S contains 10.
4. The next item is 4; push 4 onto S; S contains 10 4.
5. The next item is *; pop 4 and 10 from S; apply * to 10 and 4, giving 40; push 40 onto S; S contains 40.
6. We have reached the end of the expression; we pop S, getting 40—the result of the expression.

Note that when operands are popped from the stack, the first one popped is the second operand, and the second one popped is the first operand. This does not matter for addition and multiplication but would be important for subtraction and division. As an exercise, convert the following to postfix form and step through its evaluation using the algorithm above:

(7 - 3) * (9 - 8 / 4).

The big question, of course, is how do we convert an infix expression to postfix? Before presenting the algorithm, we observe that it will use an *operator stack*. We will also need a *precedence table* that gives the relative precedence of the operators. Given any two operators, the table will tell us whether they have the same precedence (like + and -) and, if not, which has greater precedence.

As the algorithm proceeds, it will output the postfix form of the given expression.

Here is the algorithm:

1. Initialize a stack of operators, S, to empty.
2. Get the next item, x, from the infix expression; if none, go to step 8; (x is either an operand, a left bracket, a right bracket, or an operator).
3. If x is an operand, output x.
4. If x is a left bracket, push it onto S.

5. If x is a right bracket, pop items off S and output popped items until a left bracket appears on top of S; pop the left bracket and discard.

6. If x is an operator, then do the following:

```
while (S is not empty) and
        (a left bracket is not on top of S) and
        (an operator of equal or higher precedence
         than x is on top of S)
    pop S and output popped item
push x onto S
```

7. Repeat from step 2.

8. Pop S and output the popped item until S is empty.

You are advised to step through the algorithm for the following expressions:

```
3 + 5
7 - 3 + 8
7 + 3 * 4
(7 + 3) * 4
(7 + 3) / (8 - 2 * 3)
(7 - 8 / 2 / 2) * ((7 - 2) * 3 - 6)
```

Let's write a program to read a simplified infix expression and output its postfix form. We assume that an operand is a single-digit integer. An operator can be one of +, −, *, or /. Brackets are allowed. The usual precedence of operators apply: + and − have the same precedence, which is lower than that of * and /, which have the same precedence. The left bracket is treated as an operator with very low precedence, less than that of + and −.

We will implement this as a function precedence which, given an operator, returns an integer representing its precedence. The actual value returned is not important as long as the relative precedence of the operators is maintained. We will use the following:

```
int precedence(char c) {
    if (c == '(') return 0;
    if (c == '+' || c == '-') return 3;
    if (c == '*' || c == '/') return 5;
} //end precedence
```

You could also write precedence using a switch statement as follows:

```
int precedence(char c) {
    switch (c) {
        case '(': return 0;
        case '+':
        case '-': return 3;
        case '*':
        case '/': return 5;
    }//end switch
} //end precedence
```

The actual values 0, 3, and 5 are not important. Any values can be used as long as they represent the relative precedence of the operators.

We will need a function to read the input and return the next nonblank character. The end-of-line character will indicate the end of the expression. Here is the function (we call it getToken):

```
char getToken() {
    char ch;
    while ((ch = getchar()) == ' ') ; //empty body
    return ch;
} //end getToken
```

The operator stack is simply a stack of characters that we will implement using this declaration:

```
typedef struct {
    char ch;
} StackData;
```

Step 6 of the algorithm requires us to compare the precedence of the operator on top of the stack with the current operator. This would be easy if we can "peek" at the element on top of the stack without taking it off. To do this, we write the function peek and add it to stack.h, the file containing our stack declarations/functions.

```
StackData peek(Stack S) {
    if (!empty(S)) return S -> top -> data;
    printf("\nAttempt to peek at an empty stack\n");
    exit(1);
} //end peek
```

Putting all these together, we now write Program P4.6, which implements the algorithm for converting an infix expression to postfix.

The job of reading the expression and converting to postfix is delegated to readConvert. This outputs the postfix form to a character array, post. So as not to clutter the code with error checking, we assume that post is big enough to hold the converted expression. The function returns the number of elements in the postfix expression.

The function printPostfix simply prints the postfix expression.

Program P4.6

```
#include <stdio.h>
#include <ctype.h>

typedef struct {
    char ch;
} StackData;

#include <stack.h>

int main() {
    int readConvert(char[]);
    void printPostfix(char[], int);
    char post[50];

    int n = readConvert(post);
    printPostfix(post, n);
} //end main
```

```
int readConvert(char post[]) {
    char getToken(void), token, c;
    int precedence(char);
    StackData temp;
    int h = 0;
    Stack S = initStack();
    printf("Type an infix expression and press Enter\n");
    token = getToken();
    while (token != '\n') {
        if (isdigit(token)) post[h++] = token;
        else if (token == '(') {
            temp.ch = token;
            push(S, temp);
        }
        else if (token == ')')
            while ((c = pop(S).ch) != '(') post[h++] = c;
        else {
            while (!empty(S) &&
                    precedence(peek(S).ch) >= precedence(token))
                post[h++] = pop(S).ch;
            temp.ch = token;
            push(S, temp);
        }
        token = getToken();
    } //end while

    while (!empty(S)) post[h++] = pop(S).ch;
    return h; //the size of the expression
} //end readConvert

void printPostfix(char post[], int n) {
    printf("\nThe postfix form is \n");
    for (int h = 0; h < n; h++) printf("%c ", post[h]);
    printf("\n");
} //end printPostfix

char getToken() {
    char ch;
    while ((ch = getchar()) == ' ') ; //empty body
    return ch;
} //end getToken

int precedence(char c) {
    if (c == '(') return 0;
    if (c == '+' || c == '-') return 3;
    if (c == '*' || c == '/') return 5;
} //end precedence
```

The following is a sample run of Program P4.6:

```
Type an infix expression and press Enter
(7 - 8 / 2 / 2) * ((7 - 2) * 3 - 6)

The postfix form is
7 8 2 / 2 / - 7 2 - 3 * 6 - *
```

Program P4.6 assumes that the given expression is a valid one. However, it can be easily modified to recognize some kinds of invalid expressions. For instance, if a right bracket is missing, when we reach the end of the expression, there would be a left bracket on the stack. (If the brackets match, there would be none.) Similarly, if a left bracket is missing, when a right one is encountered and we are scanning the stack for the (missing) left one, we would not find it.

You are urged to modify Program P4.6 to catch expressions with mismatched brackets. You should also modify it to handle any integer operands, not just single-digit ones. Yet another modification is to handle other operations such as %, sqrt (square root), sin (sine), cos (cosine), tan (tangent), log (logarithm), exp (exponential), and so on.

4.5.1 Evaluate Postfix Expression

Program P4.6 stores the postfix form of the expression in a character array, post. We now write a function that, given post, evaluates the expression and returns its value. The function uses the algorithm at the beginning of Section 4.5.

We will need an *integer* stack to hold the operands and intermediate results. Recall that we needed a *character* stack to hold the operators. We can neatly work with both kinds of stacks if we declare StackData as follows:

```
typedef struct {
    char ch;
    int num;
} StackData;
```

We use the char field for the operator stack and the int field for the operand stack. Here is eval:

```
int eval(char post[], int n) {
    int a, b, c;
    StackData temp;

    Stack S = initStack();
    for (int h = 0; h < n; h++) {
        if (isdigit(post[h])) {
            temp.num = post[h] - '0'; //convert to integer
            push(S, temp);
        }
        else {
            b = pop(S).num;
            a = pop(S).num;
            if (post[h] == '+') c = a + b;
            else if (post[h] == '-') c = a - b;
            else if (post[h] == '*') c = a * b;
            else c = a / b;
            temp.num = c;
            push(S, temp);
        }
    } //end for
    return pop(S).num;
} //end eval
```

We can test eval by adding it to Program P4.6 and putting its prototype, as follows, in main:

```
int eval(char[], int);
```

We change the declaration of StackData to the one shown above and add the following as the last statement in main:

```
printf("\nIts value is %d\n", eval(post, n));
```

Putting these changes together gives us Program P4.7.

Program P4.7

```
#include <stdio.h>
#include <ctype.h>

typedef struct {
    char ch;
    int num;
} StackData;

#include <stack.h>

int main() {
    int readConvert(char[]);
    void printPostfix(char[], int);
    int eval(char[], int);
    char post[50];

    int n = readConvert(post);
    printPostfix(post, n);
    printf("\nIts value is %d\n", eval(post, n));
} //end main

int readConvert(char post[]) {
    char getToken(void), token, c;
    int precedence(char);
    StackData temp;
    int h = 0;
    Stack S = initStack();
    printf("Type an infix expression and press Enter\n");
    token = getToken();
    while (token != '\n') {
        if (isdigit(token)) post[h++] = token;
        else if (token == '(') {
            temp.ch = token;
            push(S, temp);
        }
        else if (token == ')')
            while ((c = pop(S).ch) != '(') post[h++] = c;
        else {
            while (!empty(S) &&
                    precedence(peek(S).ch) >= precedence(token))
                post[h++] = pop(S).ch;
            temp.ch = token;
            push(S, temp);
        }
        token = getToken();
    } //end while
```

```
        while (!empty(S)) post[h++] = pop(S).ch;
        return h; //the size of the expression
    } //end readConvert

    void printPostfix(char post[], int n) {
        printf("\nThe postfix form is \n");
        for (int h = 0; h < n; h++) printf("%c ", post[h]);
        printf("\n");
    } //end printPostfix

    char getToken() {
        char ch;
        while ((ch = getchar()) == ' ') ; //empty body
        return ch;
    } //end getToken

    int precedence(char c) {
        if (c == '(') return 0;
        if (c == '+' || c == '-') return 3;
        if (c == '*' || c == '/') return 5;
    } //end precedence

    int eval(char post[], int n) {
        int a, b, c;
        StackData temp;

        Stack S = initStack();
        for (int h = 0; h < n; h++) {
            if (isdigit(post[h])) {
                temp.num = post[h] - '0'; //convert to integer
                push(S, temp);
            }
            else {
                b = pop(S).num;
                a = pop(S).num;
                if (post[h] == '+') c = a + b;
                else if (post[h] == '-') c = a - b;
                else if (post[h] == '*') c = a * b;
                else c = a / b;
                temp.num = c;
                push(S, temp);
            }
        } //end for
        return pop(S).num;
    } //end eval
```

The following is a sample run of the modified program:

```
Type an infix expression and press Enter
(7 - 8 / 2 / 2) * ((7 - 2) * 3 - 6)

The postfix form is
7 8 2 / 2 / - 7 2 - 3 * 6 - *

Its value is 45
```

4.6 Queues

A *queue* is a linear list in which items are added at one end and deleted from the other end. Familiar examples are queues at a bank, a supermarket, a concert, or a sporting event. People are supposed to join the queue at the rear and exit from the front. We would expect that a queue data structure would be useful for simulating these real-life queues.

Queues are also found inside the computer. There may be several jobs waiting to be executed, and they are held in a queue. For example, several people may each request something to be printed on a network printer. Since the printer can handle only one job at a time, the others have to be queued.

These are the basic operations we want to perform on a queue:

- Add an item to the queue; we say *enqueue*.
- Take an item off the queue; we say *dequeue*.
- Check whether the queue is empty.
- Inspect the item at the head of the queue.

As with stacks, we can easily implement the queue data structure using arrays or linked lists. We will use a queue of integers for illustration purposes.

4.6.1 Implement Queue Using an Array

In the array implementation of a queue (of integers), we use an integer array (QA, say) for storing the numbers and two integer variables (head and tail) that indicate the item at the head of the queue and the item at the tail of the queue, respectively.

Since we are using an array, we will need to know its size in order to declare it. We will need to have some information about the problem to determine a reasonable size for the array. We will use the symbolic constant MaxQ. In our implementation, the queue will be declared full if there are MaxQ - 1 elements in it and we attempt to add another.

We use the following to define the data type Queue:

```
typedef struct {
    int head, tail;
    int QA[MaxQ];
} QType, *Queue;
```

Valid values for head and tail will range from 0 to MaxQ - 1. When we initialize a queue, we will set head and tail to 0.

We can now declare a *queue variable*, Q, with this:

```
Queue Q;
```

Observe that Queue is declared as a pointer to the structure we call QType. So, for instance, Q is a pointer to a structure consisting of the variables head and tail and the array QA. This is necessary since head, tail, and QA would need to be changed by the enqueue and dequeue routines and the changes known to the calling function (main, say). This can be achieved by passing a pointer to them, in effect, the Queue variable.

To work with a queue, the first task is to create an empty queue. This is done by allocating storage for a QType, assigning its address to a Queue variable, and setting head and tail to 0. Later, we will see why 0 is a good value to use. We can use the following:

```
Queue initQueue() {
    Queue qp = (Queue) malloc(sizeof(QType));
    qp -> head = qp -> tail = 0;
    return qp;
}
```

In main, say, we can declare and initialize a queue, Q, with this:

```
Queue Q = initQueue();
```

When this statement is executed, the situation in memory can be represented as shown in Figure 4-5.

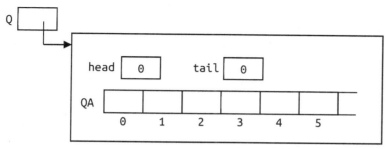

Figure 4-5. Array representation of a queue

This represents the empty queue. In working with queues, we will need a function that tells us whether a queue is empty. We can use the following:

```
int empty(Queue Q) {
    return (Q -> head == Q -> tail);
}
```

Shortly, we will see that given the way we will implement the enqueue and dequeue operations, the queue will be empty whenever head and tail have the same value. This value will not necessarily be 0. In fact, it may be any of the values from 0 to MaxQ - 1, the valid subscripts of QA.

Consider how we might add an item to the queue. In a real queue, a person joins at the tail. We will do the same here by incrementing tail and storing the item at the location indicated by tail.

For example, to add 36, say, to the queue, we increment tail to 1 and store 36 in QA[1]; head remains at 0.

If we then add 15 to the queue, it will be stored in QA[2], and tail will be 2.

If we now add 52 to the queue, it will be stored in QA[3], and tail will be 3.

Our picture in memory will look like Figure 4-6.

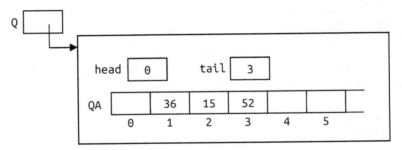

Figure 4-6. State of the queue after adding 36, 15, and 52

Note that head points "just in front of" the item that is actually at the head of the queue, and tail points at the last item in the queue.

Now consider taking something off the queue. The item to be taken off is the one at the head. To remove it, we must first increment head and then return the value pointed to by head.

For example, if we remove 36, head will become 1, and it points "just in front of" 15, the item now at the head. Note that 36 still remains in the array, but, for all intents and purposes, it is not in the queue.

Suppose we now add 23 to the queue. It will be placed in location 4, with tail being 4 and head being 1. The picture now looks like Figure 4-7.

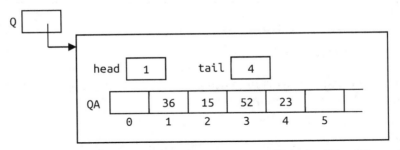

Figure 4-7. State of the queue after removing 36 and adding 23

There are three items in the queue; 15 is at the head, and 23 is at the tail.

Consider what happens if we continuously add items to the queue without taking off any. The value of tail will keep increasing until it reaches MaxQ - 1, the last valid subscript of QA. What do we do if another item needs to be added?

We *could* say that the queue is full and stop the program. However, there are two free locations, 0 and 1. It would be better to try to use one of these. This leads us to the idea of a *circular queue*. Here, we think of the locations in the array as arranged in a circle: location MaxQ - 1 is followed by location 0.

So, if tail has the value MaxQ - 1, incrementing it will set it to 0.

Suppose we had not taken off any item from the queue. The value of head would still be 0. Now, what if, in attempting to add an item, tail is incremented from MaxQ - 1 to 0? It now has the same value as head. In this situation, we declare that the queue is full.

We do this even though nothing is stored in location 0, which is, therefore, available to hold another item. The reason for taking this approach is that it simplifies our code for detecting when the queue is empty and when it is full.

To emphasize, when the queue is declared full, it contains MaxQ - 1 items.

We can now write enqueue, a function to add an item to the queue.

```
void enqueue(Queue Q, int n) {
    if (Q -> tail == MaxQ - 1) Q -> tail = 0;
    else ++(Q -> tail);
    if (Q -> tail == Q -> head) {
        printf("\nQueue is full\n");
        exit(1);
    }
    Q -> QA[Q -> tail] = n;
} //end enqueue
```

We first increment tail. If, by doing so, it has the same value as head, we declare that the queue is full. If not, we store the new item in position tail.

Consider Figure 4.7. If we delete 15 and 52, it changes to that shown in Figure 4-8.

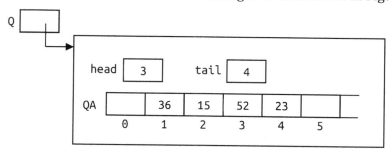

Figure 4-8. Queue after removing 15, 52

Now, head has the value 3, tail has the value 4, and there is one item in the queue, 23, in location 4. If we delete this last item, head and tail would both have the value 4, and the queue would be empty. This suggests that we have an empty queue when head has the same value as tail, as indicated earlier.

We can now write the function dequeue for removing an item from the queue.

```
int dequeue(Queue Q) {
    if (empty(Q)) {
        printf("\nAttempt to remove from an empty queue\n");
        exit(1);
    }
    if (Q -> head == MaxQ - 1) Q -> head = 0;
    else ++(Q -> head);
    return Q -> QA[Q -> head];
} //end dequeue
```

If the queue is empty, an error is reported, and the program is halted. If not, we increment head and return the value in location head. Note, again, that if head has the value MaxQ - 1, incrementing it sets it to 0.

As in the case of a stack, we can create a file called queue.h and store our declarations and functions in it so they can be used by other programs. So far, queue.h would contain the declarations shown here:

```c
#include <stdlib.h>

typedef struct {
    int head, tail;
    int QA[MaxQ];
} QType, *Queue;

Queue initQueue() {
    Queue qp = (Queue) malloc(sizeof(QType));
    qp -> head = qp -> tail = 0;
    return qp;
} //end initQueue

int empty(Queue Q) {
    return (Q -> head == Q -> tail);
} //end empty

void enqueue(Queue Q, int n) {
    if (Q -> tail == MaxQ - 1) Q -> tail = 0;
    else ++(Q -> tail);
    if (Q -> tail == Q -> head) {
        printf("\nQueue is full\n");
        exit(1);
    }
    Q -> QA[Q -> tail] = n;
} //end enqueue

int dequeue(Queue Q) {
    if (empty(Q)) {
        printf("\nAttempt to remove from an empty queue\n");
        exit(1);
    }
    if (Q -> head == MaxQ - 1) Q -> head = 0;
    else ++(Q -> head);
    return Q -> QA[Q -> head];
} //end dequeue
```

To test our queue operations, we write Program P4.8, which reads an integer and prints its digits in reverse order. For example, if 12345 is read, the program prints 54321. The digits are extracted, from the right, and stored in a queue. The items in the queue are taken off, one at a time, and printed.

Program P4.8

```c
#include <stdio.h>
#define MaxQ 10
#include <queue.h>
```

```
int main() {
    int n;
    Queue Q = initQueue();
    printf("Enter a positive integer: ");
    scanf("%d", &n);
    while (n > 0) {
        enqueue(Q, n % 10);
        n = n / 10;
    }
    printf("\nDigits in reverse order: ");
    while (!empty(Q))
        printf("%d", dequeue(Q));
    printf("\n");
} //end main
```

Note the order of the header statements. The user is free to define the value of MaxQ; this value will be used by the declarations in queue.h.

4.6.2 Implement Queue Using a Linked List

As with stacks, we can implement a queue using linked lists. This has the advantage of us not having to decide beforehand how many items to cater for. We will use two pointers, head and tail, to point to the first and last items in the queue, respectively. Figure 4-9 shows the data structure when four items (36, 15, 52, and 23) are added to the queue.

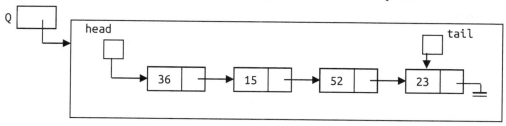

Figure 4-9. Linked list representation of a queue

We will implement the queue so that it works with a general data type that we will store in a structure called QueueData. We will use the following framework:

```
typedef struct {
    //declare all the data fields here
    int num; //for example
} QueueData;
```

Whichever kind of queue we want, we declare the data fields within the structure. In the earlier example, if we want a queue of integers, we declare one field of type int.

A linked list node will consist of two fields: a data field of type QueueData and a field that points to the next node. Here is its declaration:

```
typedef struct node {
    QueueData data;
    struct node *next;
} Node, *NodePtr;
```

We will define the Queue data type as a pointer to a structure containing two NodePtrs, head and tail, as follows:

```
typedef struct {
    NodePtr head, tail;
} QueueType, *Queue;
```

We can declare a queue as follows:

```
Queue Q;
```

The empty queue, Q, is represented as in Figure 4-10.

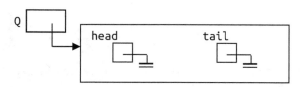

Figure 4-10. An empty queue (linked list representation)

Creating an empty queue involves allocating storage for a QueueType structure that consists of two variables, head and tail, and setting them to NULL. Here is the function, initQueue:

```
Queue initQueue() {
    Queue qp = (Queue) malloc(sizeof(QueueType));
    qp -> head = NULL;
    qp -> tail = NULL;
    return qp;
} //end initQueue
```

We can test for an empty queue with this:

```
int empty(Queue Q) {
    return (Q -> head == NULL);
} //end empty
```

This simply checks whether head is NULL.

To add an item to the queue, we need to allocate storage for a node and add it to the tail of the list. Here is enqueue:

```
void enqueue(Queue Q, QueueData d) {
    NodePtr np = (NodePtr) malloc(sizeof(Node));
    np -> data = d;
    np -> next = NULL;
    if (empty(Q)) {
        Q -> head = np;
        Q -> tail = np;
    }
```

```
    else {
        Q -> tail -> next = np;
        Q -> tail = np;
    } //end if..else
} //end enqueue
```

If the queue is empty, the new item becomes the only one in the queue; head and `tail` are set to point to it. If the queue is not empty, the item at the tail is set to point to the new one, and `tail` is updated to point to the new one.

To take an item off the queue, we first check whether the queue is empty. If it is, we print a message and end the program. If not, the item at the head of the queue is returned, and the node containing the item is deleted.

If, by removing an item, head becomes NULL, it means that the queue is empty. In this case, `tail` is also set to NULL.

Here is dequeue:

```
QueueData dequeue(Queue Q) {
    if (empty(Q)) {
        printf("\nAttempt to remove from an empty queue\n");
        exit(1);
    }
    QueueData hold = Q -> head -> data;
    NodePtr temp = Q -> head;
    Q -> head = Q -> head -> next;
    if (Q -> head == NULL) Q -> tail = NULL;
    free(temp);
    return hold;
} //end dequeue
```

As before, we can store all these declarations and functions, except QueueData, in a file called queue.h so that other programs can use them. The contents of queue.h are shown here:

```
#include <stdlib.h>

typedef struct node {
    QueueData data;
    struct node *next;
} Node, *NodePtr;

typedef struct queueType {
    NodePtr head, tail;
} QueueType, *Queue;
Queue initQueue() {
    Queue qp = (Queue) malloc(sizeof(QueueType));
    qp -> head = NULL;
    qp -> tail = NULL;
    return qp;
} //end initQueue

int empty(Queue Q) {
    return (Q -> head == NULL);
} //end empty
```

```
void enqueue(Queue Q, QueueData d) {
    NodePtr np = (NodePtr) malloc(sizeof(Node));
    np -> data = d;
    np -> next = NULL;
    if (empty(Q)) {
        Q -> head = np;
        Q -> tail = np;
    }
    else {
        Q -> tail -> next = np;
        Q -> tail = np;
    }
} //end enqueue

QueueData dequeue(Queue Q) {
    if (empty(Q)) {
        printf("\nAttempt to remove from an empty queue\n");
        exit(1);
    }
    QueueData hold = Q -> head -> data;
    NodePtr temp = Q -> head;
    Q -> head = Q -> head -> next;
    if (Q -> head == NULL) Q -> tail = NULL;
    free(temp);
    return hold;
} //end dequeue
```

To use these functions, a user program only needs to declare what he wants QueueData to be. To illustrate, we rewrite Program P4.8, which reads an integer and prints its digits in reverse order. It is shown as Program P4.9.

Program P4.9

```
#include <stdio.h>
typedef struct {
    int num;
} QueueData;

#include <queue.h>

int main() {
    int n;
    QueueData temp;
    Queue Q = initQueue();
    printf("Enter a positive integer: ");
    scanf("%d", &n);
    while (n > 0) {
        temp.num = n % 10;
        enqueue(Q, temp);
        n = n / 10;
    }
    printf("\nDigits in reverse order: ");
    while (!empty(Q))
        printf("%d", dequeue(Q).num);
    printf("\n");
} //end main
```

Note that the declaration of QueueData must come before

```
#include <queue.h>
```

Also, since enqueue expects a QueueData argument, the digits of the integer must be stored in the int field of a QueueData variable (temp is used) before being passed to enqueue.

Stacks and queues are important to systems programmers and compiler writers. We have seen how stacks are used in the evaluation of arithmetic expressions. They are also used to implement the "calling" and "return" mechanism for functions. Consider the situation where function A calls function C, which calls function B, which calls function D. When a function returns, how does the computer figure out where to return to? We show how a stack can be used to do this.

Assume we have the following situation, where a number, like 100, represents the *return address*, which is the address of the next instruction to be executed when the function returns:

```
function A        function B        function C        function D
    .                 .                 .                 .
    C;                D;                B;                .
100:              200:              300:                 .
    .                 .                 .                 .
```

When A calls C, the address 100 is pushed onto a stack, S. When C calls B, 300 is pushed onto S. When B calls D, 200 is pushed onto S. At this stage, the stack looks like the following, and control is in D:

```
(bottom of stack) 100  300  200 (top of stack)
```

When D finishes and is ready to return, the address at the top of the stack (200) is popped and execution continues at this address. Note that this is the address immediately following the call to D.

Next, when B finishes and is ready to return, the address at the top of the stack (300) is popped, and execution continues at this address. Note that this is the address immediately following the call to B.

Finally, when C finishes and is ready to return, the address at the top of the stack (100) is popped, and execution continues at this address. Note that this is the address immediately following the call to C.

Naturally, queue data structures are used in simulating real-life queues. They are also used to implement queues in the computer. In a multiprogramming environment, several jobs may have to be queued while waiting on a particular resource such as processor time or a printer.

Stacks and queues are also used extensively in working with more advanced data structures such as trees and graphs. We will discuss trees in Chapter 5 and graphs in Chapter 7.

EXERCISES 4

1. What is an *abstract data type*?

2. What is a *stack*? What are the basic operations that can be performed on a stack?

3. What is a *queue*? What are the basic operations that can be performed on a queue?

4. Modify Program P4.6 to recognize infix expressions with mismatched brackets.

5. Program P4.6 works with single-digit operands. Modify it to handle any integer operands.

6. Modify Program P4.6 to handle expressions with operations such as %, square root, sine, cosine, tangent, logarithm and exponential.

7. Write declarations/functions to implement a stack of double values.

8. Write declarations/functions to implement a queue of double values.

9. An integer array `post` is used to hold the postfix form of an arithmetic expression such that:

   a positive number represents an operand;

   -1 represents +;

   -2 represents -;

   -3 represents *;

   -4 represents /;

   0 indicates the end of the expression.

   Show the contents of post for the expression (2 + 3) * (8 / 4) - 6.

   Write a function `eval` which, given `post`, returns the value of the expression.

10. A *priority queue* is one in which items are added to the queue based on a *priority number*. Jobs with higher priority numbers are closer to the head of the queue than those with lower priority numbers. A job is added to the queue in front of all jobs of lower priority but after all jobs of greater or equal priority.

    Write declarations and functions to implement a priority queue. Each item in the queue has a job number (integer) and a priority number. Implement, at least, the following functions:

    (a) initialize an empty queue

    (b) add a job in its appropriate place in the queue

    (c) delete and dispose of the job at the head of the queue

    (d) given a job number, remove that job from the queue.

    Ensure your functions work regardless of the state of the queue.

11. An input line contains a word consisting of lowercase letters only. Explain how a stack can be used to determine if the word is a palindrome.

12. Show how to implement a queue using two stacks.

13. Show how to implement a stack using two queues.

14. A stack, S1, contains some numbers in arbitrary order. Using another stack, S2, for temporary storage, show how to sort the numbers in S1 such that the smallest is at the top of S1 and the largest is at the bottom

CHAPTER 5

■ ■ ■

Binary Trees

In this chapter, we will explain the following:

- The difference between a tree and a binary tree
- How to perform pre-order, in-order, and post-order traversals of a binary tree
- How to represent a binary tree in a computer program
- How to build a binary tree from given data
- What a binary search tree is and how to build one
- How to write a program to do a word-frequency count of words in a passage
- How to use an array as a binary tree representation
- How to write some recursive functions to obtain information about a binary tree
- How to delete a node from a binary search tree

5.1 Trees

A *tree* is a finite set of nodes such that

- There is one specially designated node called the *root* of the tree.
- The remaining nodes are partitioned into $m \geq 0$ disjoint sets $T_1, T_2, ..., T_m$, and each of these sets is a tree.

The trees $T_1, T_2, ..., T_m$, are called the *subtrees* of the root. We use a recursive definition since recursion is an innate characteristic of tree structures. Figure 5-1 illustrates a tree. By convention, the root is drawn at the top, and the tree grows downward.

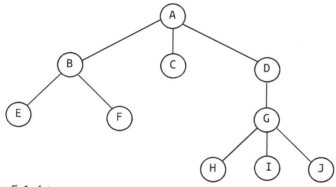

Figure 5-1. A tree

The root is A. There are three subtrees rooted at B, C, and D, respectively. The tree rooted at B has two subtrees, the one rooted at C has no subtrees, and the one rooted at D has one subtree. Each node of a tree is the root of a subtree.

The *degree* of a node is the number of subtrees of the node. Think of it as the number of lines leaving the node. For example, degree(A) = 3, degree(C) = 0, degree(D) = 1, and degree(G) = 3.

We use the terms *parent*, *child*, and *sibling* to refer to the nodes of a tree. For example, the parent A has three children, which are B, C, and D; the parent B has two children, which are E and F; and the parent D has one child, G, which has three children: H, I, and J. Note that a node may be the child of one node but the parent of another.

Sibling nodes are child nodes of the same parent. For example, B, C, and D are siblings; E and F are siblings; and H, I, and J are siblings.

In a tree, a node may have several children but, except for the root, only one parent. The root has no parent. Put another way, a nonroot node has exactly one line leading *into* it.

A *terminal* node (also called a *leaf*) is a node of degree 0. A *branch* node is a nonterminal node. In Figure 5-1, C, E, F, H, I, and J are leaves, while A, B, D, and G are branch nodes.

The *moment* of a tree is the number of nodes in the tree. The tree in Figure 5-1 has moment 10.

The *weight* of a tree is the number of leaves in the tree. The tree in Figure 5-1 has weight 6.

The *level* (or *depth*) of a node is the number of branches that must be traversed on the path to the node from the root. The root has level 0.

In the tree in Figure 5-1, B, C, and D are at level 1; E, F, and G are at level 2; and H, I, and J are at level 3. The level of a node is a measure of the depth of the node in the tree.

The *height* of a tree is the number of levels in the tree. The tree in Figure 5-1 has height 4. Note that the height of a tree is one more than its highest level.

If the relative order of the subtrees T_1, T_2, ..., T_m is important, the tree is an *ordered* tree. If order is unimportant, the tree is *oriented*.

A *forest* is a set of zero or more disjoint trees, as shown in Figure 5-2.

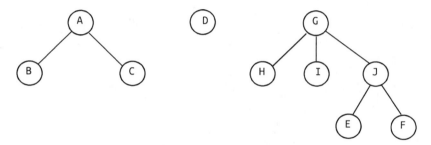

Figure 5-2. A forest of three disjoint trees

While general trees are of some interest, by far the most important kind of tree is a *binary tree*.

5.2 Binary Trees

A *binary tree* is the classic example of a nonlinear data structure—compare this to a linear list where we identify a first item, a next item, and a last item. A binary tree is a special case of the more general *tree* data structure, but it is the most useful and most widely used kind of tree. A binary tree is best defined using a recursive definition:

A *binary tree*

> (a) is empty

or

> (b) consists of a root and two subtrees—a left and a right—with each subtree being a binary tree

A consequence of this definition is that a node always has two subtrees, any of which may be empty. Another consequence is that if a node has *one* nonempty subtree, it is important to distinguish whether it is on the left or right. For example:

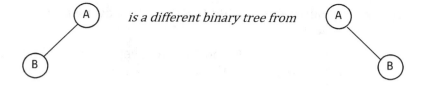

The first has an empty right subtree, while the second has an empty left subtree. However, as *trees*, they are the same.

The following are examples of binary trees.

This is a binary tree with one node, the root:

Here are binary trees with two nodes each:

These are binary trees with three nodes each:

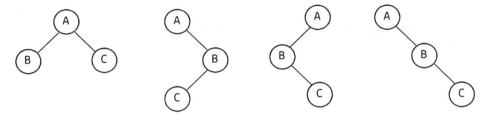

Here are binary trees with all left subtrees empty and all right subtrees empty:

This is a binary tree where each node, except the leaves, has exactly two subtrees; this is called a *complete* binary tree:

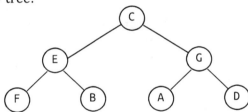

This is a general binary tree:

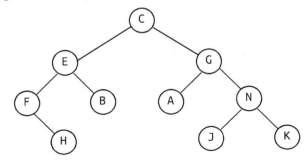

5.3 Traverse a Binary Tree

In many applications, we want to visit the nodes of a binary tree in some systematic way. For now, we'll think of "visit" as simply printing the information at the node. For a tree of n nodes, there are $n!$ ways to visit them, assuming that each node is visited once.

For example, for a tree with the three nodes A, B, and C, we can visit them in any of the following orders: ABC, ACB, BCA, BAC, CAB, and CBA. Not all of these orders are useful; we will define three—pre-order, in-order, and post-order—that are.

1. Pre-order traversal

    (a) Visit the root

    (b) Traverse the left subtree in pre-order

    (c) Traverse the right subtree in pre-order

Note that the traversal is defined recursively. In steps (b) and (c), we must re-apply the definition of pre-order traversal which says "vist the root, etc". It is useful to note that the root will always be the first node in pre-order.

The *pre-order* traversal of

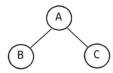

is A B C. We visit the root, **A**, followed by traversing the left subtree, **B**, then the right subtree, **C**. Using t(A) to mean "traverse the subtree rooted at A" and v(A) to mean "visit A", we can describe the complete traversal of this tree as follows:

```
t(A)                    traverse tree rooted at A
   v(A) = A                visit A
   t(B)                     traverse left subtree of A
      v(B) = B                 visit B
      t(empty)                 traverse left subtree of B
      t(empty)                 traverse right subtree of B
   t(C)                     traverse right subtree of A
      v(C) = C                 visit C
      t(empty)                 traverse left subtree of C
      t(empty)                 traverse right subtree of C
```

Since traversing a single node is the same as visiting it, we can write t(S) = S when S is a leaf. We can now describe the above traversal more simply like this:

```
t(A)                    traverse tree rooted at A
   v(A) = A                visit A
   t(B) = B                traverse left subtree of A
   t(C) = C                traverse right subtree of A
```

Now look at this tree:

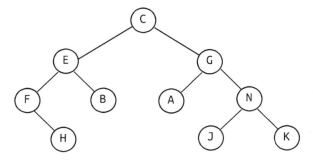

Its *pre-order* traversal is C E F H B G A N J K. Why?

- First we visit the root, **C**.
- Next, we traverse the left subtree of C. To do so, we visit the root, **E**, followed by the left subtree of E, then the right subtree of E.
- To do the left subtree of E, we visit **F**, followed by its left subtree (which is empty, so nothing to do), followed by the right subtree, **H**.
- Having traversed the left subtree of E, we now traverse its right subtree, **B**.
- We have completed the pre-order traversal of the left subtree of C. We now do its right subtree, starting with **G**.
- We continue with the left subtree of G, which is **A**, followed by the right subtree which gives us **N, J, K**.

This traversal can be described as follows:

```
t(C)                    traverse tree rooted at C
   v(C) = C                 visit C
   t(E)                     traverse left(C)
      v(E) = E                  visit E
      t(F)                      traverse left(E)
         v(F) = F                   visit F
         t(empty)                   traverse left(F)
         t(H) = H                   traverse right(F)
      t(B) = B                  traverse right(E)
   t(G)                     traverse right(C)
      v(G) = G                  visit G
      t(A) = A                  traverse left(G)
      t(N)                      traverse right(G)
         v(N) = N                   visit N
         t(J) = J                   traverse left(N)
         t(K) = K                   traverse right(N)
```

2. In-order traversal

(a) Traverse the left subtree in in-order

(b) Visit the root

(c) Traverse the right subtree in in-order

Here we traverse the left subtree first, then the root, and then the right subtree.

Consider this tree:

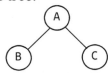

Its *in-order* traversal is B A C. We traverse the left subtree, **B**, followed by visiting the root, **A**, followed by traversing the right subtree, **C**.

In detail, this traversal can be described as follows:

```
t(A)                      traverse tree rooted at A
  t(B)                        traverse left(A)
    t(empty)                      traverse left(B)
    v(B) = B                      visit B
    t(empty)                      traverse right(B)
  v(A) = A                    visit A
  t(C)                        traverse right(A)
    t(empty)                      traverse left(C)
    v(C) = C                      visit C
    t(empty)                      traverse right(C)
```

Using t(S) = v(S) = S for a leaf node S, the traversal becomes this:

```
t(A)                      traverse tree rooted at A
  t(B) = B                    traverse left(A)
  v(A) = A                    visit A
  t(C) = C                    traverse right(A)
```

Consider this tree:

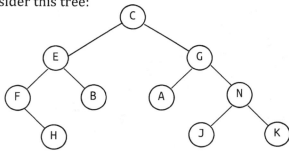

The *in-order* traversal is F H E B C A G J N K. Why?

- First we traverse the left subtree of C. This subtree has root, E. To traverse *this* subtree, we must traverse *its* left subtree, rooted at F.

- The left subtree of F is empty so there's nothing to do; we can now visit **F** and then traverse its right subtree, **H**.

- Having done the left subtree of E, we can visit **E**. We then proceed to the right subtree of E, which is rooted at B. Since B has no left subtree, we can visit **B**. Since B has no right subtree, we have completed traversing the left subtree of C.

- We visit **C**. We then traverse its right subtree, rooted at G.

- We continue by traversing the left subtree of G, which is **A**. We then visit **G**, followed by the traversal of its right subtree, which gives us **J, N, K**.

This traversal can be described as follows:

```
t(C)                        traverse tree rooted at C
    t(E)                        traverse left(C)
        t(F)                        traverse left(E)
            t(empty)                    traverse left(F)
            v(F) = F                    visit F
            t(H) = H                    traverse right(F)
        v(E) = E                    visit E
        t(B) = B                    traverse right(E)
    v(C) = C                    visit C
    t(G)                        traverse right(C)
        t(A) = A                    traverse left(G)
        v(G) = G                    visit G
        t(N)                        traverse right(G)
            t(J) = J                    traverse left(N)
            v(N) = N                    visit N
            t(K) = K                    traverse right(N)
```

It is worth noting that the first node in in-order can be found by going as far left as possible (by following left pointers from the root). The last node in in-order can be found by going as far right as possible (by following right pointers from the root).

3. Post-order traversal

(a) Traverse the left subtree in post-order

(b) Traverse the right subtree in post-order

(c) Visit the root

Here we traverse the left subtree first, followed by the right subtree and then we visit the root. It is useful to note that the root will always be the last node in post-order.

Consider this tree:

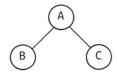

Its *post-order* traversal is B C A. We traverse the left subtree, **B**, followed by traversing the right subtree, **C**, followed by visiting the root, **A**.

In detail, this traversal can be described as follows:

```
t(A)                        traverse tree rooted at A
    t(B)                        traverse left(A)
        t(empty)                    traverse left(B)
        t(empty)                    traverse right(B)
        v(B) = B                    visit B
    t(C)                        traverse right(A)
        t(empty)                    traverse left(C)
        t(empty)                    traverse right(C)
        v(C) = C                    visit C
    v(A) = A                    visit A
```

Using t(S) = v(S) = S for a leaf node S, the traversal becomes this:

```
t(A)                    traverse tree rooted at A
    t(B) = B                traverse left(A)
    t(C) = C                traverse right(A)
    v(A) = A                visit A
```

Look at this tree:

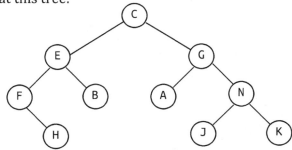

The *post-order* traversal is H F B E A J K N G C. Why?

- First we traverse the left subtree of C. This subtree has root, E. To traverse *this* subtree, we must traverse *its* left subtree, rooted at F.

- The left subtree of F is empty so there's nothing to do; we traverse its right subtree, **H**, and then visit **F**.

- Having done the left subtree of E, we proceed to the right subtree of E, which is rooted at B. We can visit **B** since it is a leaf. We can now visit **E**, completing the traversal of the left subtree of C.

- We must now traverse the right subtree of C, rooted at G.

- To do so, we traverse the left subtree of G, which is **A**. followed by the traversal of its right subtree, which gives us **J, K, N**. Having done its left and right subtrees, we can visit **G**, completing the traversal of the right subtree of C.

- Finally, having traversed its left and right subtrees, we visit **C**.

This traversal can be described as follows:

```
t(C)                    traverse tree rooted at C
    t(E)                    traverse left(C)
        t(F)                    traverse left(E)
            t(empty)                traverse left(F)
            t(H) = H                traverse right(F)
            v(F) = F                visit F
        t(B) = B                traverse right(E)
        v(E) = E                visit E
    t(G)                    traverse right(C)
        t(A) = A                traverse left(G)
        t(N)                    traverse right(G)
            t(J) = J                traverse left(N)
            t(K) = K                traverse right(N)
            v(N) = N                visit N
        v(G) = G                visit G
    v(C) = C                visit C
```

Note that the traversals derive their names from the place where we visit the root relative to the traversal of the left and right subtrees.

As another example, consider a binary tree that can represent the following arithmetic expression:

$(54 + 37) / (72 - 5 * 13)$

Here is the tree:

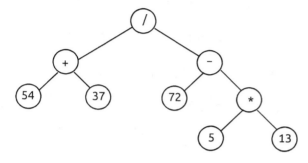

The leaves of the tree contain the operands, and the branch nodes contain the operators. Given a node containing an operator, the left subtree represents the first operand, and the right subtree represents the second operand.

The pre-order traversal is

/ + 54 37 – 72 * 5 13

The in-order traversal is

54 + 37 / 72 – 5 * 13

The post-order traversal is

54 37 + 72 5 13 * - /

The *post-order* traversal can be used in conjunction with a stack to evaluate the expression. The algorithm is as follows:

```
initialize a stack, S, to empty
while we have not reached the end of the traversal
    get the next item, x
    if x is an operand, push it onto S
    if x is an operator, pop its operands from S, apply the operator
        and push the result onto S
endwhile
pop S; // this is the value of the expression
```

Consider the post-order traversal:

54 37 + 72 5 13 * - /

It is evaluated as follows:

1. The next item is 54; push 54 onto S; S contains 54.
2. The next item is 37; push 37 onto S; S contains 54 37 (the top is on the right).

3. The next item is +; pop 37 and 54 from S; apply + to 54 and 37, giving 91; push 91 onto S; S contains 91.

4. The next item is 72; push 72 onto S; S contains 91 72.

5. The next items are 5 and 13; these are pushed onto S; S contains 91 72 5 13.

6. The next item is *; pop 13 and 5 from S; apply * to 5 and 13, giving 65; push 65 onto S; S contains 91 72 65.

7. The next item is –; pop 65 and 72 from S; apply – to 72 and 65, giving 7; push 7 onto S; S contains 91 7.

8. The next item is /; pop 7 and 91 from S; apply / to 91 and 7, giving 13; push 13 onto S; S contains 13.

9. We have reached the end of the traversal; we pop S, getting 13—the result of the expression.

Note that when operands are popped from the stack, the first one popped is the second operand, and the second one popped is the first operand. This does not matter for addition and multiplication but is important for subtraction and division.

5.4 Represent a Binary Tree

At a minimum, each node of a binary tree consists of three fields: a field containing the data at the node, a pointer to the left subtree, and a pointer to the right subtree. For example, suppose the data to be stored at each node is a word. We begin by defining a structure with three fields:

```
typedef struct treenode {
    NodeData data;
    struct treenode *left, *right;
} TreeNode, *TreeNodePtr;
```

To keep our options open, we have defined TreeNode in terms of a general data type that we call NodeData. Any program that wants to use TreeNode must provide its own definition of NodeData.

For example, if the data at a node is an integer, NodeData could be defined as follows:

```
typedef struct {
    int num;
} NodeData;
```

A similar definition can be used if the data is a character. But we are not restricted to single-field data. Any number of fields can be used. Later, we will write a program to do a frequency count of words in a passage. Each node will contain a word and its frequency count. For that program, we define NodeData as follows:

```
typedef struct {
    char word[MaxWordSize+1];
    int freq;
} NodeData;
```

In addition to the nodes of the tree, we will need to know the root of the tree. Keep in mind that once we know the root, we have access to all the nodes in the tree via the left and right pointers. Thus, a binary tree is defined solely by its root. We define a BinaryTree structure containing a single field, root, like this:

```
typedef struct {
    TreeNodePtr root;
} BinaryTree;
```

5.5 Build a Binary Tree

Let's write a function to build a binary tree. Suppose we want to build a tree consisting of a single node:

The data will be supplied as A @ @.

Each @ denotes the position of a null pointer. To build the following, we will supply the data as A B @ @ C @ @:

Each node is immediately followed by its left subtree and then its right subtree.

By comparison, to build the following, we will supply the data as A B @ C @ @ @.

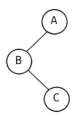

The two @s after C denote its left and right subtrees (null), and the last @ denotes the right subtree of A (null). And to build this tree:

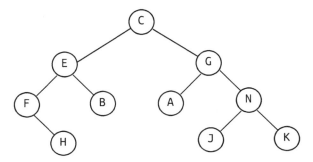

we supply the data like this: C E F @ H @ @ B @ @ G A @ @ N J @ @ K @ @.

Given data in this format, the function buildTree will build the tree and return a pointer to its root. It reads data from the file specified by in. MaxWordSize is a #defined constant.

```
TreeNodePtr buildTree(FILE * in) {
    char str[MaxWordSize+1];
    fscanf(in, "%s", str);
    if (strcmp(str, "@") == 0) return NULL;
    TreeNodePtr p = (TreeNodePtr) malloc(sizeof(TreeNode));
    strcpy(p -> data.word, str);
    p -> left = buildTree(in);
    p -> right = buildTree(in);
    return p;
} //end buildTree
```

The function uses the following definition of NodeData:

```
typedef struct {
    char word[MaxWordSize+1];
} NodeData;
```

Suppose the tree data is stored in the file btree.in. We can create a binary tree, bt, with the following code:

```
FILE * in = fopen("btree.in", "r");
BinaryTree bt;
bt.root = buildTree(in);
```

Having built the tree, we should want to check that it has been built properly. One way to do that is to perform traversals. Suppose we want to print the nodes of bt in pre-order. We could write a function as follows:

```
void preOrder(TreeNodePtr node) {
    void visit(TreeNodePtr);
    if (node != NULL) {
        visit(node);
        preOrder(node -> left);
        preOrder(node -> right);
    }
} //end preOrder
```

where visit could be written like this:

```
void visit(TreeNodePtr node) {
    printf("%s ", node -> data.word);
} //end visit
```

We could write similar functions for in-order and post-order.

Program P5.1 reads data from a file btree.in, builds a binary tree, and prints the pre-order, in-order, and post-order traversals of the tree.

Program P5.1

```
#include <stdio.h>
#include <string.h>
#include <stdlib.h>
```

```
#define MaxWordSize 20

typedef struct {
    char word[MaxWordSize+1];
} NodeData;

typedef struct treeNode {
    NodeData data;
    struct treeNode *left, *right;
} TreeNode, *TreeNodePtr;

typedef struct {
    TreeNodePtr root;
} BinaryTree;

int main() {
    TreeNodePtr buildTree(FILE *);
    void preOrder(TreeNodePtr);
    void inOrder(TreeNodePtr);
    void postOrder(TreeNodePtr);

    FILE * in = fopen("btree.in", "r");
    BinaryTree bt;
    bt.root = buildTree(in);
    printf("\nThe pre-order traversal is: ");
    preOrder(bt.root);
    printf("\n\nThe in-order traversal is: ");
    inOrder(bt.root);
    printf("\n\nThe post-order traversal is: ");
    postOrder(bt.root);
    printf("\n\n");
    fclose(in);
} // end main

TreeNodePtr buildTree(FILE * in) {
    char str[MaxWordSize+1];
    fscanf(in, "%s", str);
    if (strcmp(str, "@") == 0) return NULL;
    TreeNodePtr p = (TreeNodePtr) malloc(sizeof(TreeNode));
    strcpy(p -> data.word, str);
    p -> left = buildTree(in);
    p -> right = buildTree(in);
    return p;
} //end buildTree

void visit(TreeNodePtr node) {
    printf("%s ", node -> data.word);
} //end visit

void preOrder(TreeNodePtr node) {
    void visit(TreeNodePtr);
    if (node != NULL) {
        visit(node);
        preOrder(node -> left);
        preOrder(node -> right);
    }
} //end preOrder
```

127

```
void inOrder(TreeNodePtr node) {
    void visit(TreeNodePtr);
    if (node != NULL) {
        inOrder(node -> left);
        visit(node);
        inOrder(node -> right);
    }
} //end inOrder

void postOrder(TreeNodePtr node) {
    void visit(TreeNodePtr);
    if (node != NULL) {
        postOrder(node -> left);
        postOrder(node -> right);
        visit(node);
    }
} //end postOrder
```

Suppose btree.in contains this:

C E F @ H @ @ B @ @ G A @ @ N J @ @ K @ @

Program P5.1 builds this tree:

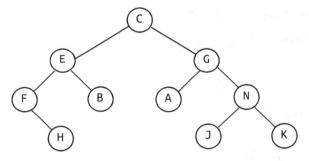

and prints this:

```
The pre-order traversal is: C E F H B G A N J K
The in-order traversal is: F H E B C A G J N K
The post-order traversal is: H F B E A J K N G C
```

The buildTree method is not restricted to single-character data; any string (not containing whitespace since we use %s to read the data) can be used.

For example, if btree.in contains this:

hat din bun @ @ fan @ @ rum kit @ @ win @ @

Program P5.1 prints the following:

```
The pre-order traversal is: hat din bun fan rum kit win
The in-order traversal is: bun din fan hat kit rum win
The post-order traversal is: bun fan din kit win rum hat
```

As an exercise, draw the tree and verify that these results are correct.

In passing, note that the in-order and pre-order traversals of a binary tree uniquely define that tree. The same holds for in-order and post-order. However, pre-order and post-order do not uniquely define the tree. In other words, it is possible to have two *different* trees A and B where the pre-order traversal of A is the same as the pre-order traversal of B, and the post-order traversal of A is the same as the post-order traversal of B. As an exercise, give an example of such a tree.

5.6 Binary Search Trees

Consider one possible binary tree built with the three-letter words shown in Figure 5-3.

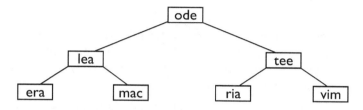

Figure 5-3. Binary search tree with some three-letter words

This is a special kind of binary tree. It has the property that, given *any* node, a word in the left subtree is "smaller," and a word in the right subtree is "greater" than the word at the node. (Here, *smaller* and *greater* refer to alphabetical order.)

Such a tree is called a *binary search tree* (BST). It facilitates the search for a given key using a method of searching similar to the binary search of a sorted array.

Consider the search for ria. Starting at the root, ria is compared with ode. Since ria is greater (in alphabetical order) than ode, we can conclude that if it is in the tree, it must be in the right subtree. It must be so since all the nodes in the left subtree are smaller than ode.

Following the right subtree of ode, we next compare ria with tee. Since ria is smaller than tee, we follow the left subtree of tee. We then compare ria with ria, and the search ends successfully.

But what if we were searching for fun?

- fun is smaller than ode, so we go left.
- fun is smaller than lea, so we go left again.
- fun is greater than era, so we must go right.

But since the right subtree of era is empty, we can conclude that fun is not in the tree. If it is necessary to add fun to the tree, note that we have also found the place where it must be added. It must be added as the right subtree of era, as shown in Figure 5-4.

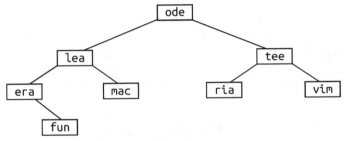

Figure 5-4. BST after adding fun

Thus, not only does the binary search tree facilitate searching, but if an item is not found, it can be easily inserted. It combines the speed advantage of a binary search with the easy insertion of an item into a linked list.

The tree drawn in Figure 5-3 is the optimal binary search tree for the seven given words. This means that it is the best possible tree for these words in the sense that no shallower binary tree can be built from these words. It gives the same number of comparisons to find a key as a binary search on a sorted linear array containing these words.

But this is not the only possible search tree for these words. Suppose the words come in one at a time, and as each word comes in, it is added to the tree in such a way that the tree remains a binary search tree. The final tree built will depend on the order in which the words come in. For example, suppose the words come in this order:

```
mac  tee  ode  era  ria  lea  vim
```

Initially the tree is empty. When mac comes in, it becomes the root of the tree.

- tee comes next and is compared with mac. Since tee is greater, it is inserted as the right subtree of mac.
- ode comes next and is greater than mac, so we go right; ode is smaller than tee, so it inserted as the left subtree of tee.
- era is next and is smaller than mac, so it is inserted as the left subtree of mac.

The tree built so far is shown in Figure 5-5.

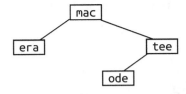

Figure 5-5. BST after adding mac, tee, ode, era

- ria is next and is greater than mac, so we go right; it is smaller than tee, so we go left; it is greater than ode, so it is inserted as the right subtree of ode.

Following this procedure, lea is inserted as the right subtree of era, and vim is inserted as the right subtree of tee, giving the final tree shown in Figure 5-6.

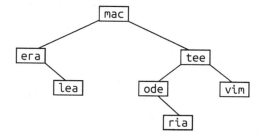

Figure 5-6. BST after adding all seven words

Note that the tree obtained is quite different from the optimal search tree. The number of comparisons required to find a given word has also changed. For instance, ria now requires four comparisons; it required three previously, and lea now requires three as opposed to two previously. But it's not all bad news; era now requires two as compared to three previously.

It can be proved that if the words come in random order, then the average search time for a given word is approximately 1.4 times the average for the optimal search tree, that is, $1.4\log_2 n$, for a tree of n nodes.

But what about the worst case? If the words come in alphabetical order, then the tree built will be that shown in Figure 5-7.

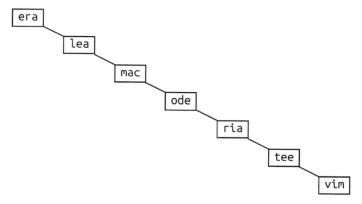

Figure 5-7. A degenerate tree

Searching such a tree is reduced to a sequential search of a linked list. This kind of tree is called a *degenerate* tree. Certain orders of the words will give some very unbalanced trees. As an exercise, draw the trees obtained for the following orders of the words:

- vim tee ria ode mac lea era
- era vim lea tee mac ria ode
- vim era lea tee ria mac ode
- lea mac vim tee era ria ode

5.7 Build a Binary Search Tree

We now write a function to find or insert an item in a binary search tree. Assuming the previous definitions of TreeNode and BinaryTree, we write the function findOrInsert. The function searches the tree for a NodeData item, d. If it is found, it returns a pointer to the node. If it is not found, the item is inserted in the tree in its appropriate place, and the function returns a pointer to the new node.

```
TreeNodePtr findOrInsert(BinaryTree bt, NodeData d) {
//searches for d; if found, return pointer to node containing d
//else insert a node containing d and return pointer to new node
    TreeNodePtr newTreeNode(NodeData);

    if (bt.root == NULL) return newTreeNode(d);
    TreeNodePtr curr = bt.root;
    int cmp;
    while ((cmp = strcmp(d.word, curr -> data.word)) != 0) {
        if (cmp < 0) { //try left
            if (curr -> left == NULL) return curr -> left = newTreeNode(d);
            curr = curr -> left;
        }
        else { //try right
            if (curr -> right == NULL) return curr -> right = newTreeNode(d);
            curr = curr -> right;
        }
    }
    //d is in the tree; return pointer to the node
    return curr;
} //end findOrInsert
```

The creation of a new node is delegated to newTreeNode.

```
TreeNodePtr newTreeNode(NodeData d) {
    TreeNodePtr p = (TreeNodePtr) malloc(sizeof(TreeNode));
    p -> data = d;
    p -> left = p -> right = NULL;
    return p;
} //end newTreeNode
```

This allocates storage for the node, stores d in the data field, and sets the left and right pointers to NULL. It returns a pointer to the node created.

5.7.1 Word Frequency Count

We will illustrate the ideas developed so far by writing a program to do a frequency count of the words in a passage. We will store the words in a binary search tree. The tree is searched for each incoming word. If the word is not found, it is added to the tree, and its frequency count is set to 1. If the word is found, then its frequency count is incremented by 1. At the end of the input, an in-order traversal of the tree gives the words in alphabetical order.

First, we must define the NodeData structure. This will consist of two fields: a word and its frequency. Here is the definition:

```
typedef struct {
    char word[MaxWordSize+1];
    int freq;
} NodeData;
```

For our program, we will define a word to be any consecutive sequence of uppercase or lowercase letters. All words are converted to lowercase before processing. We will write a function called getWord to read a word.

The gist of the algorithm for building the search tree is as follows:

```
create empty tree; set root to NULL
while (there is another word) {
    get the word
    search for word in tree; insert if necessary and set frequency to 0
    add 1 to frequency //for an old word or a newly inserted one
}
print words and frequencies
```

We now write Program P5.2 to do the frequency count of words in the file wordFreq.in. It simply reflects the algorithm.above.

Program P5.2

```
#include <stdio.h>
#include <string.h>
#include <stdlib.h>
#include <ctype.h>
#define MaxWordSize 20

typedef struct {
    char word[MaxWordSize+1];
    int freq;
} NodeData;

typedef struct treeNode {
    NodeData data;
    struct treeNode *left, *right;
} TreeNode, *TreeNodePtr;

typedef struct {
    TreeNodePtr root;
} BinaryTree;

int main() {
    int getWord(FILE *, char[]);
    TreeNodePtr newTreeNode(NodeData);
    NodeData newNodeData(char [], int);
    TreeNodePtr findOrInsert(BinaryTree, NodeData);
    void inOrder(FILE *, TreeNodePtr);

    char word[MaxWordSize+1];
    FILE * in = fopen("wordFreq.in", "r");
    FILE * out = fopen("wordFreq.out", "w");
```

```
    BinaryTree bst;
    bst.root = NULL;

    while (getWord(in, word) != 0) {
        if (bst.root == NULL)
            bst.root = newTreeNode(newNodeData(word, 1));
        else {
            TreeNodePtr node = findOrInsert(bst, newNodeData(word, 0));
            node -> data.freq++;
        }
    }

    fprintf(out, "\nWords        Frequency\n\n");
    inOrder(out, bst.root); fprintf(out, "\n\n");
    fclose(in);
    fclose(out);
} // end main

int getWord(FILE * in, char str[]) {
// stores the next word, if any, in str; word is converted to lowercase
// returns 1 if a word is found; 0, otherwise
    char ch;
    int n = 0;
    // read over non-letters
    while (!isalpha(ch = getc(in)) && ch != EOF) ; //empty while body
    if (ch == EOF) return 0;
    str[n++] = tolower(ch);
    while (isalpha(ch = getc(in)) && ch != EOF)
        if (n < MaxWordSize) str[n++] = tolower(ch);
    str[n] = '\0';
    return 1;
} // end getWord

TreeNodePtr findOrInsert(BinaryTree bt, NodeData d) {
//searches for d; if found, return pointer to node containing d
//else insert a node containing d and return pointer to new node
    TreeNodePtr newTreeNode(NodeData);

    if (bt.root == NULL) return newTreeNode(d);
    TreeNodePtr curr = bt.root;
    int cmp;
    while ((cmp = strcmp(d.word, curr -> data.word)) != 0) {
        if (cmp < 0) { //try left
            if (curr -> left == NULL) return curr -> left = newTreeNode(d);
            curr = curr -> left;
        }
        else { //try right
            if (curr -> right == NULL) return curr -> right = newTreeNode(d);
            curr = curr -> right;
        }
    } //end while
    //d is in the tree; return pointer to the node
    return curr;
} //end findOrInsert

TreeNodePtr newTreeNode(NodeData d) {
    TreeNodePtr p = (TreeNodePtr) malloc(sizeof(TreeNode));
    p -> data = d;
    p -> left = p -> right = NULL;
    return p;
} //end newTreeNode
```

```
void inOrder(FILE * out, TreeNodePtr node) {
    if (node!= NULL) {
        inOrder(out, node -> left);
        fprintf(out, "%-15s %2d\n", node -> data.word, node -> data.freq);
        inOrder(out, node -> right);
    }
} //end inOrder

NodeData newNodeData(char str[], int n) {
    NodeData temp;
    strcpy(temp.word, str);
    temp.freq = n;
    return temp;
} //end newNodeData
```

Since newTreeNode and findOrInsert require NodeData structures as arguments, we must create a NodeData structure from a given word to pass as the argument. The function newNodeData stores a given word and frequency in a NodeData structure and returns the structure. It is used as shown in the while loop in main.

An in-order traversal of the search tree yields the words in alphabetical order.

Suppose the file wordFreq.in contains the following data (from *If* by *Rudyard Kipling*):

```
If you can dream—and not make dreams your master;
    If you can think—and not make thoughts your aim;
If you can meet with Triumph and Disaster
    And treat those two impostors just the same...
If you can fill the unforgiving minute
    With sixty seconds' worth of distance run,
Yours is the Earth...
```

When Program P5.2 was run with this data, it sent the following output to the file worFreq.out:

Words	Frequency
aim	1
and	4
can	4
disaster	1
distance	1
dream	1
dreams	1
earth	1
fill	1
if	4
impostors	1
is	1
just	1
make	2
master	1
meet	1
minute	1
not	2
of	1

```
run             1
same            1
seconds         1
sixty           1
the             3
think           1
those           1
thoughts        1
treat           1
triumph         1
two             1
unforgivin      1
with            2
worth           1
you             4
your            2
yours           1
```

5.8 A Cross-Reference Program

We now consider a slightly more difficult problem than keeping a count of word frequencies. Given an English passage, we want to create a cross-reference listing of the words in the passage. More specifically, the output consists of the lines in the passage, numbered starting at 1; this is followed by an alphabetical listing of the words, and each word is followed by the line number(s) in which it appears. If it appears more than once on a given line, the line number is repeated. For example, given the following passage from *The Prophet* by Kahlil Gibran (shown here with the lines numbered, which must be done by the program):

```
 1.        Farewell to you and the youth I have
 2.    spent with you.
 3.        It was but yesterday we met in a dream.
 4.        You have sung to me in my aloneness,
 5.    and I of your longings have built a tower
 6.    in the sky.
 7.        But now our sleep has fled and our dream
 8.    is over, and it is no longer dawn.
 9.        The noontide is upon us and our half
10.    waking has turned to fuller day, and we
11.    must part.
12.        If in the twilight of memory we should
13.    meet once more, we shall speak again together
14.    and you shall sing to me a deeper song.
15.        And if our hands should meet in another
16.    dream we shall build another tower in the
17.    sky.
```

the program must produce the following output:

Words	Line numbers
a	3, 5, 14
again	13
aloneness	4

and	1, 5, 7, 8, 9, 10, 14, 15
another	15, 16
build	16
built	5
but	3, 7
dawn	8
day	10
deeper	14
dream	3, 7, 16
farewell	1
fled	7
fuller	10
half	9
hands	15
has	7, 10
have	1, 4, 5
i	1, 5
if	12, 15
in	3, 4, 6, 12, 15, 16
is	8, 8, 9
it	3, 8
longer	8
longings	5
me	4, 14
meet	13, 15
memory	12
met	3
more	13
must	11
my	4
no	8
noontide	9
now	7
of	5, 12
once	13
our	7, 7, 9, 15
over	8
part	11
shall	13, 14, 16
should	12, 15
sing	14
sky	6, 17
sleep	7
song	14
speak	13
spent	2
sung	4
the	1, 6, 9, 12, 16
to	1, 4, 10, 14
together	13
tower	5, 16
turned	10
twilight	12
upon	9
us	9
waking	10
was	3
we	3, 10, 12, 13, 16
with	2
yesterday	3

```
you                    1,  2,  4,  14
your                   5
youth                  1
```

We will use a binary search tree to store the words. This will facilitate searching for a word as well as printing the words in alphabetical order. Compared to the word frequency program, the new problem here is how to store the line numbers.

What complicates matters is that some words may appear on several lines while others may appear on just one or two. Our solution is to keep a linked list of line numbers for each word. Thus each node of the tree will contain a pointer to a linked list node containing the first line number in which the word occurs. The line number nodes will have the format

lineNum	next

where next points to the cell containing the next line number in which the word occurs (NULL, if none). To use such nodes, we declare a structure ListNode as follows:

```
typedef struct listNode {
    int lineNum;
    struct listNode *next;
} ListNode, *ListNodePtr;
```

Now the 'node data' for the tree will consist of two fields, as follows:

```
typedef struct {
    char word[MaxWordSize+1];
    ListNodePtr firstLine;
} NodeData;
```

The function newNodeData now becomes this:

```
NodeData newNodeData(char str[]) {
    NodeData temp;
    strcpy(temp.word, str);
    temp.firstLine = NULL;
    return temp;
} //end newNodeData
```

Assume the data is stored in a file, passage.in. We can read a line of data from the file with this:

```
FILE * in = fopen("passage.in", "r");
fgets(line, max, in);
```

fgets is used to read an entire string from the file in, up to, and including, the next newline character. The character array line must have at least max elements. Characters are read from in and stored in line until *newline* is encountered or max-1 characters have been stored, whichever comes first. If *newline* is encountered and max-1 characters have not yet been stored, \n is added to line. In either case, line is terminated with \0.

If at least one character (other than \0) is stored in line, fgets returns line (which is, in effect, a pointer to the characters stored). If end-of-file is encountered and no characters have been stored in line, fgets returns NULL.

The following code will read the passage and number the lines:

```
while (fgets(line, MaxLine, in) != NULL)
//MaxLine is a #defined constant
    fprintf(out, "%3d. %s", ++currentLine, line);
    //currentLine = 0, initially
```

Having read a line of input, we will use a modified version of getWord to get the words, one at a time, from the line. We will use an int variable p to keep track of our position in line. We declare it as static so that it retains its value between calls to getWord. When the end of the line is reached, p is reset to 0.

The following code will process the words on a line:

```
while (getWord(line, word) != 0) {
    if (bst.root == NULL)
        bst.root = node = newTreeNode(newNodeData(word));
    else
        node = findOrInsert(bst, newNodeData(word));
    ListNodePtr ptr = newListNode(currentLine);
    ptr -> next = node -> data.firstLine;
    node -> data.firstLine = ptr;
}
```

This fetches the next word on the line and checks for it in the binary search tree. A ListNode with the current line number is created and added at the *head* of the list of line numbers for the word. Thus the line numbers are stored in reverse order. However, we will *print* them in the correct order by printing the line number list in reverse order.

The output is produced by doing an in-order traversal of the search tree. All the details are shown in Program P5.3.

Program P5.3

```
#include <stdio.h>
#include <ctype.h>
#include <string.h>
#define MaxWordSize 20
#define MaxLine 101

typedef struct listNode {
    int lineNum;
    struct listNode *next;
} ListNode, *ListNodePtr;

typedef struct {
    char word[MaxWordSize+1];
    ListNodePtr firstLine;
} NodeData;

typedef struct treeNode {
    NodeData data;
    struct treeNode *left, *right;
} TreeNode, *TreeNodePtr;

typedef struct {
    TreeNodePtr root;
} BinaryTree;
```

```
int main() {
    int getWord(char[], char[]);
    TreeNodePtr newTreeNode(NodeData);
    NodeData newNodeData(char []);
    TreeNodePtr findOrInsert(BinaryTree, NodeData), node;
    ListNodePtr newListNode(int);
    void inOrder(FILE *, TreeNodePtr);
    char word[MaxWordSize+1];
    char line[MaxLine];
    int currentLine = 0;

    FILE * in = fopen("passage.in", "r");
    FILE * out = fopen("passage.out", "w");
    BinaryTree bst;
    bst.root = NULL;

    while (fgets(line, MaxLine, in) != NULL) {
        fprintf(out, "%3d. %s", ++currentLine, line);
        //extract words from the current line
        while (getWord(line, word) != 0) {
            if (bst.root == NULL)
                bst.root = node = newTreeNode(newNodeData(word));
            else
                node = findOrInsert(bst, newNodeData(word));
            ListNodePtr ptr = newListNode(currentLine);
            ptr -> next = node -> data.firstLine;
            node -> data.firstLine = ptr;
        }
    }
    fprintf(out, "\nWords                    Line numbers\n\n");
    inOrder(out, bst.root);
    fclose(in); fclose(out);
} // end main

int getWord(char line[], char str[]) {
// finds the next word in line and stores it in str
// returns 1 if a word is found; 0, otherwise
    static int p = 0; //p retains its value between calls to getWord
    char ch;
    int n = 0;
    // skip over non-letters
    while (line[p] != '\0' && !isalpha(line[p])) p++;
    if (line[p] == '\0') return p = 0; //reset p for next line
    str[n++] = tolower(line[p++]);
    while (isalpha(line[p])) {
        if (n < MaxWordSize) str[n++] = tolower(line[p]);
        p++;
    }
    str[n] = '\0';
    return 1;
} // end getWord

TreeNodePtr findOrInsert(BinaryTree bt, NodeData d) {
//searches for d; if found, return pointer to node containing d
//else insert a node containing d and return pointer to new node
    TreeNodePtr newTreeNode(NodeData);

    if (bt.root == NULL) return newTreeNode(d);
    TreeNodePtr curr = bt.root;
```

```
      int cmp;
      while ((cmp = strcmp(d.word, curr -> data.word)) != 0) {
          if (cmp < 0) { //try left
              if (curr -> left == NULL) return curr -> left = newTreeNode(d);
              curr = curr -> left;
          }
          else { //try right
              if (curr -> right == NULL) return curr -> right = newTreeNode(d);
              curr = curr -> right;
          }
      }
      //d is in the tree; return pointer to the node
      return curr;
} //end findOrInsert

TreeNodePtr newTreeNode(NodeData d) {
      TreeNodePtr p = (TreeNodePtr) malloc(sizeof(TreeNode));
      p -> data = d;
      p -> left = p -> right = NULL;
      return p;
} //end newTreeNode

void inOrder(FILE * out, TreeNodePtr node) {
      void printAWord(FILE *, TreeNodePtr);
      if (node!= NULL) {
          inOrder(out, node -> left);
          printAWord(out, node);
          inOrder(out, node -> right);
      }
} //end inOrder

void printAWord(FILE * out, TreeNodePtr pt) {
      void printLineNumbers(FILE *, ListNodePtr);
      fprintf(out, "%-20s", pt -> data.word);
      printLineNumbers(out, pt -> data.firstLine -> next); //print all except first
      fprintf(out, "%3d\n", pt -> data.firstLine -> lineNum); //print first
} //end printAWord

void printLineNumbers(FILE * out, ListNodePtr top) {
//line numbers are in reverse order; print list reversed
      if (top != NULL) {
          printLineNumbers(out, top -> next);
          fprintf(out, "%3d,", top -> lineNum);
      }
} //end printLineNumbers

NodeData newNodeData(char str[]) {
      NodeData temp;
      strcpy(temp.word, str);
      temp.firstLine = NULL;
      return temp;
} //end newNodeData

ListNodePtr newListNode(int lineNo) {
      ListNodePtr p = (ListNodePtr) malloc(sizeof(ListNode));
      p -> lineNum = lineNo;
      p -> next = NULL;
      return p;
} //end newListNode
```

5.9 Non-Recursive Traversals

So far, we have written pre-order, in-order and post-order traversals using recursive methods. We now perform these traversals using non-recursive algorithms. We start with in-order.

As we move down the tree, we will need some way to get back up the tree. One way to do this is to stack the nodes on the way down. When needed, we will take nodes off the stack to retrace our steps. Here is the algorithm:

Algorithm for in-order traversal

```
initialize a stack S to empty
curr = root
finished = false
while (not finished) {
    while (curr != null) {
        push curr onto S
        curr = left(curr)
    }
    if (S is empty) finished = true
    else {
        pop S into curr
        visit curr
        curr = right(curr)
    } //endif
} //endwhile
```

Given this tree:

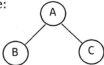

the algorithm will traverse it as follows:

We set S to empty, curr to A (actually a pointer to A but we will ignore the difference in the example) and finished to false.

- curr is not null; we push A onto S and set curr to left(A), that is, B; S contains A.
- curr is not null; we push B onto S and set curr to left(B), that is, null; S contains A B.
- Since curr is null, we exit the while and check if S is empty; it is not, so we pop B into curr and visit B; we then set curr to right(B), that is, null; S contains A.
- Control goes to the outer while and then to the inner while; since curr is null, we exit the loop immediately and check if S is empty; it is not, so we pop A into curr and visit A; we then set curr to right(A), that is, C; S is empty.
- Control goes to the outer while and then to the inner while; curr is C, so we push C onto S and set curr to left(C), that is, null; S contains C.
- Since curr is null, we exit the while and check if S is empty; it is not, so we pop C into curr and visit C; we then set curr to right(C), that is, null; S is empty.

- Control goes to the outer `while` and then to the inner `while`; since `curr` is `null`, we exit the loop immediately and check if S is empty; it is, so we set `finished` to `true` and the algorithm terminates having visited the nodes in the order B A C.

The algorithm can be easily modified to perform a pre-order traversal. Just move `visit curr` so it becomes the first statement in the inner `while` loop, which should now read:

```
while (curr != null) {
    visit curr
    push curr onto S
    curr = left(curr)
}
```

As an exercise, walk through the algorithm to do a pre-order traversal of this tree:

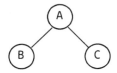

Post-order is a bit more difficult. For instance, in the above tree, we meet A as we go down the left and we meet A when we come back up from the left. However, we cannot visit A until we have traversed its right subtree. So A has to be stacked again to be met (and visited) when we come back up from the right subtree.

In other words, A will be taken off the stack twice and can only be visited after the second time. We need to distinguish between the first and the second time.

One solution is to push (A, 0) onto S the first time. When we pop an item, we check the second argument. If it is 0, we replace it by 1 and push the item back onto S. If it is 1, we are seeing the item for the second time so we visit it. Here is the algorithm:

Algorithm for post-order traversal

```
initialize a stack S to empty
curr = root
finished = false
while (not finished) {
    while (curr != null) {
        push (curr, 0) onto S
        curr = left(curr)
    }
    if (S is empty) finished = true
    else {
        pop S into (temp, t)
        if (t == 1) visit temp
        else {
            push (temp, 1) onto S
            curr = right(temp)
        }
    } //end else
} //end while (not finished)
```

5.9.1 Implement Post-Order

We now write a program to perform a non-recursive post-order traversal of a binary tree. We will assume the stack implementation described in Section 4.4 is stored in an "include" file, stack.h.

What kind of stack items would we need? As indicated in the algorithm above, each stack item consists of two fields: a TreeNodePtr and an integer. We define StackData as follows:

```
typedef struct {
    TreeNodePtr tnode;
    int meet;
} StackData;
```

Given these, we write Program P5.4 to build a binary tree and perform a *non-recursive post-order traversal.* It uses the buildTree function from Section 5.5. For this program, a tree node consists of just a string so NodeData is defined accordingly.

Program P5.4

```
#include <stdio.h>
#include <string.h>
#define MaxWordSize 20

typedef struct {
    char word[MaxWordSize+1];
} NodeData;

typedef struct treeNode {
    NodeData data;
    struct treeNode *left, *right;
} TreeNode, *TreeNodePtr;

typedef struct {
    TreeNodePtr root;
} BinaryTree;

typedef struct {
    TreeNodePtr tnode;
    int meet;
} StackData;

#include <stack.h>

int main() {
    TreeNodePtr buildTree(FILE *);
    void postOrder(TreeNodePtr);

    FILE * in = fopen("btree.in", "r");
    BinaryTree bt;
    bt.root = buildTree(in);

    printf("\nThe post-order traversal is: ");
    postOrder(bt.root);
    printf("\n\n");
    fclose(in);
} //end main
```

```
void postOrder(TreeNodePtr root) {
    StackData newStackData(TreeNodePtr, int);
    Stack S = initStack();
    TreeNodePtr curr = root;
    int finished = 0;
    while (!finished) {
        while (curr != NULL) {
            push(S, newStackData(curr, 0));
            curr = curr -> left;
        }
        if (empty(S)) finished = 1;
        else {
            StackData temp = pop(S);
            if (temp.meet == 1) printf("%s ", temp.tnode -> data.word);
            else {
                push(S, newStackData(temp.tnode, 1));
                curr = temp.tnode -> right;
            }
        } //end else
    } //end while (!finished)
} //end postOrder

StackData newStackData(TreeNodePtr tnp, int n) {
    StackData temp;
    temp.tnode = tnp;
    temp.meet = n;
    return temp;
} //end newStackData

TreeNodePtr buildTree(FILE * in) {
    char str[MaxWordSize+1];
    fscanf(in, "%s", str);
    if (strcmp(str, "@") == 0) return NULL;
    TreeNodePtr p = (TreeNodePtr) malloc(sizeof(TreeNode));
    strcpy(p -> data.word, str);
    p -> left = buildTree(in);
    p -> right = buildTree(in);
    return p;
} //end buildTree
```

Suppose btree.in contains this: C E F @ H @ @ B @ @ G A @ @ N J @ @ K @ @

Program P5.4 builds this tree:

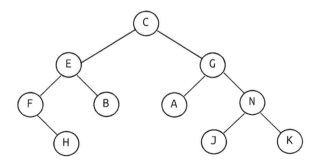

and prints this: The post-order traversal is: H F B E A J K N G C

5.10 Build Binary Tree with Parent Pointers

We have seen how to perform pre-order, in-order and post-order traversals using recursion (which is implemented using a stack) or an explicit stack. We now look at a third possibility. First, let us build the tree so that it contains "parent" pointers.

Each node now contains an additional field—a pointer to its parent. The parent field of the root will be null. For example, in the tree below, H's parent field points to F, A's parent field points to G and G's parent field points to C.

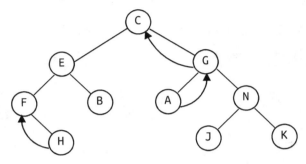

To accommodate parent pointers, we declare TreeNode as follows:

```
typedef struct treeNode {
    NodeData data;
    struct treeNode *left, *right, *parent;
} TreeNode, *TreeNodePtr;
```

We rewrite buildTree as follows:

```
TreeNodePtr buildTree(FILE * in) {
    char str[MaxWordSize+1];
    fscanf(in, "%s", str);
    if (strcmp(str, "@") == 0) return NULL;
    TreeNodePtr p = (TreeNodePtr) malloc(sizeof(TreeNode));
    strcpy(p -> data.word, str);
    p -> left = buildTree(in);
    if (p -> left != null) p -> left -> parent = p;
    p -> right = buildTree(in);
    if (p -> right != null) p -> right -> parent = p;
    return p;
} //end buildTree
```

After we build the left subtree of a node p, we check if it is null. If it is, there is nothing further to do. If it is not, and q is its root, we set the parent of q to p. Similar remarks apply to the right subtree.

With parent fields, we can do traversals without needing a stack. For example, we can perform an in-order traversal as follows:

```
get the first node in in-order; call it "node"
while (node is not null) {
    visit node
    get next node in in-order
}
```

Given the non-null root of a tree, we can find the first node in in-order with this:

```
TreeNodePtr node = root;
while (node -> left != NULL) node = node -> left;
```

We go as far left as possible. When we can't go any further, we have reached the first node in in-order. Here, node will point to the first node in in-order.

The main problem to solve is the following: given a pointer to any node, return a pointer to its *in-order successor* (that is, the node which comes after it in in-order), if any. The last node in in-order will have no successor.

There are two cases to consider:

1. If the node has a non-empty right subtree, then its in-order successor is the first node in in-order of that right subtree. We can find it with the following code:

   ```
   if (node -> right != NULL) {
       node = node -> right;
       while (node -> left != NULL) node = node -> left;
       return node;
   }
   ```

   For example, consider the following tree:

   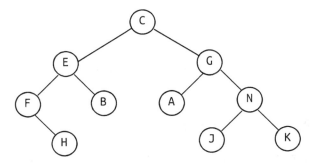

   The in-order successor of G is found by going right once (to N) and then as far left as possible (to J). J is the in-order successor of G.

2. If the node has an empty right subtree, then its in-order successor is one of its ancestors. Which one? It's the lowest ancestor for which the given node is in its *left* subtree. For example, what is the in-order successor of B?

   We look at B's parent, E. Since B is in the right subtree of E, it is not E.

   We then look at E's parent, C. Since E (and hence, B) is in the left subtree of C, we conclude that C is the in-order successor of B.

   Note, however, that K, being the last node in in-order, has no successor. If we follow parent pointers from K, we never find one with K in its left subtree. In this case, our function will return NULL.

Using these ideas, we write inOrder and inOrderSuccessor to perform an in-order traversal of a binary tree with parent pointers:

```
void inOrder(TreeNodePtr node) {
    TreeNodePtr inOrderSuccessor(TreeNodePtr);
    if (node == NULL) return;
    //find first node in in-order
    while (node -> left != NULL) node = node -> left;
    while (node != NULL) {
        printf("%s ", node -> data.word);
        node = inOrderSuccessor(node);
    }
} //end inOrder

TreeNodePtr inOrderSuccessor(TreeNodePtr node) {
    if (node -> right != NULL) {
        node = node -> right;
        while (node -> left != NULL) node = node -> left;
        return node;
    }
    //node has no right subtree; search for the lowest ancestor of
    //the node for which the node is in the ancestor's left subtree
    //return NULL if there is no successor
    //(node is the last in in-order)
    TreeNodePtr parent = node -> parent;
    while (parent != NULL && parent -> right == node) {
        node = parent;
        parent = node -> parent;
    }
    return parent;
} //end inOrderSuccessor
```

As an exercise, write similar functions to perform pre-order and post-order traversals. We will write a program to test these functions in the next section.

5.10.1 Build BST with Parent Pointers

Previously, we wrote a function findOrInsert to build a binary *search* tree. We now re-write the function to build a *search* tree with parent pointers.

```
TreeNodePtr findOrInsert(BinaryTree bt, NodeData d) {
//Searches the tree for d; if found, returns a pointer to the node.
//If not found, d is added and a pointer to the new node returned.
//The parent field of d is set to point to its parent.
    TreeNodePtr newTreeNode(NodeData), curr, node;
    int cmp;
    if (bt.root == NULL) {
        node = newTreeNode(d);
        node -> parent = NULL;
        return node;
    }
    curr = bt.root;
```

```
    while ((cmp = strcmp(d.word, curr -> data.word)) != 0) {
        if (cmp < 0) { //try left
            if (curr -> left == NULL) {
                curr -> left  = newTreeNode(d);
                curr -> left -> parent = curr;
                return curr -> left;
            }
            curr = curr -> left;
        }
        else { //try right
            if (curr -> right == NULL)  {
                curr -> right = newTreeNode(d);
                curr -> right -> parent = curr;
                return curr -> right;
            }
            curr = curr -> right;
        } //end else
    } //end while
    //d is in the tree; return pointer to the node
    return curr;
} //end findOrInsert
```

When we need to add a node (N, say) to the tree, if curr points to the node from which N will hang, we simply set the parent field of N to curr.

We can test findOrInsert and inOrder with Program P5.5. It simply reads words from a file words.in, builds the search tree and performs an in-order traversal to print the words in alphabetical order.

For example, if words.in contains the following:

mac tee ode era ria lea vim

Program P5.5 builds the binary search tree, with parent pointers, like this:

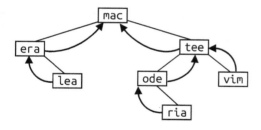

and prints

The in-order traversal is: era lea mac ode ria tee vim

Program P5.5

```
#include <stdio.h>
#include <string.h>
#define MaxWordSize 20

typedef struct {
    char word[MaxWordSize+1];
} NodeData;
```

```
typedef struct treeNode {
    NodeData data;
    struct treeNode *left, *right, *parent;
} TreeNode, *TreeNodePtr;

typedef struct {
    TreeNodePtr root;
} BinaryTree;

int main() {
    TreeNodePtr newTreeNode(NodeData);
    NodeData newNodeData(char []);
    TreeNodePtr findOrInsert(BinaryTree, NodeData);
    void inOrder(TreeNodePtr);

    char word[MaxWordSize+1];

    FILE * in = fopen("words.in", "r");

    BinaryTree bst;
    bst.root = NULL;

    while (fscanf(in, "%s", word) == 1)
        if (bst.root == NULL) bst.root = newTreeNode(newNodeData(word));
        else findOrInsert(bst, newNodeData(word));

    printf("\nThe in-order traversal is: ");
    inOrder(bst.root);
    printf("\n\n");
    fclose(in);
} //end main

TreeNodePtr newTreeNode(NodeData d) {
    TreeNodePtr p = (TreeNodePtr) malloc(sizeof(TreeNode));
    p -> data = d;
    p -> left = p -> right = p -> parent = NULL;
    return p;
} //end newTreeNode

NodeData newNodeData(char str[]) {
    NodeData temp;
    strcpy(temp.word, str);
    return temp;
} //end newNodeData

TreeNodePtr findOrInsert(BinaryTree bt, NodeData d) {
//Searches the tree for d; if found, returns a pointer to the node.
//If not found, d is added and a pointer to the new node returned.
//The parent field of d is set to point to its parent.

    TreeNodePtr newTreeNode(NodeData), curr, node;
    int cmp;
    if (bt.root == NULL) {
        node = newTreeNode(d);
        node -> parent = NULL;
        return node;
    }
    curr = bt.root;
```

```
        while ((cmp = strcmp(d.word, curr -> data.word)) != 0) {
            if (cmp < 0) { //try left
                if (curr -> left == NULL) {
                    curr -> left  = newTreeNode(d);
                    curr -> left -> parent = curr;
                    return curr -> left;
                }
                curr = curr -> left;
            }
            else { //try right
                if (curr -> right == NULL)  {
                    curr -> right = newTreeNode(d);
                    curr -> right -> parent = curr;
                    return curr -> right;
                }
                curr = curr -> right;
            } //end else
        } //end while
        //d is in the tree; return pointer to the node
        return curr;
} //end findOrInsert

void inOrder(TreeNodePtr node) {
    TreeNodePtr inOrderSuccessor(TreeNodePtr);
    if (node == NULL) return;
    //find first node in in-order
    while (node -> left != NULL) node = node -> left;
    while (node != NULL) {
        printf("%s ", node -> data.word);
        node = inOrderSuccessor(node);
    }
} //end inOrder

TreeNodePtr inOrderSuccessor(TreeNodePtr node) {
    if (node -> right != NULL) {
        node = node -> right;
        while (node -> left != NULL) node = node -> left;
        return node;
    }
    //node has no right subtree; search for the lowest ancestor of the
    //node for which the node is in the ancestor's left subtree
    //return NULL if there is no successor (node is the last in in-order)
    TreeNodePtr parent = node -> parent;
    while (parent != NULL && parent -> right == node) {
        node = parent;
        parent = node -> parent;
    }
    return parent;
} //end inOrderSuccessor
```

5.11 Level-Order Traversal

In addition to pre-order, in-order and post-order, another useful order is *level-order*. Here we traverse the tree level by level, starting at the root. At each level, we traverse the nodes from left to right. For example, given this tree:

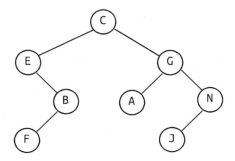

The level-order traversal is C E G B A N F J.

To perform a level-order traversal, we will need to use a queue. The following algorithm shows how:

```
add the root to the queue, Q
while (Q is not empty) {
    remove item at the head of Q and store in p
    visit p
    if (left(p) is not null) add left(p) to Q
    if (right(p) is not null) add right(p) to Q
}
```

For the tree above, the following occurs:

- Put C on Q.
- Q is not empty, so remove and visit C; add E and G to Q which now has E G.
- Q is not empty, so remove and visit E; add B to Q which now has G B.
- Q is not empty; remove and visit G; add A and N to Q which now has B A N.
- Q is not empty; remove and visit B; add F to Q which now has A N F.
- Q is not empty; remove and visit A; add nothing to Q which now has N F.
- Q is not empty; remove and visit N; add J to Q which now has F J.
- Q is not empty; remove and visit F; add nothing to Q which now has J.
- Q is not empty; remove and visit J; add nothing to Q which is now empty.
- Q is empty; the traversal ends having visited C E G B A N F J.

We will use the Queue header file from Section 4.6.2. To use it, we will define QueueData like this:

```
typedef struct {
    TreeNodePtr tnode;
} QueueData;
```

and create a QueueData structure with this:

```
QueueData newQueueData(TreeNodePtr tnp) {
    QueueData temp;
    temp.tnode = tnp;
    return temp;
} //end newQueueData
```

Using Queue and QueueData, we can write levelOrder as follows:

```c
void levelOrder(TreeNodePtr root) {
    QueueData newQueueData(TreeNodePtr);
    Queue Q = initQueue();
    enqueue(Q, newQueueData(root));
    while (!empty(Q)) {
        QueueData temp = dequeue(Q);
        printf("%s ", temp.tnode -> data.word);;
        if (temp.tnode -> left != NULL)
            enqueue(Q, newQueueData(temp.tnode -> left));
        if (temp.tnode -> right != NULL)
            enqueue(Q, newQueueData(temp.tnode -> right));
    } //end while
} //end levelOrder
```

We can test levelOrder with Program P5.6.

Program P5.6

```c
#include <stdio.h>
#define MaxWordSize 20

typedef struct {
    char word[MaxWordSize+1];
} NodeData;

typedef struct treeNode {
    NodeData data;
    struct treeNode *left, *right;
} TreeNode, *TreeNodePtr;

typedef struct {
    TreeNodePtr root;
} BinaryTree;

typedef struct {
    TreeNodePtr tnode;
} QueueData;

#include <queue.h>

int main() {
    TreeNodePtr buildTree(FILE *);
    void levelOrder(TreeNodePtr);
    FILE * in = fopen("btree.in", "r");
    BinaryTree bt;
    bt.root = buildTree(in);
    printf("\nThe level-order traversal is: ");
    levelOrder(bt.root);
    printf("\n\n");
    fclose(in);
}

TreeNodePtr buildTree(FILE * in) {
    char str[MaxWordSize+1];
    fscanf(in, "%s", str);
```

```
    if (strcmp(str, "@") == 0) return NULL;
    TreeNodePtr p = (TreeNodePtr) malloc(sizeof(TreeNode));
    strcpy(p -> data.word, str);
    p -> left = buildTree(in);
    p -> right = buildTree(in);
    return p;
} //end buildTree

QueueData newQueueData(TreeNodePtr tnp) {
    QueueData temp;
    temp.tnode = tnp;
    return temp;
} //end newQueueData

void levelOrder(TreeNodePtr root) {
    QueueData newQueueData(TreeNodePtr);
    Queue Q = initQueue();
    enqueue(Q, newQueueData(root));
    while (!empty(Q)) {
        QueueData temp = dequeue(Q);
        printf("%s ", temp.tnode -> data.word);;
        if (temp.tnode -> left != NULL)
            enqueue(Q, newQueueData(temp.tnode -> left));
        if (temp.tnode -> right != NULL)
            enqueue(Q, newQueueData(temp.tnode -> right));
    } //end while
} //end levelOrder
```

Suppose btree.in contains the following (the description of the tree shown at the start of this section):

```
C E @ B F @ @ @ G A @ @ N J @ @ @
```

The program will print this:

```
The level-order traversal is: C E G B A N F J
```

5.12 Some Useful Binary Tree Functions

We will now show you how to write some functions that return information about a binary tree. The functions are all recursive, reflecting the recursive nature of a binary tree.

The first counts the number of nodes in a tree.

```
int numNodes(TreeNodePtr root) {
    if (root == NULL) return 0;
    return 1 + numNodes(root -> left) + numNodes(root -> right);
} //end numNodes
```

If bt is a BinaryTree, numNodes(bt.root) returns the number of nodes in the tree.

The next function returns the number of leaves in the tree:

```
int numLeaves(TreeNodePtr root) {
    if (root == NULL) return 0;
    if (root-> left == NULL && root-> right == NULL) return 1;
    return numLeaves(root-> left) + numLeaves(root-> right);
} //end numLeaves
```

And the next returns the height of the tree:

```
int height(TreeNodePtr root) {
    if (root == NULL) return 0;
    return 1 + max(height (root-> left), height (root-> right));
} //end height
```

max can be defined as follows:

```
#define max(a, b) ((a) > (b) ? (a) : (b))
```

You are advised to test these functions on some sample trees to verify that they return the correct values.

5.13 Binary Search Tree Deletion

Consider the problem of deleting a node from a binary search tree (BST) so that it remains a BST. There are three cases to consider.

1. The node is a leaf
2. (a) The node has no left subtree

   (b) The node has no right subtree
3. The node has non-empty left and right subtrees

We illustrate these cases using the BST shown in Figure 5-8.

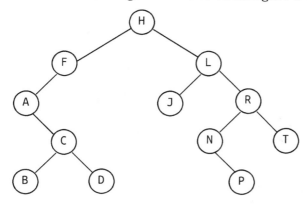

Figure 5-8. A binary search tree

Case 1 is easy. For example, to delete P, we simply set the right subtree of N to null. Case 2 is also easy. To delete A (no left subtree), we replace it by C, its right subtree. And to delete F (no right subtree), we replace it by A, its left subtree.

155

Case 3 is a bit more difficult since we have to worry about what to do with two subtrees. For example, how do we delete L? One approach is to replace L by its in-order successor, N, which *must* have an empty left subtree. Why? Because, by definition, the in-order successor of a node is the first node (in in-order) in its right subtree. And this first node (in any non-empty tree) is found by going as far left as possible.

Since N has no left subtree, we will set its left link to the left subtree of L. We will set the left link of the parent of N (R in this case) to point to P, the right subtree of N. Finally, we will set the right link of N to point to the right subtree of L, giving the tree shown in Figure 5-9.

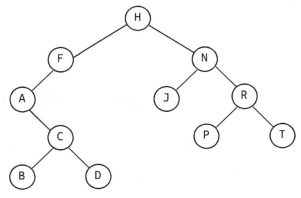

Figure 5-9 BST after deletion of L in BST 5.8

Another way to look at it is to imagine the contents of node N being copied into node L. And the left link of the parent of N (that is, R) is set to point to the right subtree of N (that is, P).

We will treat the node to be deleted as the root of a subtree. We will delete the root and return a pointer to the root of the reconstructed tree. The following is a function, written in pseudocode, to perform this task:

```
deleteNode(TreeNode T) {
    if (T == null) return null
    if (right(T) == null) return left(T)  //cases 1 and 2b
    R = right(T)
    if (left(T) == null) return R //case 2a

    if (left(R) == null) {
        left(R) == left(T
        return R
    }

    while (left(R) != null) {//loop executed at least once
        P = R
        R = left(R)
    }
```

```
//R is pointing to the in-order successor of T;
//P is its parent
left(R) = left(T)
left(P) = right(R)
right(R) = right(T)
return R
```

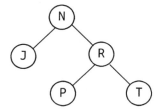

} //end deleteNode

Suppose we call deleteNode with a pointer to the node L in Figure 5-14 as argument. The function will delete L and return a pointer to the following tree:

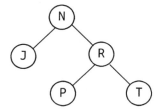

Since L was the right subtree of H, we can now set the right subtree of H to point to this tree.

5.14 Create 'Best' BST from Sorted Keys

Previously, we saw that if keys come in sorted order, the binary search tree algorithm creates a degenerate tree. In this section, we show how to create a 'best' binary search tree if we *know* that the keys come in order.

Consider the following complete binary tree of 15 nodes:

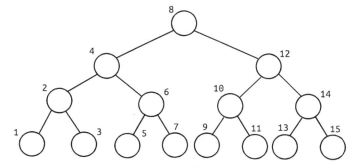

The nodes are labelled in *in-order* sequence. Note the following:

- The leaves are labelled with odd numbers.
- The nodes at the next level up start with 2; the difference between their labels is 4.
- The nodes at the next level up start with 4; the difference between their labels is 8.
- The node at the next level up is the root and is labelled 8.

For the purpose of this discussion, we consider the leaves to be at level 0 and the level increases as we go *up* the tree. Thus the root is at level 3.

Important observation: the level of a node is the highest power of two that divides its label. Thus,

- The highest power of 2 that divides odd numbers is 0; the leaves are at level 0.
- The highest power of 2 that divides 2, 6, 10, 14 is 1; these nodes are at level 1.
- The highest power of 2 that divides 4 and 12 is 2; these nodes are at level 2.
- The highest power of 2 that divides 8 is 3; this node is at level 3.

It follows that if we know the position of an item in the in-order sequence, we can calculate its level in the final tree. The following function will do this:

```
int getNodeLevel(int n) {
//returns the highest power of 2 that divides n
    int level = 0;
    while (n % 2 == 0) {
        level++;
        n /= 2;
    }
    return level;
} //end getNodeLevel
```

In order to build the search tree, we will need to keep track of the last node processed at each level. We will use an array lastNode for this. We will let MaxHeight represent the highest tree that we will cater for; a value of 20 will let us build a tree with just over a million nodes ($2^{20} - 1 = 1,048,575$, to be exact).

Initially, we will set all the entries in lastNode to NULL, indicating that no nodes have been processed at any level. We will use the following algorithm to build a search tree of integers:

```
numNodes = 0
while (there is another integer) {
    read next integer, num
    TreeNodePtr tp = newTreeNode(num)
    ++numNodes
    level = getNodeLevel(numNodes)
    //if the new node is a leaf, its left pointer
    //is set to null (already done)
    //else its left pointer is set to the entry
    //in lastNode one level lower
    if (level > 0) tp -> left = lastNode[level - 1]
    //if lastNode[level+1] exists and has a null right link,
    //set it to new node
    if (lastNode[level+1] != NULL && lastNode[level+1] -> right == NULL)
        lastNode[level+1] -> right = tp
    //the current node is the last node processed at this level
    lastNode[level] = tp
} //end while
the root of the tree is the last non-null entry in lastNode
```

Consider how this algorithm will build a search tree with the following 7 integers:

```
12  17  24  31  36  42  47
```

When 12 is read, numNodes is set to 1 so level is 0. None of the if conditions is true since level is 0 and lastNode[1] is NULL. We have a tree of 1 node:

and lastNode[0] is set to point to this node; we will use the notation ^12 to refer to the node containing 12. Note that when the node is created, its left and right pointers are set to null.

Next, 17 is read, numNodes is set to 2 so level is 1. Since level is greater than 0, the left pointer of the new node is set to lastNode[0], that is, ^12.

We have a tree of 2 nodes:

lastNode[0] is ^12 and lastNode[1] is ^17. These are the last nodes processed at levels 0 and 1, respectively.

Next, 24 is read, numNodes is set to 3 so level is 0. Since lastNode[1] is not null and the right link of ^17 *is* null, we set the right link of ^17 to ^24, the new node. We have a tree of 3 nodes:

lastNode[0] is now ^24 and lastNode[1] is still ^17.

Next, 31 is read, numNodes is set to 4 so level is 2. Since level is greater than 0, the left pointer of the new node is set to lastNode[1], that is, ^17.

We have a tree of 4 nodes:

lastNode[0] is ^24, lastNode[1] is ^17 and lastNode[2] is ^31.

Next, 36 is read, numNodes is set to 5 so level is 0. Now, lastNode[1] is not null but its right link is *not* null, so nothing further happens. We have this:

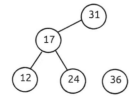

lastNode[0] is ^36, lastNode[1] is ^17 and lastNode[2] is ^31.

Next, 42 is read, numNodes is set to 6 so level is 1. Since level is greater than 0, the left pointer of the new node is set to lastNode[0], that is, ^36. Since lastNode[2] is not null and the right link of ^31 *is* null, we set the right link of ^31 to ^42, the new node.We have the following:

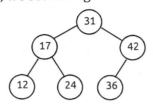

lastNode[0] is ^36, lastNode[1] is ^42 and lastNode[2] is ^31.

Finally, 47 is read, numNodes is set to 7 so level is 0. Since lastNode[1] is not null and the right link of ^42 *is* null, we set the right link of ^42 to ^47, the new node. We now have the tree:

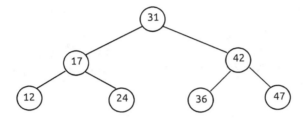

lastNode[0] is ^47, lastNode[1] is ^42 and lastNode[2] is ^31.

Since there are no more numbers, the algorithm terminates with the root of the tree being set to lastNode[2], the last non-null entry in lastNode. Thus, ^31 is properly designated as the root of the final tree.

The algorithm has built the best possible binary search tree for the 7 integers.

5.14.1 Build Best Almost Complete BST

As given, the algorithm will create the best possible binary search tree if the number of nodes is exactly $2^n - 1$, for some n. In other words, we will get the best tree if the number of nodes is the right amount for creating a *complete* binary tree.

If it is not, there may be some unconnected or isolated nodes after the last number is processed and we will have to do some extra work to tie them into the final tree.

For example, above, after 36 is processed, we have this situation:

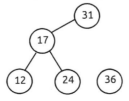

If there are no more numbers, we can complete the job by setting the right link of ^31 to ^36.

We can 'finalize' the tree after the algorithm above terminates using the following:

```
find the highest node, n, whose right subtree is null;
this right link is set to the highest node in lastNode
that is not already in the left subtree of n.
```

In this example, 'the highest node whose right subtree is null' is ^31; it is at level 2. Since lastNode[1] (^17) is in the left subtree of ^31 and lastNode[0] (^36) is not in the left subtree of ^31, the right link of ^31 is set to ^36.

For a more involved example, consider a tree being built with 21 integers. After the last integer has been processed, we will have the following:

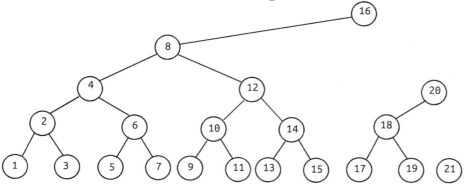

lastNode[0] is ^21, lastNode[1] is ^18, lastNode[2] is ^20, lastNode[3] is ^8 and lastNode[4] is ^16.

We will finalize this tree as follows:

- The highest node with a null right link is ^16; the highest node in lastNode that is not in the left subtree of ^16 is ^20; so the right link of ^16 is set to ^20.

We continue the process with node ^20, now the highest node with a null right link.

- The highest node in lastNode that is not in the left subtree of ^20 is ^21; so the right link of ^20 is set to ^21.

The process would normally continue with ^21 but this is a leaf so nothing further needs to be done.

The tree is now finalized with the root being ^16, the highest non-null entry in lastNode.

Based on the algorithm given earlier, we can write the function insertBestBST. It is shown as part of Program P5.7. The program also shows the function finalizeBestBST which finalizes the search tree. The program reads some sorted integers from a file, bestBST.in, creates the binary search tree based on the above discussion, and prints the pre-order, in-order and post-order traversals of the tree.

Program P5.7

```
#include <stdio.h>
#include <string.h>
#define MaxHeight 20
```

```
typedef struct {
    int num;
} NodeData;

typedef struct treeNode {
    NodeData data;
    struct treeNode *left, *right;
} TreeNode, *TreeNodePtr;

typedef struct {
    TreeNodePtr root;
} BinaryTree;

int main() {
    void preOrder(TreeNodePtr);
    void inOrder(TreeNodePtr);
    void postOrder(TreeNodePtr);
    void insertBestBST(int, TreeNodePtr[]);
    TreeNodePtr finalizeBestBST(TreeNodePtr []);
    int n;
    TreeNodePtr lastNode[MaxHeight];

    for (n = 0; n < MaxHeight; n++) lastNode[n] = NULL;

    FILE * in = fopen("bestBST.in", "r");
    BinaryTree bst;

    while (fscanf(in, "%d", &n) == 1)
        insertBestBST(n, lastNode);

    bst.root = finalizeBestBST(lastNode);

    printf("\nThe pre-order traversal is: ");
    preOrder(bst.root);
    printf("\n\nThe in-order traversal is: ");
    inOrder(bst.root);
    printf("\n\nThe post-order traversal is: ");
    postOrder(bst.root);
    printf("\n\n");
    fclose(in);
} // end main

int getNodeLevel(int n) {
//returns the highest power of 2 that divides n
    int level = 0;
    while (n % 2 == 0) {
        level++;
        n /= 2;
    }
    return level;
} //end getNodeLevel

void insertBestBST(int n, TreeNodePtr lastNode[]) {
    int getNodeLevel(int);
    TreeNodePtr newTreeNode(NodeData);
    NodeData newNodeData(int);
    static int numNodes = 0;

    TreeNodePtr p = newTreeNode(newNodeData(n));
    numNodes++;
```

```
        int level = getNodeLevel(numNodes);
        // left pointer of new node is null if it is a leaf
        // else it's the entry in lastNode one level lower than new node
        if (level > 0) p -> left = lastNode[level-1];
        // if lastNode[level+1] exists and has a null right link,
        // set it to the new node
        if (lastNode[level+1] != NULL)
            if (lastNode[level+1] -> right == NULL)
                lastNode[level+1] -> right = p;
        // the current node is the last node processed at this level
        lastNode[level] = p;
    } //end insertBestBST

    TreeNodePtr newTreeNode(NodeData d) {
        TreeNodePtr p = (TreeNodePtr) malloc(sizeof(TreeNode));
        p -> data = d;
        p -> left = p -> right = NULL;
        return p;
    } //end newTreeNode

    NodeData newNodeData(int n) {
        NodeData temp;
        temp.num = n;
        return temp;
    } //end newNodeData

    TreeNodePtr finalizeBestBST(TreeNodePtr lastNode[]) {
        int m, n = MaxHeight - 1;
        // find the last entry in lastNode that is non-null
        // this is the root
        while (n > 0 && lastNode[n] == NULL) n--;
        TreeNodePtr root = lastNode[n];

        while (n > 0) {
            // find the highest node, n, whose right subtree is null;
            // this right child is set to the highest node in lastNode
            // that is not already in the left subtree of n.
            if (lastNode[n] -> right != NULL) n--;
            else {
                // need to check left(n) and all right subtrees from there
                TreeNodePtr tn = lastNode[n] -> left;
                m = n - 1;
                // check if the node, tn, in left subtree is the same as
                // the last node processed at that level, lastNode[m]
                while (m >= 0 && tn == lastNode[m]) {
                    tn = tn -> right;
                    m--;
                }
                if (m >= 0) lastNode[n] -> right = lastNode[m];
                n = m;
            } //end else
        } //end while
        return root;
    } //end finalizeBST

    void visit(TreeNodePtr node) {
        printf("%d ", node -> data.num);
    } //end visit
```

```
void preOrder(TreeNodePtr node) {
   void visit(TreeNodePtr);
   if (node != NULL) {
      visit(node);
      preOrder(node -> left);
      preOrder(node -> right);
   }
} //end preOrder

void inOrder(TreeNodePtr node) {
   void visit(TreeNodePtr);
   if (node != NULL) {
      inOrder(node -> left);
      visit(node);
      inOrder(node -> right);
   }
} //end inOrder

void postOrder(TreeNodePtr node) {
   void visit(TreeNodePtr);
   if (node != NULL) {
      postOrder(node -> left);
      postOrder(node -> right);
      visit(node);
   }
} //end postOrder
```

Suppose bestBST.in contains these numbers: 10 15 23 32 41 46 52 59 63 71 84. Program P5.7 will build this tree:

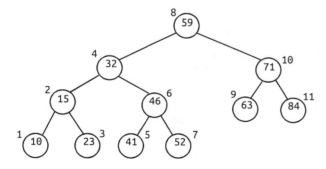

and print the following:

```
The pre-order traversal is: 59 32 15 10 23 46 41 52 71 63 84

The in-order traversal is: 10 15 23 32 41 46 52 59 63 71 84

The post-order traversal is: 10 23 15 41 52 46 32 63 84 71 59
```

If the numbers are given in sorted order, Program P5.7 builds a binary *search* tree. However, if the numbers are not in order, the program still builds the best binary tree but it will not be a search tree. It will be a tree whose in-order traversal is the same as the given order.

5.14.2 Build Best BST for Items in Random Order

Consider the problem of building the best binary search tree if the data items come in random order. We can do this as follows:

- Build a BST for the given order; this may or may not be a 'good' tree but it does not matter. All we want is a way to get the nodes in sorted order.
- Perform an in-order traversal of this BST; this will give the nodes in sorted order. As we 'visit' each node, pass it to `insertBestBST` which will build the best tree for items which come in sorted order.
- Call `finalizeBestBST` to 'finalize' the tree.

5.15 Array as Binary Tree Representation

A *complete* binary tree is one in which every nonleaf node has two nonempty subtrees and all leaves are at the same level. Figure 5-10 shows some complete binary trees.

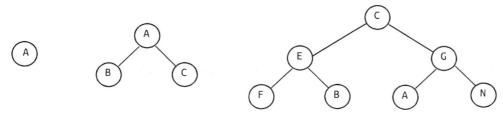

Figure 5-10. Complete binary trees

The first is a complete binary tree of height 1, the second is a complete binary tree of height 2, and the third is a complete binary tree of height 3. For a complete binary tree of height n, the number of nodes in the tree is $2^n - 1$.

Consider the third tree. Let's number the nodes as shown in Figure 5-11.

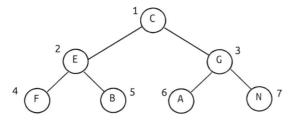

Figure 5-11. Numbering the nodes, level by level

Starting from 1 at the root, we number the nodes in order from top to bottom and from left to right at each level.

Observe that if a node has label n, its left subtree has label $2n$, and its right subtree has label $2n + 1$.

Suppose the nodes are stored in an array T[1..7], like this:

T

C	E	G	F	B	A	N
1	2	3	4	5	6	7

- T[1] is the root.
- The left subtree of T[i] is T[2i] if 2i <= 7 and null otherwise.
- The right subtree of T[i] is T[2i+1] if 2i+1 <= 7 and null otherwise.
- The parent of T[i] is T[i/2] (integer division).

Based on this, the array is a representation of a complete binary tree. In other words, given the array, we can easily construct the binary tree it represents.

An array represents a *complete* binary tree if the number of elements in the array is $2^n - 1$, for some n. If the number of elements is some other value, the array represents an *almost complete binary tree*.

An almost complete binary tree is one in which

    (a) All levels, except possibly the lowest, are completely filled.

    (b) The nodes at the lowest level (all leaves) are as far left as possible.

If the nodes are numbered as above, then all leaves will be labeled with consecutive numbers from $n/2 + 1$ to n. The last *nonleaf* node will have label $n/2$. For example, consider the tree with ten nodes drawn and labeled as in Figure 5-12.

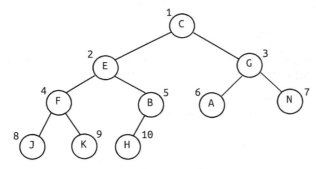

Figure 5-12. A tree of ten nodes labeled level by level

Note that the leaves are numbered from 6 to 10. If, for instance, H were the right subtree of B instead of the left, the tree would not be "almost complete" since the leaves on the lowest level would not be "as far left as possible".

The following array of size 10 can represent this almost complete binary tree:

T

C	E	G	F	B	A	N	J	K	H
1	2	3	4	5	6	7	8	9	10

In general, if the tree is represented by an array T[1..n], then

- T[1] is the root.

- The left subtree of T[i] is T[2i] if 2i <= n and null otherwise.
- The right subtree of T[i] is T[2i+1] if 2i+1 <= n and null otherwise.
- The parent of T[i] is T[i/2] (integer division).

Looked at another way, there is exactly one almost complete binary tree with *n* nodes, and an array of size *n* represents this tree.

An almost complete binary tree has no "holes" in it; there is no room to add a node between existing nodes. The only place to add a node is after the last one.

The tree in Figure 5-13 is not "almost complete" since there is a "hole" at the right subtree of B.

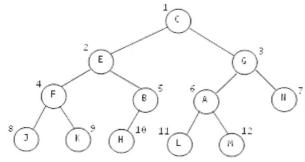

Figure 5-13. Empty right subtree of B makes this not "almost complete"

With the hole, the left subtree of A (in position 6) is *not* now in position 6*2 = 12, and the right subtree is not in position 6*2+1 =13. This relationship holds only when the tree is almost complete.

Given an array T[1..n] representing an almost complete binary tree with *n* nodes, we can perform an in-order traversal of the tree with the call inOrder(1, n) of the following function:

```
void inOrder(int h, int n) {
    if (h <= n) {
        inOrder(h * 2, n);
        visit(h); //or visit(T[h]), if you wish
        inOrder(h * 2 + 1, n);
    }
} //end inOrder
```

We can write similar functions for pre-order and post-order traversals.

By comparison to a complete binary tree, a *full binary tree* is one in which every node, except a leaf, has exactly two nonempty subtrees. Figure 5-14 is an example of a full binary tree.

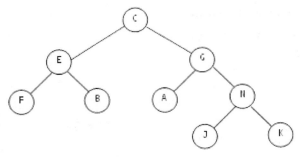

Figure 5-14. A full binary tree

Note that a complete binary tree is always full, but as shown in Figure 5-14, a full binary tree is not necessarily complete. An almost complete binary tree may or may not be full.

The tree in Figure 5-15 is almost complete but not full (G has *one* non-empty subtree).

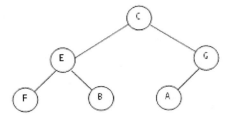

Figure 5-15. An almost complete but not full binary tree

However, if node A is removed, the tree will be almost complete *and* full.

In the next chapter, we will explain how to sort an array, using a method called *heapsort*, by interpreting it as an almost complete binary tree.

5.15.1 Represent General Binary Tree in Array

We can use an array to represent an arbitrary binary tree if we "fill out" the tree to make it (almost) complete. Consider the following tree:

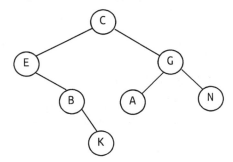

Wherever there is a null pointer we put an imaginary node, as shown here:

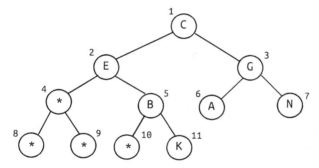

A node with an asterisk denotes an imaginary node. Note the imaginary node to the left of E. This, in turn, gives rise to two more in order to make the tree almost complete. The number at a node indicates the position in the array in which the node would be stored. Normally, we would add imaginary nodes to A and N but we omit them here since these would all come at the end of the array. In other words, the last element in the array would be the last real node (K, in this case).

If n (11 in the example) is the last entry in the array T, we have the following:

- T[1] is the root.
- The left subtree of T[i] is T[2i] unless 2i > n or T[2i] contains *, in which case the left subtree is empty.
- The right subtree of T[i] is T[2i+1] unless 2i+1 > n or T[2i+1] contains *, in which case the right subtree is empty.
- For nodes in the tree, the parent of T[i] is T[i/2] (integer division).

In the example, we use 11 array locations to store a tree consisting of 7 nodes. While *some* storage is used for imaginary nodes, the representation is compact and it is easy to find the left child, the right child and the parent of a node.

5.15.2 Build Binary Tree in an Array

We now show how to build a binary tree in an array. Given that data for the tree is in the same format as described in Section 5.5 (using @ to represent a null pointer), we write buildTree as follows:

```
int buildTree(FILE * in, char T[][MaxWordSize+1], int root) {
    char str[MaxWordSize+1];
    static int lastNode = 0;

    fscanf(in, "%s", str);
    if (strcmp(str, "@") == 0) {
        if (root <= MaxNodes) strcpy(T[root], "*");
        return;
    }
    if (root > MaxNodes) {
        printf("\nArray is too small to hold tree\n");
        exit(1);
    }
    if (root > lastNode) lastNode = root;
    strcpy(T[root], str);
```

```
    buildTree(in, T, root * 2);       //build the left subtree
    buildTree(in, T, root * 2 + 1);   //build the right subtree
    return lastNode;
} //end buildTree
```

Initially, root is 1. MaxNodes is the maximum number of nodes we cater for; we will store node values in T[1] to T[MaxNodes]. As the tree is built, the variable lastNode holds the last used position in T. When the tree is completely built, this value is returned by buildTree. A null pointer (indicated by *) is stored only if its position falls within MaxNodes.

For example, suppose we want to build the following tree:

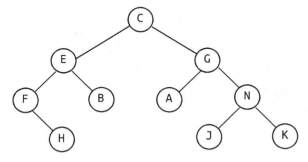

The data must be supplied as follows:

C E F @ H @ @ B @ @ G A @ @ N J @ @ K @ @

The function will create the following array:

T

C	E	G	F	B	A	N	*	H	*	*	*	*	J	K
1	2	3	4	5	6	7	8	9	10	11	12	13	14	15

But, for example, if the left subtree of G is null (A is not present), buildTree will create this:

T

C	E	G	F	B	*	N	*	H	*	*	?	?	J	K
1	2	3	4	5	6	7	8	9	10	11	12	13	14	15

T[12] and T[13], which would normally hold the children of the left subtree of G, are undefined since no values are ever stored there. However, this is not a problem since, in *processing* the tree (for example, doing a traversal) these locations will never be accessed.

Program P5.8 shows how to build a binary tree and perform a pre-order traversal.

Program P5.8

```
#include <stdio.h>
#include <string.h>
#define MaxWordSize 20
#define MaxNodes 100
int main() {
    int buildTree(FILE *, char[][MaxWordSize+1], int);
    void preOrder(char[][MaxWordSize+1], int, int);
```

```
    FILE * in = fopen("btree.in", "r");
    char T[MaxNodes+1][MaxWordSize+1];

    int n = buildTree(in, T, 1);
    printf("\nThe pre-order traversal is: ");
    preOrder(T, 1, n);
    printf("\n\n");
    fclose(in);
} // end main

int buildTree(FILE * in, char T[][MaxWordSize+1], int root) {
    char str[MaxWordSize+1];
    static int lastNode = 0;

    fscanf(in, "%s", str);
    if (strcmp(str, "@") == 0) {
        if (root <= MaxNodes) strcpy(T[root], "*");
        return;
    }
    if (root > MaxNodes) {
        printf("\nArray is too small to hold tree\n");
        exit(1);
    }
    if (root > lastNode) lastNode = root;
    strcpy(T[root], str);
    buildTree(in, T, root * 2);          //build the left subtree
    buildTree(in, T, root * 2 + 1);      //build the right subtree
    return lastNode;
} //end buildTree

void visit(char T[][MaxWordSize+1], int node) {
    printf("%s ", T[node]);
} //end visit

void preOrder(char T[][MaxWordSize+1], int root, int n) {
    //tree is stored in T[1] to T[n]
    void visit(char[][MaxWordSize+1], int);
    if (root <= n && strcmp(T[root], "*") != 0) { //if not null
        visit(T, root);
        preOrder(T, root * 2, n);
        preOrder(T, root * 2 + 1, n);
    }
} //end preOrder
```

Suppose btree.in contains this:

C E F @ H @ @ B @ @ G A @ @ N J @ @ K @ @

Program P5.8 will build the representation of the binary tree, above, and print this:

The pre-order traversal is: C E F H B G A N J K

You are urged to write functions for the other traversals.

EXERCISES 5

1. A binary tree consists of an integer key field and pointers to the left subtree, right subtree and parent. Write the declarations required for building a tree and code to create an empty tree.

2. Each node of a binary tree has fields `left`, `right`, key and `parent`.

    (a) Write a function to return the in-order successor of any given node x. Hint: if the right subtree of node x is empty and x has a successor y, then y is the lowest ancestor of x which contains x in its left subtree.

    (b) Write a function to return the pre-order successor of any given node x.

    (c) Write a function to return the post-order successor of any given node x.

    (d) Using these functions, write functions to perform the in-order, pre-order and post-order traversals of a given binary tree.

3. Do exercise 2 assuming the tree is stored in an array.

4. Write functions to implement the in-order and pre-order traversals of a binary tree using non-recursive algorithms.

5. Write a function which, given the root of a binary search tree, deletes the smallest node and returns a pointer to the root of the reconstructed tree.

6. Write a function which, given the root of a binary search tree, deletes the largest node and returns a pointer to the root of the reconstructed tree.

7. Write a function which, given the root of a binary search tree, deletes the root and returns a pointer to the root of the reconstructed tree. Write the function replacing the root by (i) its in-order successor and (ii) its in-order predecessor.

8. Store the following integers in an array `bst[1..15]` such that `bst` represents a complete binary search tree: 34 23 45 46 37 78 90 2 40 20 87 53 12 15 91.

    A function F1 outputs the in-order traversal of the above tree to a file and another function F2 reads the numbers from the file, one at a time, and reconstructs the tree. Write F1 and F2.

9. Draw a non-degenerate binary tree of 5 nodes such that the pre-order and level-order traversals produce identical results.

10. Write a function which, given the root of binary tree, returns the width of the tree, that is, the maximum number of nodes at any level.

11. Assume that the following keys are inserted in a binary search tree (BST) in the order given:
    56 30 61 39 47 35 75 13 21 64 26 73 18

    (a) Draw the tree obtained.

    (b) There is one almost complete BST for the above keys. Draw it.

    (c) List the keys in an order which will produce the almost complete BST.

    (d) Assuming that the almost complete tree is stored in a one-dimensional array `num[1..13]`, write a recursive function for printing the integers in post-order.

12. A binary search tree contains integers. For each of the following sequences, state whether it could be the sequence of values examined in searching for the number 36. If it cannot, state why.

    7 25 42 40 33 34 39 36
    92 22 91 24 89 20 35 36
    95 20 90 24 92 27 30 36
    7 46 41 21 26 39 37 24 36

13. An imaginary 'external' node is attached to each null pointer of a binary tree of n nodes. How many external nodes are there?

    If I is the sum of the levels of the original tree nodes and E is the sum of the levels of the external nodes, prove that $E - I = 2n$. (I is called the *internal path length*.)

    Write a recursive function which, given the root of a binary tree, returns I.

    Write a non-recursive function which, given the root of a binary tree, returns I.

14. Draw the binary tree whose in-order and post-order traversals of the nodes are as follows:

    In-order: G D P K E N F A T L

    Post-order: G P D K F N T A L E

15. Draw the binary tree whose in-order and pre-order traversals of the nodes are as follows:

    In-order: G D P K E N F A T L

    Pre-order: N D G K P E T F A L

16. Draw binary trees, T1 and T2, such that the pre-order traversal of T1 is the same as the pre-order traversal of T2 and the post-order traversal of T1 is the same as the post-order traversal of T2.

17. Write a recursive function which, given the root of a binary tree and a key, searches for the key using (i) a pre-order (ii) an in-order (iii) a post-order traversal. If found, return the node containing the key; otherwise, return null.

18. Each node of a *binary search tree* contains three fields—left, right and data—with their usual meanings; data is a positive integer field. Write an *efficient* function which, given the root of the tree and key, returns the *smallest* number in the tree which is *greater* than key. If there is no such number, return -1.

19. Write a program which takes a C program as input and outputs the program, numbering the lines, followed by an alphabetical cross-reference listing of all user identifiers; that is, a user identifier is followed by the numbers of all lines in which the identifier appears. If an identifier appears more than once in a given line, the line number must be repeated the number of times it appears.

    The cross-reference listing must not contain C reserved words, words within character strings or words within comments.

CHAPTER 6

■ ■ ■

Sorting

In this chapter, we will explain the following:

- How to sort a list of items using selection and insertion sort
- How to add a new item to a sorted list so that the list remains sorted
- How to sort an array of strings
- How to sort related (parallel) arrays
- How to search a sorted list using *binary search*
- How to search an array of strings
- How to write a program to do a frequency count of words in a passage
- How to merge two sorted lists to create one sorted list

6.1 Sorting

In this chapter, we discuss several methods for sorting a list of items. For completeness, we start with a brief review of the 'simple' methods—selection and insertion sort. We then take a detailed look at some faster methods—heapsort, mergesort, quicksort and Shell (diminishing increment) sort.

Sorting is the process by which a set of values are arranged in ascending or descending order. There are many reasons to sort. Sometimes we sort in order to produce more readable output (for example, to produce an alphabetical listing). A teacher may need to sort her students in order by name or by average score. If we have a large set of values and we want to identify duplicates, we can do so by sorting; the repeated values will come together in the sorted list.

Another advantage of sorting is that some operations can be performed faster and more efficiently with sorted data. For example, if data is sorted, it is possible to search it using binary search—this is much faster than using a sequential search. Also, merging two separate lists of items can be done much faster than if the lists were unsorted.

6.2 Selection Sort

Consider the following array:

num

57	48	79	65	15	33	52
0	1	2	3	4	5	6

Sorting num in ascending order using selection sort proceeds as follows:

1st pass

- Find the smallest number in positions 0 to 6; the smallest is 15, found in position 4.
- Interchange the numbers in positions 0 and 4. We get this:

num

15	48	79	65	57	33	52
0	1	2	3	4	5	6

2nd pass

- Find the smallest number in positions 1 to 6; the smallest is 33, found in position 5.
    - Interchange the numbers in positions 1 and 5. We get this:

num

15	33	79	65	57	48	52
0	1	2	3	4	5	6

3rd pass

- Find the smallest number in positions 2 to 6; the smallest is 48, found in position 5.
- Interchange the numbers in positions 2 and 5. We get this:

num

15	33	48	65	57	79	52
0	1	2	3	4	5	6

4th pass

- Find the smallest number in positions 3 to 6; the smallest is 52, found in position 6.
- Interchange the numbers in positions 3 and 6. We get this:

num

15	33	48	52	57	79	65
0	1	2	3	4	5	6

5th pass

- Find the smallest number in positions 4 to 6; the smallest is 57, found in position 4.
- Interchange the numbers in positions 4 and 4. We get this (no change):

num						
15	33	48	52	57	79	65
0	1	2	3	4	5	6

6th pass

- Find the smallest number in positions 5 to 6; the smallest is 65, found in position 6.
- Interchange the numbers in positions 5 and 6. We get this:

num						
15	33	48	52	57	65	79
0	1	2	3	4	5	6

and the array is now completely sorted.

If we let h go from 0 to 5, on each pass:

- We find the smallest number from positions h to 6.
- If the smallest number is in position s, we interchange the numbers in positions h and s.
- For an array of size n, we make n-1 passes. In our example, we sorted 7 numbers in 6 passes.

The following is an outline of the algorithm:

```
for h = 0 to n - 2
    s = position of smallest number from num[h] to num[n-1]
    swap num[h] and num[s]
endfor
```

We will need a function to return the position of the smallest number in an integer array. Here it is:

```
//find position of smallest from num[lo] to num[hi]
int getSmallest(int num[], int lo, int hi) {
    int small = lo;
    for (int h = lo + 1; h <= hi; h++)
        if (num[h] < num[small]) small = h;
    return small;
} //end getSmallest
```

We will also need a function to swap two elements in an *integer* array:

```
//swap elements num[i] and num[j]
void swap(int num[], int i, int j) {
    int hold = num[i];
    num[i] = num[j];
    num[j] = hold;
} //end swap
```

With getSmallest and swap, we can code the algorithm, above, as a function selectionSort. To emphasize that we can use any names for our parameters, we write the function to sort an integer array called list. To make it general, we also tell the function which *portion* of the array to sort by specifying subscripts lo and hi. Instead of the loop going from 0 to n-2 as in the algorithm, it now goes from lo to hi-1, just a minor change for greater flexibility.

```c
//sort list[lo] to list[hi] in ascending order
void selectionSort(int list[], int lo, int hi) {
    int getSmallest(int [], int, int);
    void swap(int [], int, int);
    for (int h = lo; h < hi; h++) {
        int s = getSmallest(list, h, hi);
        swap(list, h, s);
    }
} //end selectionSort
```

We now write Program P6.1 to test whether selectionSort works properly. The program requests up to 10 numbers (since the array is declared to be of size 10), stores them in the array num, calls selectionSort, then prints the sorted list.

Program P6.1

```c
#include <stdio.h>
#define MaxNum 10

int main() {
    void selectionSort(int [], int, int);
    int v, num[10];
    printf("Type up to 10 numbers followed by 0\n");
    int n = 0;
    scanf("%d", &v);
    while (v != 0 && n < MaxNum) {
        num[n++] = v;
        scanf("%d", &v);
    }
    //n numbers are stored from num[0] to num[n-1]
    selectionSort(num, 0, n-1);
    printf("\nThe sorted numbers are\n");
    for (int h = 0; h < n; h++) printf("%d ", num[h]);
    printf("\n");
} //end main

void selectionSort(int list[], int lo, int hi) {
//sort list[lo] to list[hi] in ascending order
    int getSmallest(int [], int, int);
    void swap(int [], int, int);
    for (int h = lo; h < hi; h++) {
        int s = getSmallest(list, h, hi);
        swap(list, h, s);
    }
} //end selectionSort

int getSmallest(int num[], int lo, int hi) {
//find position of smallest from num[lo] to num[hi]
    int small = lo;
    for (int h = lo + 1; h <= hi; h++)
        if (num[h] < num[small]) small = h;
    return small;
} //end getSmallest
```

```
void swap(int num[], int i, int j) {
//swap elements num[i] and num[j]
    int hold = num[i];
    num[i] = num[j];
    num[j] = hold;
} //end swap
```

The following is a sample run of the program:

```
Type up to 10 numbers followed by 0
57 48 79 65 15 33 52 0

The sorted numbers are
15 33 48 52 57 65 79
```

Comments on Program P6.1

As written, if the user enters more than 10 numbers before entering 0, only the first 10 will be sorted. To cater for more numbers, just change the value of MaxNum..

We have sorted an array in *ascending* order. We can sort num[0] to num[n-1] in *descending* order with the following algorithm:

```
for h = 0 to n - 2
    b = position of biggest number from num[h] to num[n-1]
    swap num[h] and num[b]
endfor
```

To find the *biggest* number in an array, we just need to change < to > in the function getSmallest (which should be renamed getBiggest, say) and change the variable small to big.

6.2.1 Analysis of Selection Sort

To find the smallest of k items, we make k-1 comparisons. On the first pass, we make n-1 comparisons to find the smallest of n items. On the second pass, we make n-2 comparisons to find the smallest of n-1 items. And so on, until the last pass where we make one comparison to find the smaller of two items. In general, on the kth pass, we make n-k comparisons to find the smallest of n-k+1 items. Hence:

total number of comparisons $= 1 + 2 + ... + n\text{-}1 = \frac{1}{2} n(n\text{-}1) \approx \frac{1}{2} n^2$

We say selection sort is of order $O(n^2)$ ("big O n squared"). The constant ½ is not important in "big O" notation since, as n gets very big, the constant becomes insignificant.

On each pass, we swap two items using three assignments. Since we make n-1 passes, we make $3(n\text{-}1)$ assignments in all. Using "big O" notation, we say that the number of assignments is $O(n)$. The constants 3 and 1 are not important as n gets large.

Does selection sort perform any better if there is order in the data? No. One way to find out is to give it a sorted list and see what it does. If you work through the algorithm, you will see that the method is oblivious to order in the data. It will make the same number of comparisons every time, regardless of the data.

As we will see, some sorting methods, such as *quicksort* and *mergesort* (see Sections 6.8 and 6.9) require extra array storage to implement them. Note that selection sort is performed "in place" in the given array and does not require additional storage.

As an exercise, modify the programming code so that it counts the number of comparisons and assignments made in sorting a list using selection sort.

6.3 Insertion Sort

Consider the same array as before:

num

57	48	79	65	15	33	52
0	1	2	3	4	5	6

Think of the numbers as cards on a table and picked up one at a time in the order in which they appear in the array. Thus, we first pick up 57, then 48, then 79, and so on, until we pick up 52. However, as we pick up each new number, we add it to our hand in such a way that the numbers in our hand are all sorted.

When we pick up 57, we have just one number in our hand. We consider one number to be sorted.

When we pick up 48, we add it in front of 57 so our hand contains

48 57

When we pick up 79, we place it after 57 so our hand contains

48 57 79

When we pick up 65, we place it after 57 so our hand contains

48 57 65 79

At this stage, four numbers have been picked up and our hand contains them in sorted order.

When we pick up 15, we place it before 48 so our hand contains

15 48 57 65 79

When we pick up 33, we place it after 15 so our hand contains

15 33 48 57 65 79

Finally, when we pick up 52, we place it after 48 so our hand contains

15 33 48 52 57 65 79

The numbers have been sorted in ascending order.

The method described illustrates the idea behind *insertion* sort. The numbers in the array will be processed one at a time, from left to right. This is equivalent to picking up the numbers from the table, one at a time. Since the first number, by itself, is sorted, we will process the numbers in the array starting from the second.

When we come to process num[h], we can assume that num[0] to num[h-1] are sorted. We then attempt to insert num[h] among num[0] to num[h-1] so that num[0] to num[h] are sorted. We will then go on to process num[h+1]. When we do so, our assumption that elements num[0] to num[h] are sorted will be true.

Sorting num in ascending order using insertion sort proceeds as follows:

1st pass

- Process num[1], that is, 48. This involves placing 48 so that the first two numbers are sorted; num[0] and num[1] now contain the following:

num

48	57
0	1

The rest of the array remains unchanged.

2nd pass

- Process num[2], that is, 79. This involves placing 79 so that the first three numbers are sorted; num[0] to num[2] now contain the following:

num

48	57	79
0	1	2

The rest of the array remains unchanged.

3rd pass

- Process num[3], that is, 65. This involves placing 65 so that the first four numbers are sorted; num[0] to num[3] now contain the following:

num

48	57	65	79
0	1	2	3

The rest of the array remains unchanged.

4th pass

- Process num[4], that is, 15. This involves placing 15 so that the first five numbers are sorted. To simplify the explanation, think of 15 as being taken out and stored in a simple variable (key, say) leaving a "hole" in num[4]. We can picture this as follows:

key

15

num

48	57	65	79		33	52
0	1	2	3	4	5	6

The insertion of 15 in its correct position proceeds as follows:

- Compare 15 with 79; it is smaller, so move 79 to location 4, leaving location 3 free. This gives the following:

key

15

num

48	57	65		79	33	52
0	1	2	3	4	5	6

- Compare 15 with 65; it is smaller, so move 65 to location 3, leaving location 2 free. This gives the following:

key

| 15 |

num

48	57		65	79	33	52
0	1	2	3	4	5	6

- Compare 15 with 57; it is smaller, so move 57 to location 2, leaving location 1 free. This gives the following:

key

| 15 |

num

48		57	65	79	33	52
0	1	2	3	4	5	6

- Compare 15 with 48; it is smaller, so move 48 to location 1, leaving location 0 free. This gives the following:

key

| 15 |

num

	48	57	65	79	33	52
0	1	2	3	4	5	6

- There are no more numbers to compare with 15, so it is inserted in location 0, giving the following:

key

| 15 |

num

15	48	57	65	79	33	52
0	1	2	3	4	5	6

We can express the logic of placing 15 (key) by comparing it with the numbers to its left, starting with the nearest one, like this. As long as key is less than num[k], for some k, we move num[k] to position num[k+1] and move on to consider num[k-1], providing it exists. It won't exist when k is actually 0. In this case, the process stops, and key is inserted in position 0.

5th pass

- Process num[5], that is, 33. This involves placing 33 so that the first six numbers are sorted. This is done as follows:
  - Store 33 in key, leaving location 5 free.
  - Compare 33 with 79; it is smaller, so move 79 to location 5, leaving location 4 free.
  - Compare 33 with 65; it is smaller, so move 65 to location 4, leaving location 3 free.
  - Compare 33 with 57; it is smaller, so move 57 to location 3, leaving location 2 free.
  - Compare 33 with 48; it is smaller, so move 48 to location 2, leaving location 1 free.
  - Compare 33 with 15; it is bigger, so insert 33 in location 1. This gives the following:

key

| 33 |

num

15	33	48	57	65	79	52
0	1	2	3	4	5	6

We can express the logic of placing 33 (key) by comparing it with the numbers to its left, starting with the nearest one, like this. As long as key is less than num[k], for some k, we move num[k] to position num[k+1] and move on to consider num[k-1], providing it exists. If key is greater than or equal to num[k] for some k, then key is inserted in position k+1. Here, 33 is greater than num[0] and so is inserted into num[1].

6th pass

- Process num[6], that is, 52. This involves placing 52 so that the first seven (all) numbers are sorted. This is done as follows:

  - Store 52 in key, leaving location 6 free.

  - Compare 52 with 79; it is smaller, so move 79 to location 6, leaving location 5 free.

  - Compare 52 with 65; it is smaller, so move 65 to location 5, leaving location 4 free.

  - Compare 52 with 57; it is smaller, so move 57 to location 4, leaving location 3 free.

  - Compare 52 with 48; it is bigger, so insert 52 in location 3. This gives the following:

key		num						
33		15	33	48	52	57	65	79
		0	1	2	3	4	5	6

The array is now completely sorted.

The following is an outline to sort the first n elements of an array, num, using insertion sort:

```
for h = 1 to n - 1 do
    insert num[h] among num[0] to num[h-1] so that
    num[0] to num[h] are sorted
endfor
```

Using this outline, we write the function insertionSort using the parameter list.

```
void insertionSort(int list[], int n) {
//sort list[0] to list[n-1] in ascending order
    for (int h = 1; h < n; h++) {
        int key = list[h];
        int k = h - 1; //start comparing with previous item
        while (k >= 0 && key < list[k]) {
            list[k + 1] = list[k];
            --k;
        }
        list[k + 1] = key;
    } //end for
} //end insertionSort
```

The while statement is at the heart of the sort. It states that as long as we are within the array (k >= 0) and the current number (key) is less than the one in the array (key < list[k]), we move list[k] to the right (list[k+1] = list[k]) and move on to the next number on the left (--k).

We exit the while loop if k is equal to -1 or if key is greater than or equal to list[k], for some k. In either case, key is inserted into list[k+1].

If k is -1, it means that the current number is smaller than all the previous numbers in the list and must be inserted in list[0]. But list[k+1] *is* list[0] when k is -1, so key is inserted correctly in this case.

The function sorts in ascending order. To sort in descending order, all we have to do is change < to > in the while condition, like this:

```
while (k >= 0 && key > list[k])
```

Now, a key moves to the left if it is *bigger*.

We write Program P6.2 to test whether insertionSort works correctly.

Program P6.2

```c
#include <stdio.h>
int main() {
    void insertionSort(int [], int);
    int v, num[10];
    printf("Type up to 10 numbers followed by 0\n");
    int n = 0;
    scanf("%d", &v);
    while (v != 0) {
        num[n++] = v;
        scanf("%d", &v);
    }
    //n numbers are stored from num[0] to num[n-1]
    insertionSort(num, n);
    printf("\nThe sorted numbers are\n");
    for (int h = 0; h < n; h++) printf("%d ", num[h]);
    printf("\n");
} //end main

void insertionSort(int list[], int n) {
//sort list[0] to list[n-1] in ascending order
    for (int h = 1; h < n; h++) {
        int key = list[h];
        int k = h - 1; //start comparing with previous item
        while (k >= 0 && key < list[k]) {
            list[k + 1] = list[k];
            --k;
        }
        list[k + 1] = key;
    } //end for
} //end insertionSort
```

The program requests up to 10 numbers (since the array is declared to be of size 10), stores them in the array num, calls insertionSort, then prints the sorted list. The following is a sample run of P9.2:

```
Type up to 10 numbers followed by 0
57 48 79 65 15 33 52 0

The sorted numbers are
15 33 48 52 57 65 79
```

Note that if the user enters more than ten numbers, the program will recognize this and sort only the first ten.

We could easily generalize insertionSort to sort a *portion* of a list. To illustrate, we rewrite insertionSort (calling it insertionSort1) to sort list[lo] to list[hi] where lo and hi are passed as arguments to the function.

Since element lo is the first one, we start processing elements from lo + 1 until element hi. This is reflected in the for statement. Also now, the lowest subscript is lo, rather than 0. This is reflected in the while condition k >= lo. Everything else remains the same as before.

```
void insertionSort1(int list[], int lo, int hi) {
    //sort list[lo] to list[hi] in ascending order
    for (int h = lo + 1; h <= hi; h++) {
        int key = list[h];
        int k = h - 1; //start comparing with previous item
        while (k >= lo && key < list[k]) {
            list[k + 1] = list[k];
            --k;
        }
        list[k + 1] = key;
    } //end for
} //end insertionSort1
```

6.3.1 Analysis of Insertion Sort

In processing item j, we can make as few as one comparison (if num[j] is bigger than num[j-1]) or as many as j-1 comparisons (if num[j] is smaller than all the previous items). For random data, we would expect to make $\frac{1}{2}(j-1)$ comparisons, on average. Hence, the average total number of comparisons to sort n items is as follows:

$$\sum_{j=2}^{n} \frac{1}{2}(j-1) = \frac{1}{2}\{1 + 2 + ...+ n\text{-}1\} = \frac{1}{4}\,n(n\text{-}1) \approx \frac{1}{4}\,n^2$$

We say insertion sort is of order $O(n^2)$ ("big O n squared"). The constant $\frac{1}{4}$ is not important as n gets large.

Each time we make a comparison, we also make an assignment. Hence, the total number of assignments is also $\frac{1}{4}\,n(n\text{-}1) \approx \frac{1}{4}\,n^2$.

We emphasize that this is an average for random data. Unlike selection sort, the actual performance of insertion sort depends on the data supplied. If the given array is already sorted, insertion sort will quickly determine this by making n-1 comparisons. In this case, it runs in $O(n)$ time. One would expect that insertion sort will perform better the more order there is in the data.

If the given data is in descending order, insertion sort performs at its worst since each new number has to travel all the way to the beginning of the list. In this case, the number of comparisons is $\frac{1}{2}\,n(n\text{-}1) \approx \frac{1}{2}\,n^2$. The number of assignments is also $\frac{1}{2}\,n(n\text{-}1) \approx \frac{1}{2}\,n^2$.

Thus, the number of comparisons made by insertion sort ranges from n-1 (best) to $\frac{1}{4}\,n^2$ (average) to $\frac{1}{2}\,n^2$ (worst). The number of assignments is always the same as the number of comparisons.

As with selection sort, insertion sort does not require extra array storage for its implementation.

As an exercise, modify the programming code so that it counts the number of comparisons and assignments made in sorting a list using insertion sort.

6.3.2 Insert an Element in Place

Insertion sort uses the idea of adding a new element to an already sorted list so that the list remains sorted. We can treat this as a problem in its own right (nothing to do with insertion sort). Specifically, given a sorted list of items from list[m] to list[n], we want to add a new item (newItem, say) to the list so that list[m] to list[n + 1] are sorted.

Adding a new item increases the size of the list by 1. We assume that the array has room to hold the new item. We write the function insertInPlace to solve this problem.

```
void insertInPlace(int newItem, int list[], int m, int n) {
//list[m] to list[n] are sorted
//insert newItem so that list[m] to list[n+1] are sorted
    int k = n;
    while (k >= m && newItem < list[k]) {
        list[k + 1] = list[k];
        --k;
    }
    list[k + 1] = newItem;
} //end insertInPlace
```

Using insertInPlace, we can rewrite insertionSort (calling it insertionSort2) as follows:

```
void insertionSort2(int list[], int lo, int hi) {
//sort list[lo] to list[hi] in ascending order
    void insertInPlace(int, int [], int, int);
    for (int h = lo + 1; h <= hi; h++)
        insertInPlace(list[h], list, lo, h - 1);
} //end insertionSort2
```

Note that the prototype for insertionSort2 is now this:

void insertionSort2(int [], int, int);

and to sort an array num of n items, we must call it like this:

insertionSort2(num, 0, n-1);

6.4 Heapsort

Heapsort is a method of sorting that *interprets* the elements in an array as an almost complete binary tree. Consider the following array, which is to be sorted in ascending order:

num

37	25	43	65	48	84	73	18	79	56	69	32
1	2	3	4	5	6	7	8	9	10	1	1

We can think of this array as an almost complete binary tree with 12 nodes, as shown in Figure 6-1.

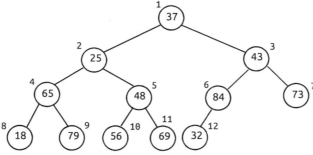

Figure 6-1. A binary tree view of the array

Suppose we now require that the value at each node be greater than or equal to the values in its left and right subtrees, if present. As it is, only node 6 and the leaves have this property. Shortly, we will see how to rearrange the nodes so that *all* nodes satisfy this condition. But, first, we give this condition a name:

> A **heap** is an almost complete binary tree such that the value at the root is greater than or equal to the values at the left and right children, and the left and right subtrees are also heaps.

An immediate consequence of this definition is that the largest value is at the root. Such a heap is referred to as a *max-heap*. We define a *min-heap* with the word *greater* replaced by *smaller*. In a min-heap, the *smallest* value is at the root.

Let's now convert the binary tree in Figure 6-1 into a max-heap.

6.4.1 Convert Binary Tree to Max-Heap

First, we observe that all the leaves are heaps since they have no children.

Starting at the last nonleaf node (6, in the example), we convert the tree rooted there into a max-heap. If the value at the node is greater than its children, there is nothing to do. This is the case with node 6, since 84 is bigger than 32.

Next, we move on to node 5. The value here, 48, is smaller than at least one child (both, in this case, 56 and 69). We first find the larger child (69) and interchange it with node 5. Thus, 69 ends up in node 5, and 48 ends up in node 11.

Next, we go to node 4. The larger child, 79, is moved to node 4, and 65 is moved to node 9. At this stage, the tree looks like that in Figure 6-2.

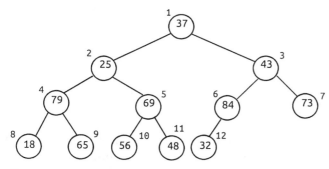

Figure 6-2. After nodes 6, 5, and 4 have been processed

Continuing at node 3, 43 must be moved. The larger child is 84, so we interchange the values at nodes 3 and 6. The value now at node 6 (43) is bigger than its child (32), so there is nothing more to do. Note, however, that if the value at node 6 were 28, say, it would have had to be exchanged with 32.

Moving to node 2, 25 is exchanged with its larger child, 79. But 25 now in node 4 is smaller than 65, its right child in node 9. Thus, these two values must be exchanged.

Finally, at node 1, 37 is exchanged with its larger child, 84. It is further exchanged with its (new) larger child, 73, giving the tree, which is now a heap, shown in Figure 6-3.

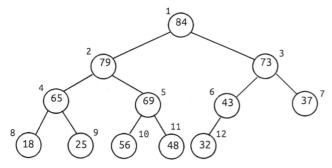

Figure 6-3. The final tree, which is now a heap

6.4.2 The Sorting Process

After conversion to a heap, note that the largest value, 84, is at the root of the tree. Now that the values in the array form a heap, we can sort them in ascending order as follows:

- Store the last item, 32, in a temporary location. Next, move 84 to the last position (node 12), freeing node 1. Then, imagine 32 is in node 1 and move it so that items 1 to 11 become a heap. This will be done as follows:
  - 32 is exchanged with its bigger child, 79, which now moves into node 1. 32 is further exchanged with its (new) bigger child, 69, which moves into node 2.
  - Finally, 32 is exchanged with 56, giving us Figure 6-4.

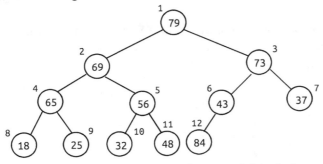

Figure 6-4. After placing 84 and reorganizing the heap

At this stage, the second largest number, 79, is in node 1. This is placed in node 11, and 48 is "sifted down" from node 1 until items 1 to 10 form a heap. Now, the third largest number, 73, will be at the root. This is placed in node 10, and so on. The process is repeated until the array is sorted.

After the initial heap is built, the sorting process can be described with the following:

```
for k = n downto 2 do
     item = num[k]      //extract current last item
     num[k] = num[1]    //move top of heap to current last node
     siftDown(item, num, 1, k-1)  //restore heap properties from 1 to k-1
end for
```

where

```
siftDown(item, num, 1, k-1)
```

assumes that the following holds:

- num[1] is empty;
- num[2] to num[k-1] form a heap;
- Starting at position 1, item is inserted so that num[1] to num[k-1] form a heap.

In the sorting process described above, each time through the loop, the value in the current last position (k) is stored in item. The value at node 1 is moved to position k; node 1 becomes empty (available), and nodes 2 to k-1 all satisfy the heap property.

The call

```
siftDown(item, num, 1, k-1)
```

will add item so that num[1] to num[k-1] contain a heap. This ensures that the next highest number is at node 1.

The nice thing about siftDown (when we write it) is that it can be used to create the initial heap from the given array. Recall the process of creating a heap described in Section 6.4.1. At each node (h, say), we "sifted the value down" so that we formed a heap rooted at h. To use siftDown in this situation, we generalize it as follows:

```
void siftDown(int key, int num[], int root, int last)
```

where

- num[root] is empty;
- num[root+1] to num[last] form a heap;
- Starting at root, key is inserted so that num[root] to num[last] form a heap.

Given an array of values num[1] to num[n], we could build the heap with this:

```
for h = n/2 downto 1 do // n/2 is the last non-leaf node
    siftDown(num[h], num, h, n)
```

We now show how to write siftDown.

Consider Figure 6-5.

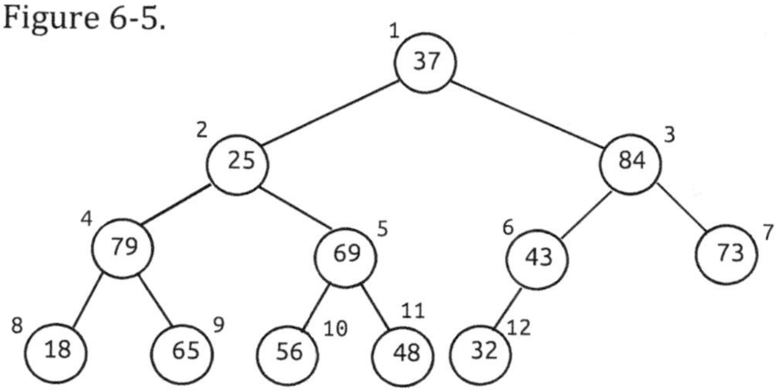

Figure 6-5. A heap, except for nodes 1 and 2

Except for nodes 1 and 2, all the other nodes satisfy the heap property that they are bigger than or equal to their children. Suppose we want to make node 2 the root of a heap. As it is, the value 25 is smaller than its children (79 and 69). We want to write siftDown so that the call siftDown(25, num, 2, 12) will do the job. Here, 25 is the key, num is the array, 2 is the root, and 12 is the position of the last node.

After this, each of nodes 2 to 12 will be the root of a heap, and the call

siftDown(37, num, 1, 12)

will ensure that the entire array contains a heap.

The gist of siftDown is as follows:

```
find the larger child of num[root]; //suppose it is in node m
if (key >= num[m]) we are done; put key in num[root]
//key is smaller than the bigger child
store num[m] in num[root]   //promote bigger child
set root to m
```

The process is repeated until the value at root is bigger than its children or there are no children. Here is siftDown:

```
void siftDown(int key, int num[], int root, int last) {
    int bigger = 2 * root;
    while (bigger <= last) { //while there is at least one child
        if (bigger < last) //there is a right child; find the bigger
            if (num[bigger+1] > num[bigger]) bigger++;
        //'bigger' holds the index of the bigger child
        if (key >= num[bigger]) break;
        //key is smaller; promote num[bigger]
        num[root] = num[bigger];
        root = bigger;
        bigger = 2 * root;
    } //end while
    num[root] = key;
} //end siftDown
```

We can now write heapSort as follows:

```
void heapSort(int num[], int n) {
//sort num[1] to num[n]
    void siftDown(int, int[], int, int);
    //convert the array to a heap
    for (int h = n / 2; h >= 1; h--) siftDown(num[h], num, h, n);

    for (int k = n; k > 1; k--) {
        int item = num[k]; //extract current last item
        num[k] = num[1];    //move top of heap to current last node
        siftDown(item, num, 1, k-1); //restore heap properties from 1 to k-1
    }
} //end heapSort
```

We can test heapSort with Program P6.3.

Program P6.3

```
#include <stdio.h>
int main() {
    void heapSort(int[], int);
    int num[] = {0, 37, 25, 43, 65, 48, 84, 73, 18, 79, 56, 69, 32};
    int n = 12;
    heapSort(num, n);
    for (int h = 1; h <= n; h++) printf("%d ", num[h]);
    printf("\n");
} //end main

void heapSort(int num[], int n) {
//sort num[1] to num[n]
    void siftDown(int, int[], int, int);
    //convert the array to a heap
    for (int h = n / 2; h >= 1; h--) siftDown(num[h], num, h, n);

    for (int k = n; k > 1; k--) {
        int item = num[k]; //extract current last item
        num[k] = num[1];    //move top of heap to current last node
        siftDown(item, num, 1, k-1); //restore heap, 1 to k-1
    }
} //end heapSort

void siftDown(int key, int num[], int root, int last) {
    int bigger = 2 * root;
    while (bigger <= last) { //while there is at least one child
        if (bigger < last) //there is a right child; find the bigger
            if (num[bigger+1] > num[bigger]) bigger++;
        //'bigger' holds the index of the bigger child
        if (key >= num[bigger]) break;
        //key is smaller; promote num[bigger]
        num[root] = num[bigger];
        root = bigger;
        bigger = 2 * root;
    } //end while
    num[root] = key;
} //end siftDown
```

When run, this program produces the following output (num[1] to num[12] sorted):

18 25 32 37 43 48 56 65 69 73 79 84

Programming note: As written, heapSort sorts an array assuming that *n* elements are stored from subscripts 1 to *n*. If they are stored from 0 to *n*-1, appropriate adjustments would have to be made. They would be based mainly on the following observations:

- The root is stored in num[0].
- The left child of node h is node 2h+1 if 2h+1 < n.
- The right child of node h is node 2h+2 if 2h+2 < n.
- The parent of node h is node (h−1)/2 (integer division).
- The last nonleaf node is (n−2)/2 (integer division).

You can verify these observations using the tree (*n* = 12) shown in Figure 6-6.

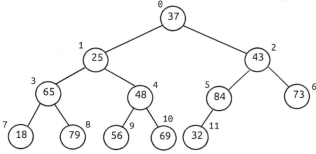

Figure 6-6. A binary tree stored starting at 0

You are urged to rewrite heapSort so that it sorts the array num[0..n-1]. As a hint, note that the only change required in siftDown is in the calculation of bigger. Instead of 2 * root, we now use 2 * root + 1.

6.5 Build a Heap Using siftUp

Consider the problem of adding a new node to an existing heap. Specifically, suppose num[1] to num[n] contain a heap. We want to add a new number, newKey, so that num[1] to num[n+1] contain a heap that includes newKey. We assume the array has room for the new key.

For example, suppose we have the heap shown in Figure 6-7 and we want to add 40 to the heap. When the new number is added, the heap will contain 13 elements. We imagine 40 is placed in num[13] (but do not store it there, as yet) and compare it with its parent 43 in num[6]. Since 40 is smaller, the heap property is satisfied; we place 40 in num[13], and the process ends.

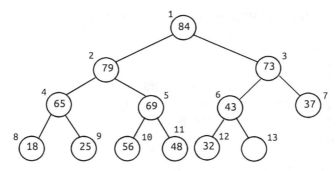

Figure 6-7. A heap to which we will add a new item

But suppose we want to add 80 to the heap. We imagine 80 is placed in num[13] (but do not actually store it there, as yet) and compare it with its parent 43 in num[6]. Since 80 is bigger, we move 43 to num[13] and imagine 80 being placed in num[6].

Next, we compare 80 with its parent 73 in num[3]. It is bigger, so we move 73 to num[6] and imagine 80 being placed in num[3].

We then compare 80 with its parent 84 in num[1]. It is smaller, so we place 80 in num[3], and the process ends.

Note that if we were adding 90 to the heap, 84 would be moved to num[3], and 90 would be inserted in num[1]. It is now the largest number in the heap.

Figure 6-8 shows the heap after 80 is added.

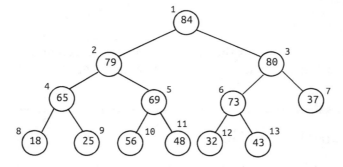

Figure 6-8. The heap after 80 is added

The following algorithm adds newKey to a heap stored in num[1] to num[n]:

```
child = n + 1;
parent = child / 2;
while (parent > 0) {
    if (newKey <= num[parent]) break;
    num[child] = num[parent]; //move down parent
    child = parent;
    parent = child / 2;
}
num[child] = newKey;
n = n + 1;
```

The process described is usually referred to as *sifting up*. We can rewrite the previous algorithm as a function siftUp. We assume that siftUp is given an array heap[1..n] such that heap[1..n-1] contains a heap and heap[n] is to be sifted up so that heap[1..n] contains a heap. In other words, heap[n] plays the role of newKey in the previous algorithm.

We show siftUp as part of Program P6.4, which creates a heap out of numbers stored in a file, heap.in.

Program P6.4

```c
#include <stdio.h>
#include <stdlib.h>
#define MaxHeapSize 100
int main() {
    void siftUp(int[], int);
    int num[MaxHeapSize + 1];
    int n = 0, number;
    FILE * in = fopen("heap.in", "r");

    while (fscanf(in, "%d", &number) == 1) {
        if (n < MaxHeapSize) { //check if array has room
            num[++n] = number;
            siftUp(num, n);
        }
        else {
            printf("\nArray too small\n");
            exit(1);
        }
    }
    for (int h = 1; h <= n; h++) printf("%d ", num[h]);
    printf("\n");
    fclose(in);
} //end main

void siftUp(int heap[], int n) {
//sifts up the value in heap[n] so that heap[1..n] contains a heap
    int siftItem = heap[n];
    int child = n;
    int parent = child / 2;

    while (parent > 0) {
        if (siftItem <= heap[parent]) break;
        heap[child] = heap[parent]; //move down parent
        child = parent;
        parent = child / 2;
    }
    heap[child] = siftItem;
} //end siftUp
```

If heap.in contains the following:

37 25 43 65 48 84 73 18 79 56 69 32

Program P6.4 will build the heap (described next) and print the following:

84 79 73 48 69 37 65 18 25 43 56 32

After 37, 25, and 43 are read, we will have Figure 6-9.

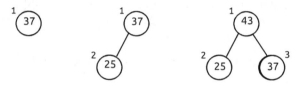

Figure 6-9. Heap after processing 37, 25, 43

After 65, 48, 84, and 73 are read, we will have Figure 6-10.

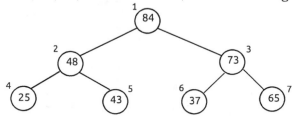

Figure 6-10. Heap after processing 65, 48, 84, 73

And after 18, 79, 56, 69, and 32 are read, we will have the final heap shown in Figure 6-11.

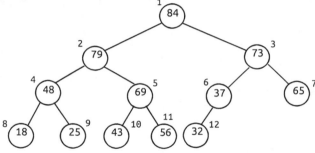

Figure 6-11. Final heap after processing 18, 79, 56, 69, 32

Note that the heap in Figure 6-11 is different from that of Figure 6-3 even though they are formed from the same numbers. What hasn't changed is that the largest value, 84, is at the root.

If the values are already stored in an array num[1..n], we can create a heap with the following:

```
for (int k = 2; k <= n; k++) siftUp(num, k);
```

6.6 Analysis of Heapsort

Is siftUp or siftDown better for creating a heap? Keep in mind that the most times any node will ever have to move is $\log_2 n$.

In siftDown, we process $n/2$ nodes, and at each step, we make two comparisons: one to find the bigger child and one to compare the node value with the bigger child. In a simplistic analysis, in the worst case, we will need to make $2*n/2*\log_2 n = n\log_2 n$ comparisons. However, a more careful analysis will show that we need to make, at most, only $4n$ comparisons.

In siftUp, we process n-1 nodes. At each step, we make one comparison: the node with its parent. In a simplistic analysis, in the worst case, we make $(n-1)\log_2 n$ comparisons. However, it is possible that all the leaves may have to travel all the way to the top of the tree. In this case, we have $n/2$ nodes having to travel a distance of $\log_2 n$, giving a total of $(n/2)\log_2 n$ comparisons. And that's only for the leaves. In the end, a more careful analysis still gives us approximately $n\log_2 n$ comparisons for siftUp.

The difference in performance is hinged on the following: in siftDown, there is no work to do for half the nodes (the leaves); siftUp has the most work to do for these nodes.

Whichever method we use for creating the initial heap, heapsort will sort an array of size n making at most $2n\log_2 n$ comparisons and $n\log_2 n$ assignments. This is very fast. In addition, heapsort is *stable* in the sense that its performance is always at worst $2n\log_2 n$, regardless of the order of the items in the given array. (We also use the term *stable sorting method* to refer to a method in which equal keys in the given list retain their relative order in the sorted list.)

To give an idea of how fast heapsort (and all sorting methods that are of order $O(n\log_2 n)$, such as *quicksort* and *mergesort*) is, let's compare it with selection sort, which makes roughly $\frac{1}{2}n^2$ comparisons to sort n items.

n	select(comp)	heap(comp)	select(sec)	heap(sec)
100	5,000	1,329	0.005	0.001
1,000	500,000	19,932	0.5	0.020
10,000	50,000,000	265,754	50	0.266
100,000	5,000,000,000	3,321,928	5,000	3.322
1,000,000	500,000,000,000	39,863,137	500,000	39.863

The second and third columns show the number of comparisons that each method makes. The last two columns show the running time of each method (in seconds) assuming that the computer can process 1 million comparisons per second. For example, to sort 1 million items, selection sort will take 500,000 seconds (almost 6 days!), whereas heapsort will do it in less than 40 seconds.

6.7 Heaps and Priority Queues

A *priority queue* is one in which each item is assigned some "priority" and its position in the queue is based on this priority. The item with top priority is placed at the head of the queue. The following are some typical operations that may be performed on a priority queue:

- Remove (serve) the item with the highest priority
- Add an item with a given priority
- Remove (delete without serving) an item from the queue
- Change the priority of an item, adjusting its position based on its new priority

We can think of priority as an integer—the bigger the integer, the higher the priority.

Immediately, we can surmise that if we implement the queue as a max-heap, the item with the highest priority will be at the root, so it can be easily removed. Reorganizing the heap will simply involve "sifting down" the last item, starting from the root.

Adding an item will involve placing the item in the position after the current last one and sifting it up until it finds its correct position.

To delete an arbitrary item from the queue, we will need to know its position. Deleting it will involve replacing it with the current last item and sifting it up or down to find its correct position. The heap will shrink by one item.

If we change the priority of an item, we may need to sift it either up or down to find its correct position. Of course, it may also remain in its original position, depending on the change.

In many situations (for example, a job queue on a multitasking computer), the priority of a job may increase over time so that it eventually gets served. In these situations, a job moves closer to the top of the heap with each change; thus, only sifting up is required.

In a typical situation, information about the items in a priority queue is held in another structure that can be quickly searched, for example a binary search tree. One field in the node will contain the index of the item in the array used to implement the priority queue.

Using the job queue example, suppose we want to add an item to the queue. We can search the tree by job number, say, and add the item to the tree. Its priority number is used to determine its position in the queue. This position is stored in the tree node.

If, later, the priority changes, the item's position in the queue is adjusted, and this new position is stored in the tree node. Note that adjusting this item may also involve changing the position of other items (as they move up or down the heap), and the tree will have to be updated for these items as well.

6.8 Quicksort

At the heart of quicksort is the notion of *partitioning* the list with respect to one of the values called a *pivot*. For example, suppose we are given the following list of n elements ($n = 10$) to be sorted:

num

53	12	98	63	18	32	80	46	72	21
0	1	2	3	4	5	6	7	8	9

We can *partition* it with respect to the first value, 53. This means placing 53 in such a position that all *values to the left of it are smaller* and all *values to the right are greater* than or equal to it. Shortly, we will describe an algorithm that will partition num as follows:

num

21	12	18	32	46	53	80	98	72	63
0	1	2	3	4	5	6	7	8	9

The value 53 is used as the *pivot*. It is placed in position 5. All values to the left of 53 are smaller than 53, and all values to the right are greater. The location in which the pivot is placed is called the *division point* (dp, say). By definition, 53 is in its final sorted position.

If we can sort num[0..dp-1] and num[dp+1..n-1], we would have sorted the entire list. But we can use the same process to sort these pieces, indicating that a recursive procedure is appropriate.

Assuming a function `partition` is available that partitions a given section of an array and returns the division point, we can write `quicksort` as follows:

```
void quicksort(int A[], int lo, int hi) {
//sorts A[lo] to A[hi] in ascending order
    int partition(int[], int, int);
    if (lo < hi) {
        int dp = partition(A, lo, hi);
        quicksort(A, lo, dp-1);
        quicksort(A, dp+1, hi);
    }
} //end quicksort
```

The call

```
quicksort(num, 0, n-1)
```

will sort `num[0..n-1]` in ascending order.

We now look at how `partition` may be written. Consider the following array:

num

53	12	98	63	18	32	80	46	72	21
0	1	2	3	4	5	6	7	8	9

We will partition it with respect to `num[0]`, 53 (the pivot) by making *one pass* through the array. We will look at each number in turn. If it is bigger than the pivot, we do nothing. If it is smaller, we move it to the left side of the array. Initially, we set the variable `lastSmall` to 0; as the method proceeds, `lastSmall` will be the index of the last item that is known to be smaller than the pivot. We partition `num` as follows:

1. Compare 12 with 53; it is smaller, so add 1 to `lastSmall` (making it 1) and swap `num[1]` with itself.
2. Compare 98 with 53; it is bigger, so move on.
3. Compare 63 with 53; it is bigger, so move on.
4. Compare 18 with 53; it is smaller, so add 1 to `lastSmall` (making it 2) and swap `num[2]`, 98, with 18.

At this stage, we have this:

num

53	12	18	63	98	32	80	46	72	21
0	1	2	3	4	5	6	7	8	9

5. Compare 32 with 53; it is smaller, so add 1 to `lastSmall` (making it 3) and swap `num[3]`, 63, with 32.
6. Compare 80 with 53; it is bigger, so move on.
7. Compare 46 with 53; it is smaller, so add 1 to `lastSmall` (making it 4) and swap `num[4]`, 98, with 46.

We now have the following:

num

53	12	18	32	46	63	80	98	72	21
0	1	2	3	4	5	6	7	8	9

8. Compare 72 with 53; it is bigger, so move on.

9. Compare 21 with 53; it is smaller, so add 1 to lastSmall (making it 5) and swap num[5], 63, with 21.

10. We have come to the end of the array; swap num[0] and num[lastSmall]; this moves the pivot, 53, into its final position.

We end up with this:

num

21	12	18	32	46	53	80	98	72	63
0	1	2	3	4	5	6	7	8	9

The division point is denoted by lastSmall (5).

We can express the procedure just described as a function partition1.

```
int partition1(int A[], int lo, int hi) {
//partition A[lo] to A[hi] using A[lo] as the pivot
    void swap(int[], int, int);
    int pivot = A[lo];
    int lastSmall = lo, h;
    for (h = lo + 1; h <= hi; h++)
        if (A[h] < pivot) {
            ++lastSmall;
            swap(A, lastSmall, h);
        }
    //end for
    swap(A, lo, lastSmall);
    return lastSmall;   //return the division point
} //end partition1

void swap(int list[], int i, int j) {
//swap list[i] and list[j]
    int hold = list[i];
    list[i] = list[j];
    list[j] = hold;
} //end swap
```

We can test quicksort and partition1 with Program P6.5.

Program P6.5

```
#include <stdio.h>
int main() {
    void quicksort(int[], int, int);
    int num[] = {53, 12, 98, 63, 18, 32, 80, 46, 72, 21};
    int n = 10;
    quicksort(num, 0, n-1);
    for (int h = 0; h < n; h++) printf("%d ", num[h]);
    printf("\n");
} //end main
```

```
void quicksort(int A[], int lo, int hi) {
//sorts A[lo] to A[hi] in ascending order
    int partition1(int[], int, int);
    if (lo < hi) {
        int dp = partition1(A, lo, hi);
        quicksort(A, lo, dp-1);
        quicksort(A, dp+1, hi);
    }
} //end quicksort

int partition1(int A[], int lo, int hi) {
//partition A[lo] to A[hi] using A[lo] as the pivot
    void swap(int[], int, int);
    int pivot = A[lo];
    int lastSmall = lo, h;
    for (h = lo + 1; h <= hi; h++)
        if (A[h] < pivot) {
            ++lastSmall;
            swap(A, lastSmall, h);
        }
    //end for
    swap(A, lo, lastSmall);
    return lastSmall;  //return the division point
} //end partition1

void swap(int list[], int i, int j) {
//swap list[i] and list[j]
    int hold = list[i];
    list[i] = list[j];
    list[j] = hold;
} //end swap
```

When run, this program produces the following output (num[0] to num[9] sorted):

```
12 18 21 32 46 53 63 72 80 98
```

6.8.1 Analysis of Quicksort

Quicksort is one of those methods whose performance can range from very fast to very slow. Typically, it is of order $O(n\log_2 n)$, and for random data, the number of comparisons varies between $n\log_2 n$ and $3n\log_2 n$. However, things can get worse.

The idea behind partitioning is to break up the given portion into two fairly equal pieces. Whether this happens depends, to a large extent, on the value that is chosen as the pivot.

In the function, we choose the first element as the pivot. This will work well in most cases, especially for random data. However, if the first element happens to be the smallest, the partitioning operation becomes almost useless since the division point will simply be the first position. The "left" piece will be empty, and the "right" piece will be only one element smaller than the given sublist. Similar remarks apply if the pivot is the largest element.

While the algorithm will still work, it will be slowed considerably. For example, if the given array is sorted, quicksort will become as slow as selection sort.

To avoid this problem, choose a random element as the pivot, not always the first one. While it is still possible that this method will choose the smallest (or the largest), that result will be merely by chance, not deliberate, and should not occur often.

Yet another method is to choose the median of the first (A[lo]), last (A[hi]), and middle (A[(lo+hi)/2]) items as the pivot.

You are advised to experiment with various ways of choosing the pivot.

Our experiments showed that choosing a random element as the pivot was simple and effective, even for sorted data. In fact, in many cases, the method ran faster with sorted data than with random data, an unusual result for quicksort.

One possible disadvantage of quicksort is that, depending on the actual data being sorted, the overhead of the recursive calls may be high. We will see how to minimize this in Section 6.8.3. On the plus side, quicksort uses very little extra storage. On the other hand, mergesort (which is also recursive) needs extra storage (the same size as the array being sorted) to facilitate the merging of sorted pieces. Heapsort has neither of these disadvantages. It is *not* recursive and uses very little extra storage. And, as noted in Section 6.6, heapsort is *stable* in that its performance is always at worst $2n\log_2 n$, regardless of the order of the items in the given array.

6.8.2 Another Way to Partition

There are many ways to achieve the goal of partitioning—splitting the list into two parts such that the elements in the left part are smaller than the elements in the right part. Our first method, shown earlier, placed the pivot in its final position. For variety, we will look at another way to partition. While this method still partitions with respect to a pivot, it does *not* place the pivot in its final sorted position. As we will see, this is not a problem.

Consider, again, the array num[0..n-1] where *n* = 10.

num

53	12	98	63	18	32	80	46	72	21
0	1	2	3	4	5	6	7	8	9

We choose 53 as the pivot. The general idea is to *scan from the right* looking for a key that is smaller than, or equal to, the pivot. We then *scan from the left* for a key that is greater than, or equal to, the pivot. We swap these two values; this process effectively puts smaller values to the left and bigger values to the right.

We use two variables, lo and hi, to mark our positions on the left and right. Initially, we set lo to - 1 and hi to 10 (n). We then loop as follows:

1. Subtract 1 from hi (making it 9).
2. Compare num[hi], 21, with 53; it is smaller, so stop scanning from the right with hi = 9.
3. Add 1 to lo (making it 0).
4. Compare num[lo], 53, with 53; it is not smaller, so stop scanning from the left with lo = 0.
5. lo (0) is less than hi (9), so swap num[lo] and num[hi].
6. Subtract 1 from hi (making it 8).
7. Compare num[hi], 72, with 53; it is bigger, so decrease hi (making it 7). Compare num[hi], 46, with 53; it is smaller, so stop scanning from the right with hi = 7.
8. Add 1 to lo (making it 1).

9. Compare num[lo], 12, with 53; it is smaller, so add 1 to lo (making it 2). Compare num[lo], 98, with 53; it is bigger, so stop scanning from the left with lo = 2.

10. lo (2) is less than hi (7), so swap num[lo] and num[hi].

At this stage, we have lo = 2, hi = 7 and num as follows:

num

21	12	46	63	18	32	80	98	72	53
0	1	2	3	4	5	6	7	8	9

11. Subtract 1 from hi (making it 6).

12. Compare num[hi], 80, with 53; it is bigger, so decrease hi (making it 5). Compare num[hi], 32, with 53; it is smaller, so stop scanning from the right with hi = 5.

13. Add 1 to lo (making it 3).

14. Compare num[lo], 63, with 53; it is bigger, so stop scanning from the left with lo = 3.

15. lo (3) is less than hi (5), so swap num[lo] and num[hi], giving this:

num

21	12	46	32	18	63	80	98	72	53
0	1	2	3	4	5	6	7	8	9

16. Subtract 1 from hi (making it 4).

17. Compare num[hi], 18, with 53; it is smaller, so stop scanning from the right with hi = 4.

18. Add 1 to lo (making it 4).

19. Compare num[lo], 18, with 53; it is smaller, so add 1 to lo (making it 5). Compare num[lo], 63, with 53; it is bigger, so stop scanning from the left with lo = 5.

20. lo (5) is not less than hi (4), so the algorithm ends.

The value of hi is such that the values in num[0..hi] are smaller than those in num[hi+1..n-1]. Here, the values in num[0..4] are smaller than those in num[5..9]. Note that 53 is not in its final sorted position. However, this is not a problem since, to sort the array, all we need to do is sort num[0..hi] and num[hi+1..n-1].

We can write the procedure just described as partition2:

```
int partition2(int A[], int lo, int hi) {
//return dp such that A[lo..dp] <= A[dp+1..hi]
   void swap(int[], int, int);
   int pivot = A[lo];
   --lo; ++hi;
   while (lo < hi) {
      do --hi; while (A[hi] > pivot);
      do ++lo; while (A[lo] < pivot);
      if (lo < hi) swap(A, lo, hi);
   }
   return hi;
} //end partition2
```

With this version of partition, we can write quicksort2 as follows:

```
void quicksort2(int A[], int lo, int hi) {
//sorts A[lo] to A[hi] in ascending order
    int partition2(int[], int, int);
    if (lo < hi) {
        int dp = partition2(A, lo, hi);
        quicksort2(A, lo, dp);
        quicksort2(A, dp+1, hi);
    }
} //end quicksort2
```

In partition2, we choose the first element as the pivot. However, as discussed earlier, choosing a random element will give better results. We can do this with the following:

```
swap(A, lo, random(lo, hi));
int pivot = A[lo];
```

where random can be written as shown in Program P6.6.

Note the declaration of the the prototype of random in partition2 and the addition of the following statement since random uses rand and RAND_MAX, which are declared in stdlib.h:

```
#include <stdlib.h>
```

Program P6.6

```
#include <stdio.h>
#include <stdlib.h>

int main() {
    void quicksort2(int[], int, int);
    int num[] = {53, 12, 98, 63, 18, 32, 80, 46, 72, 21};
    int n = 10;
    quicksort2(num, 0, n-1);
    for (int h = 0; h < n; h++) printf("%d ", num[h]);
    printf("\n");
} //end main

void quicksort2(int A[], int lo, int hi) {
//sorts A[lo] to A[hi] in ascending order
    int partition2(int[], int, int);
    if (lo < hi) {
        int dp = partition2(A, lo, hi);
        quicksort2(A, lo, dp);
        quicksort2(A, dp+1, hi);
    }
} //end quicksort2

int partition2(int A[], int lo, int hi) {
//return dp such that A[lo..dp] <= A[dp+1..hi]
    void swap(int[], int, int);
    int random(int, int);
    swap(A, lo, random(lo, hi)); //choose a random element as the pivot
    int pivot = A[lo];
    --lo; ++hi;
    while (lo < hi) {
        do --hi; while (A[hi] > pivot);
        do ++lo; while (A[lo] < pivot);
        if (lo < hi) swap(A, lo, hi);
    }
    return hi;
} //end partition2
```

```
void swap(int list[], int i, int j) {
//swap list[i] and list[j]
    int hold = list[i];
    list[i] = list[j];
    list[j] = hold;
} //end swap

int random(int m, int n) {
//returns a random integer from m to n, inclusive
    int offset = rand()/(RAND_MAX + 1.0) * (n - m + 1);
    return m + offset;
} //end random
```

When run, Program P6.6 prints the following:

```
12 18 21 32 46 53 63 72 80 98
```

6.8.3 Non-recursive Quicksort

In the versions of quicksort shown earlier, after a sublist is partitioned, we call quicksort with the left part followed by the right part. For most cases, this will work fine. However, it is possible that, for a large n, the number of pending recursive calls can get so large so as to generate a "recursive stack overflow" error.

In our experiments, this occurred with n = 7000 if the given data was already sorted and the first element was chosen as the pivot. However, there was no problem even for n = 100000 if a random element was chosen as the pivot.

Another approach is to write quicksort nonrecursively. This would require us to stack the pieces of the list that remain to be sorted. It can be shown that when a sublist is subdivided, if we process the *smaller* sublist first, the number of stack elements will be restricted to at most $\log_2 n$.

For example, suppose we are sorting A[1..99] and the first division point is 40. Assume we are using partition2, which does not put the pivot in its final sorted position. Thus, we must sort A[1..40] and A[41..99] to complete the sort. We will stack (41, 99) and deal with A[1..40] (the shorter sublist) first.

Suppose the division point for A[1..40] is 25. We will stack (1, 25) and process A[26..40] first. At this stage we have two sublists—(41, 99) and (1, 25)—on the stack that remain to be sorted. Attempting to sort A[26..40] will cause another sublist to be added to the stack, and so on. In our implementation, we will also add the shorter sublist to the stack, but this will be taken off immediately and processed.

The result mentioned above assures us that there will never be more than $\log_2 99 = 7$ (rounded up) elements on the stack at any given time. Even for n = 1,000,000, we are guaranteed that the number of stack items will not exceed 20.

Of course, we will have to manipulate the stack ourselves. Each stack element will consist of two integers (left and right, say), meaning that the portion of the list from left to right remains to be sorted. We will assume the stack implementation described in Chapter 4 is stored in an include file, stack.h.

We define StackData and newStackData as follows:

```
typedef struct {
    int left, right;
} StackData;

StackData newStackData(int a, int b) {
    StackData temp;
    temp.left = a;
    temp.right = b;
    return temp;
} //end newStackData
```

We now write quicksort3 based on the previous discussion.

```
void quicksort3(int A[], int lo, int hi) {
    int partition2(int[], int, int);
    StackData newStackData(int, int);
    Stack S = initStack();
    push(S, newStackData(lo, hi));
    int stackItems = 1, maxStackItems = 1;
    while (!empty(S)) {
        --stackItems;
        StackData d = pop(S);
        if (d.left < d.right) { //if the sublist is > 1 element
            int dp = partition2(A, d.left, d.right);
            if (dp - d.left + 1 < d.right - dp) { //compare sublists
                push(S, newStackData(dp+1, d.right));
                push(S, newStackData(d.left, dp));
            }
            else {
                push(S, newStackData(d.left, dp));
                push(S, newStackData(dp+1, d.right));
            }
            stackItems += 2;    //two items added to stack
        } //end if
        if (stackItems > maxStackItems) maxStackItems = stackItems;
    } //end while
    printf("Max stack items: %d\n\n", maxStackItems);
} //end quicksort3
```

When partition2 returns, the lengths of the two sublists are compared, and the longer one is placed on the stack first followed by the shorter one. This ensures that the shorter one will be taken off first and processed before the longer one.

We also added statements to quicksort3 to keep track of the maximum number of items on the stack at any given time. When used to sort 100,000 integers, the maximum number of stack items was 13; this is less than the theoretical maximum $\log_2 100000 = 17$, rounded up.

As written, even if a sublist consists of two items only, the method will go through the whole process of calling partition2, checking the lengths of the sublists, and stacking the two sublists. This seems an awful lot of work to sort two items.

We can make quicksort more efficient by using a simple method (insertion sort, say) to sort sublists that are shorter than some predefined length (8, say). You are urged to write quicksort with this change and experiment with different values of the predefined length.

6.8.4 Find the kth Smallest Number

Consider the problem of finding the kth smallest number in a list of n numbers. One way to do this is to sort the n numbers and pick out the kth one. If the numbers are stored in an array A[1..n], we simply retrieve A[k] after sorting.

Another, more efficient way is to use partitioning. We will use the version of partition that places the pivot in its final sorted position. Consider an array A[1..99], and suppose a call to partition returns a division point of 40. This means the pivot has been placed in A[40] with smaller numbers to the left and bigger numbers to the right. In other words, the 40th smallest number has been placed in A[40]. So, if k is 40, we have our answer immediately.

What if k was 59? We know the 40 smallest numbers occupy A[1..40]. So, the 59th must be in A[41..99]; we can confine our search to this part of the array. In other words, with one call to partition, we eliminate 40 numbers from consideration. The idea is similar to binary search.

Suppose the next call to partition returns 65. We now know the 65th smallest number and the 59th will be in A[41..64]; we have eliminated A[66..99] from consideration. We repeat this process, each time reducing the size of the part that contains the 59th smallest number. Eventually, partition will return 59, and we will have our answer.

The following is one way to write kthSmall; it uses partition1:

```
int kthSmall(int A[], int k, int lo, int hi) {
//returns the kth smallest from A[lo] to A[hi]
    int partition1(int[], int, int);
    int kShift = lo + k - 1; //shift k to the given portion, A[lo..hi]
    if (kShift < lo || kShift > hi) return -9999;
    int dp = partition1(A, lo, hi);
    while (dp != kShift) {
        if (kShift < dp) hi = dp - 1; //kth smallest in the left part
        else lo = dp + 1;            //kth smallest in the right part
        dp = partition1(A, lo, hi);
    }
    return A[dp];
} //end kthSmall
```

For instance, the call

kthSmall(num, 59, 1, 99)

will return the 59th smallest number from num[1..99]. Note, however, that the call

kthSmall(num, 10, 30, 75)

will return the 10th smallest number from num[30..75].

As an exercise, write the recursive version of kthSmall.

6.9 Mergesort

Mergesort uses an idea similar to quicksort—the idea of splitting the list in two. We can express it as follows:

```
sort a list {
    sort the first half of the list
    sort the second half of the list
    merge the sorted halves
}
```

In quicksort, partitioning breaks up the given sublist into two parts which can be quite different in size. Mergesort breaks up the list into two approximately equal parts, sorts the parts and then merges them into one sorted list.

Of course, the question arises: how do we sort the first half (and the second half)? Well, we use the same method! To sort the first half, we break it up into two equal pieces, sort the pieces and merge the pieces into one sorted list. And we repeat the process for each piece. We stop breaking up a piece when it is a single element which, by definition, is sorted.

For example, given the following array to be sorted:

53	12	98	63	18	32	80	46	72	21
0	1	2	3	4	5	6	7	8	9

we sort the first 5 and the second 5 elements separately, getting this:

12	18	53	63	98	21	32	46	72	80
0	1	2	3	4	5	6	7	8	9

We then merge the two sorted halves to get the final sorted array:

12	18	21	32	46	53	63	72	80	98
0	1	2	3	4	5	6	7	8	9

But to sort the first 5 numbers, we apply the same method: we sort the first two, getting 12 53; then we sort the next three, getting 18 63 98. We merge these two pieces to get 12 18 53 63 98.

And to sort the first two, we must break it up into two pieces. Now, the pieces consist of just one element each, which is considered sorted. Merging the two will give us two sorted values.

We can write mergeSort as follows:

```
void mergeSort(int A[], int lo, int hi) {
//sort elements A[lo..hi]
    void merge(int[], int, int, int);
    if (lo < hi) { //list contains at least 2 elements
        int mid = (lo + hi) / 2; //get the mid-point subscript
        mergeSort(A, lo, mid); //sort first half
        mergeSort(A, mid + 1, hi); //sort second half
        merge(A, lo, mid, hi); //merge sorted halves
    }
} //end mergeSort
```

The call

merge(A, lo, mid, hi)

merges the sorted pieces A[lo..mid] and A[mid+1..hi] into one sorted piece A[lo..hi]. Here is merge:

```
void merge(int A[], int lo, int mid, int hi) {
//A[lo..mid] and A[mid+1..hi] are sorted;
//merge the pieces so that A[lo..hi] are sorted
   static int T[MaxNum]; //"static" so storage for T is allocated once
   int i = lo;
   int j = mid + 1;
   int k = lo;
   while (i <= mid || j <= hi) {
      if (i > mid) T[k++] = A[j++];    //A[lo..mid]  completely processed
      else if (j > hi) T[k++] = A[i++];    // A[mid+1..hi]  completely processed
      else if (A[i] < A[j]) T[k++] = A[i++]; //neither part completed
      else T[k++] = A[j++];
   }
   for (i = lo; i <= hi; i++) A[i] = T[i]; //copy merged elements from T to A
} //end merge
```

It is not possible to merge the pieces "in place" without overwriting some of the numbers. So the pieces are merged into a temporary array T and, at the end, copied back into A. This need for extra storage is one disadvantage of mergesort; the size of T is the same as A. The time taken to copy elements is also a minor drawback.

However, mergesort is fast; its running time is of order $O(n\log_2 n)$, on par with heapsort and quicksort.

We test mergesort with Program P6.7.

Program P6.7

```
#include <stdio.h>
#define MaxNum 100
int main() {
   void mergeSort(int[], int, int);
   int num[] = {53, 12, 98, 63, 18, 32, 80, 46, 72, 21};
   int n = 10;
   mergeSort(num, 0, n-1);
   for (int h = 0; h < n; h++) printf("%d ", num[h]);
   printf("\n");
} //end main

void mergeSort(int A[], int lo, int hi) {
   void merge(int[], int, int, int);
   if (lo < hi) { //list contains at least 2 elements
      int mid = (lo + hi) / 2; //get the mid-point subscript
      mergeSort(A, lo, mid); //sort first half
      mergeSort(A, mid + 1, hi); //sort second half
      merge(A, lo, mid, hi); //merge sorted halves
   }
} //end mergeSort
```

```
void merge(int A[], int lo, int mid, int hi) {
//A[lo..mid] and A[mid+1..hi] are sorted;
//merge the pieces so that A[lo..hi] are sorted
    static int T[MaxNum];
    int i = lo;
    int j = mid + 1;
    int k = lo;
    while (i <= mid || j <= hi) {
        if (i > mid) T[k++] = A[j++]; //A[lo..mid] completely processed
        else if (j > hi) T[k++] = A[i++];              //A[mid+1..hi] completely
        processed
        else if (A[i] < A[j]) T[k++] = A[i++]; //neither part completed
        else T[k++] = A[j++];
    }
    for (i = lo; i <= hi; i++) A[i] = T[i]; //copy values from T to A
} //end merge
```

When run, the program produces the following output (num[0] to num[9] sorted):

12 18 21 32 46 53 63 72 80 98

6.10 Shell (Diminishing Increment) Sort

Shell sort (named after Donald Shell) uses a series of *increments* to govern the sorting process. It makes several passes over the data, with the last pass being the same as insertion sort. For the other passes, elements that are a fixed distance apart (for instance, five apart) are sorted using the same technique as insertion sort.

For example, to sort the following array, we can use three increments—8, 3, and 1:

num

67	90	28	84	29	58	25	32	16	64	13	71	82	10	51	57
0	1	2	3	4	5	6	7	8	9	10	11	12	13	14	15

The increments decrease in size (hence the term *diminishing increment sort*), with the last one being 1.

Using increment 8, we *eight-sort* the array. This means we sort the elements that are eight apart. We sort elements 0 and 8, 1 and 9, 2 and 10, 3 and 11, 4 and 12, 5 and 13, 6 and 14, and 7 and 15. The 8-sort will transform num into this:

num

16	64	13	71	29	10	25	32	67	90	28	84	82	58	51	57
0	1	2	3	4	5	6	7	8	9	10	11	12	13	14	15

Next, we *three-sort* the array; that is, we sort elements that are three apart. We sort elements (0, 3, 6, 9, 12, 15), (1, 4, 7, 10, 13), and (2, 5, 8, 11, 14). This gives us the following:

num

16	28	10	25	29	13	57	32	51	71	58	67	82	64	84	90
0	1	2	3	4	5	6	7	8	9	10	11	12	13	14	15

Note that, at each step, the array is a little closer to being sorted. Finally, we perform a *one-sort*, sorting the entire list, giving this:

num

10	13	16	25	28	29	32	51	57	58	64	67	71	82	84	90
0	1	2	3	4	5	6	7	8	9	10	11	12	13	14	15

You may ask, why didn't we just do a one-sort from the beginning and sort the entire list? The idea here is that when we reach the stage of doing a one-sort, the array is more or less in order, and if we use a method that works better with partially ordered data (such as insertion sort), then the sort can proceed quickly.

When the increment is large, the pieces to sort are small. In the example, when the increment is eight, each piece consists of two elements only. Presumably, we can sort a small list quickly. When the increment is small, the pieces to sort are bigger. However, by the time we get to the small increments, the data is partially sorted, and we can sort the pieces quickly if we use a method that takes advantage of order in the data.

We will use a slightly modified version of insertion sort to sort elements that are h apart rather than 1 apart.

Recall that, in insertion sort, when we come to process num[k], we assume that num[0..k-1] are sorted and insert num[k] among the previous items so that num[0..k] are sorted.

Suppose the increment is h and consider how we might process num[k] where k is any valid subscript. Remember, our goal is to sort items that are h apart. So, we must sort num[k] with respect to num[k-h], num[k-2h], num[k-3h], and so on, provided these elements fall within the array. When we come to process num[k], if the previous items that are h apart are sorted among themselves, we must simply insert num[k] among those items so that the sublist ending at num[k] is sorted.

To illustrate, suppose h = 3 and k = 3. There is only one element before num[3] that is three away; that is num[0]. So, when we come to process num[3], we can assume that num[0], by itself, is sorted. We insert num[3] relative to num[0] so that num[0] and num[3] are sorted.

Similarly, there is only one element before num[4] that is three away; that is num[1]. So, when we come to process num[4], we can assume that num[1], by itself, is sorted. We insert num[4] relative to num[1] so that num[1] and num[4] are sorted. Similar remarks apply to num[2] and num[5].

When we get to num[6], the two items before num[6] (num[0] and num[3]) are sorted. We insert num[6] such that num[0], num[3], and num[6] are sorted.

When we get to num[7], the two items before num[7] (num[1] and num[4]) are sorted. We insert num[7] such that num[1], num[4], and num[7] are sorted.

When we get to num[8], the two items before num[8] (num[2] and num[5]) are sorted. We insert num[8] such that num[2], num[5], and num[8] are sorted.

When we get to num[9], the three items before num[9] (num[0], num[3], and num[6]) are sorted. We insert num[9] such that num[0], num[3], num[6], and num[9] are sorted.

And so on. Starting at h, we step through the array processing each item with respect to previous items that are multiples of h away.

In the example, when h = 3, we said we must sort elements (0, 3, 6, 9, 12, 15), (1, 4, 7, 10, 13), and (2, 5, 8, 11, 14). This is true, but our algorithm will not sort items (0, 3, 6, 9, 12, 15), followed by items (1, 4, 7, 10, 13) followed by items (2, 5, 8, 11, 14).

Rather, it will sort them in parallel by sorting the pieces in the following order: (0, 3), (1, 4), (2, 5), (0, 3, 6), (1, 4, 7), (2, 5, 8), (0, 3, 6, 9), (1, 4, 7, 10), (2, 5, 8, 11), (0, 3, 6, 9, 12), (1, 4, 7, 10, 13), (2, 5, 8, 11, 14), and finally (0, 3, 6, 9, 12, 15). This may sound more difficult, but it is actually easier to code.

The following will perform an h-sort on A[0..n-1]:

```
void hsort(int A[], int n, int h) {
//perform an h-sort on A[0..n-1]
    for (int k = h; k < n; k++) {
        int j = k - h; //j will index elements k - h, k - 2h, k - 3h, etc
        int key = A[k];
        while (j >= 0 && key < A[j]) {
            A[j + h] = A[j];
            j = j - h;
        }
        A[j + h] = key;
    }
} //end hsort
```

Alert readers will realize that if we set h to 1, this becomes insertion sort.

Given a series of increments $h_t, h_{t-1}, ..., h_1 = 1$, we simply call hsort with each increment, from largest to smallest, to effect the sort. How to do this is shown in Program P6.8. It assumes the numbers to be sorted are stored in a file shell.in. Suppose the file contains the numbers used in the example above (in any order):

```
67 90 28 84 29 58 25 32
16 64 13 71 82 10 51 57
```

Program P6.8 will produce the following output (the numbers in sorted order):

```
10 13 16 25 28 29 32 51 57 58 64 67 71 82 84 90
```

Program P6.8

```
#include <stdio.h>
#include <stdlib.h>
#define MaxSize 100

int main() {
    void hsort(int[], int, int);
    int num[MaxSize];
    int n = 0, number;
    FILE * in = fopen("shell.in", "r");

    while (fscanf(in, "%d", &number) == 1) {
        if (n < MaxSize) num[n++] = number;
        else {
            printf("\nArray too small\n");
            exit(1);
        }
    }
    //perform Shell sort with increments 8, 3 and 1
    hsort(num, n, 8);
    hsort(num, n, 3);
    hsort(num, n, 1);
```

```
    for (int h = 0; h < n; h++) printf("%d ", num[h]);
    printf("\n");
    fclose(in);
} //end main
void hsort(int A[], int n, int h) {
//perform an h-sort on A[0..n-1]
    for (int k = h; k < n; k++) {
        int j = k - h; //j will index elements k - h, k - 2h, k - 3h, etc
        int key = A[k];
        while (j >= 0 && key < A[j]) {
            A[j + h] = A[j];
            j = j - h;
        }
        A[j + h] = key;
    }
} //end hsort
```

We note that our code would be more flexible if the increments are stored in an array (incr, say) and hsort is called with each element of the array in turn. For example, suppose incr[0] contains the number of increments (m, say), and incr[1] to incr[m] contain the increments in decreasing order with incr[m] = 1. We could call hsort with each increment as follows:

```
for (int i = 1; i <= incr[0]; i++) hsort(num, n, incr[i]);
```

One question that arises is how do we decide which increments to use for a given n? Many methods have been proposed. The following gives reasonable results:

```
let h₁ = 1
generate hₛ₊₁ = 3hₛ + 1, for s = 1, 2, 3,...
and stop when hₜ ≥ n.
Use increments h₁ to hₜ₋₂
```

For example, if $n = 100$, we generate $h_1 = 1$, $h_2 = 4$, $h_3 = 13$, $h_4 = 40$, $h_5 = 121$. Since $h_5 > 100$, we use h_1, h_2, and h_3 as the increments to sort 100 items.

The performance of Shell sort lies somewhere between the simple $O(n^2)$ methods (insertion, selection) and the $O(n\log_2 n)$ methods (heapsort, quicksort, mergesort). Its order is approximately $O(n^{1.3})$ for n in a practical range tending to $O(n(\log_2 n)^2)$ as n tends to infinity.

As an exercise, write a program to sort a list using Shell sort, counting the number of comparisons and assignments made in sorting the list. Your program should determine the increments to be used in the sort.

EXERCISES 6

---

1. Write a program to compare the performance of the sorting methods discussed in this chapter with respect to "number of comparisons" and "number of assignments". For quicksort, compare the performance of choosing the first element as the pivot with choosing a random element.

    (a) Run the program to sort 10, 100, 1000, 10000 and 100000 elements supplied in random order.

    (b) Run the program to sort 10, 100, 1000, 10000 and 100000 elements which are already sorted.

2. A function makeHeap is passed an integer array A. If A[0] contains n, then A[1] to A[n] contain numbers in arbitrary order. Write makeHeap such that A[1] to A[n] contain a max-heap (largest value at the root). Your function must create the heap by processing the elements in the order A[2], A[3],...,A[n].

3. A heap is stored in a one-dimensional integer array num[1..n] with the largest value in position 1. Give an efficient algorithm which deletes the root and rearranges the other elements so that the heap now occupies num[1] to num[n-1].

4. A heap is stored in a one-dimensional integer array A[0..max] with the largest value in position 1. A[0] specifies the number of elements in the heap at any time. Write a function to add a new value v to the heap. Your function should work if the heap is initially empty and should print a message if there is no room to store v.

5. Write code to read a set of positive integers (terminated by 0) and create a heap in an array H with the *smallest* value at the top of the heap. As each integer is read, it is inserted among the existing items such that the heap properties are maintained. At any time, if n numbers have been read then H[1..n] must contain a heap. Assume that H is large enough to hold all the integers.

    You are given the following data: 51 26 32 45 38 89 29 58 34 23 0

    Using the method above, show the contents of H after each number has been read and processed.

6. A function is given an integer array A and two subscripts m and n. The function must rearrange the elements A[m] to A[n] and return a subscript d such that all elements to the left of d are less than or equal to A[d] and all elements to the right of d are greater than A[d].

7. Write a function which, given an integer array num and an integer n, sorts the elements num[1] to num[n] using Shell sort. The function must return the number of key comparisons made in performing the sort. You may use any reasonable method for determining increments.

8. Write a recursive function for finding the kth smallest number in an array of *n* numbers.

9. A single integer array A[1..n] contains the following: A[1..k] contains a min-heap and A[k+1..n] contains arbitrary values. Write efficient code to merge the two portions so that A[1..n] contains one min-heap. Do not use any other array.

10. Write insertion sort using a binary search to determine the position in which A[i] will be inserted among the sorted sublist A[1..i-1].

11. An *integer* max-heap is stored in an array (A, say) such that the size of the heap (n, say) is stored in A[0] and A[1] to A[n] contain the elements of the heap with the largest value in A[1].

    (a) Write a function deleteMax which, given an array like A, deletes the largest element and reorganizes the array so that it remains a heap.

    (b) Given two arrays A and B containing heaps as described above, write programming code to merge the elements of A and B into another array C such that C is in ascending order. Your method must proceed by comparing an element of A with one in B. You may assume that deleteMax is available.

12. A sorting algorithm is said to be *stable* if equal keys retain their original relative order after sorting. Which of the sorting methods discussed in this chapter are stable?

13. You are given a list of *n* numbers. Write efficient algorithms to find (i) the smallest (ii) the largest (iii) the mean (iv) the median (the middle value) and (v) the mode (the value that appears most often).

    Write one efficient algorithm to find all five values.

14. It is known that every number in a list of *n distinct* numbers is between 100 and 9999.

    (a) Devise an efficient method for sorting the numbers.

    (b) Modify the method to sort the list if it may contain duplicate numbers.

15. Modify mergesort and quicksort so that if a sublist to be sorted is smaller than some pre-defined size, it is sorted using insertion sort.

16. You are given a list of *n* numbers and another number x. You must find the smallest number in the list that is greater than or equal to x. You must then delete this number from the list and replace it by a new number y, retaining the list structure. Devise ways of solving this problem using (i) an unsorted array (ii) a sorted array (iii) a sorted linked list (iv) a binary search tree (v) a heap.

    Which of these is the most efficient?

17. You are given a (long) list of English words. Write a program to determine which of those words are anagrams of each other. Output consists of each group of anagrams (two or more words) followed by a blank line. Two words are anagrams if they consist of the same letters, e.g. (teacher, cheater), (sister, resist).

18. Each value in A[1..n] is either 1, 2 or 3. You are required to find the minimal number of exchanges to sort the array. For example, the array

2	2	1	3	3	3	2	3	1
1	2	3	4	5	6	7	8	9

can be sorted with 4 exchanges, in order: (1, 3) (4, 7) (2, 9) (5, 9). Another solution is (1, 3) (2, 9) (4, 7) (5, 9). This array cannot be sorted with less than 4 exchanges.

CHAPTER 7

■ ■ ■

Graphs

In this chapter, we will explain:

- Some graph terminology
- How to perform *depth-first* and *breadth-first* traversals of a graph
- How to represent a graph in a computer program
- How to build a graph representation from given data
- How to classify the edges in a graph
- How to perform a *topological sort* of a graph
- How to derive minimum-cost paths from a source node to all other nodes using Dijkstra's algorithm (edge weights must be non-negative)
- How to derive minimum-cost paths from a source node to all other nodes using the Bellman-Ford algorithm (edge weights can be negative)
- How to construct a minimum-cost spanning tree using Prim's algorithm
- How to represent disjoint sets
- How to construct a minimum-cost spanning tree using Kruskal's algorithm

7.1 Graph Terminology

In this chapter, we discuss a general-purpose data structure—the graph. We have seen how useful trees can be but a tree is just a special case of a graph. We should expect that, with a graph, we can model much more complex situations than we can with a tree.

A *graph* G is a pair $(\mathcal{V}, \mathcal{E})$ where $\mathcal{V}$ is a finite set and $\mathcal{E}$ is a binary relation on $\mathcal{V}$. Each element of $\mathcal{V}$ is called a *vertex* or *node* and each element of $\mathcal{E}$ is called an *edge*. $\mathcal{V}$ is called the *vertex set* and $\mathcal{E}$ is called the *edge set*. The number of vertices is denoted by $|\mathcal{V}|$ and the number of edges by $|\mathcal{E}|$.

For example, if $\mathcal{V}$ is the set {A, B, H, K, N} and $\mathcal{E}$ is the set {(A, H), (H, B), (B, K), (B, A), (N, H), (N, B)}, we have a graph with 5 vertices (nodes) and 6 edges which we can draw as shown in Figure 7-1.

214

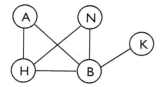

Figure 7-1. A graph (undirected) with 5 nodes and 6 edges

If $\mathcal{E}$ consists of *unordered* pairs of vertices, the graph is *undirected*. Given the edge (u, v) ε $\mathcal{E}$, we simply say there is an edge connecting u and v. We consider that the edge goes *from* u to v or *from* v to u, so an undirected edge is sometimes called *bidirectional*.

If $\mathcal{E}$ consists of *ordered* pairs of vertices, the graph is *directed*. We call it a directed graph or *digraph*. Given the directed edge (u, v) ε $\mathcal{E}$, we say there is an edge *from* u *to* v (depicted as u → v). We sometimes refer to u as the *parent* and v as the *child*. There is *no* implication that there is automatically an edge from v to u; there will be an edge from v to u only if the edge (v, u) is also in $\mathcal{E}$.

In the above graph, suppose the same set of edges were directed. That is, suppose $\mathcal{E}$ = {(A, H), (H, B), (B, K), (B, A), (N, H), (N, B)} where (u, v) ε $\mathcal{E}$ means that there is an edge from u to v but not vice versa. We can draw *this* graph as in Figure 7-2.

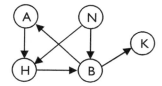

Figure 7-.2. A directed graph with 5 nodes and 6 edges

To represent a directed edge (u, v), we draw an arrowed line from u to v. If, in addition, there is a directed edge (K, B), we could draw the graph as in Figure 7-3.

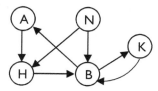

Figure 7-3. Graph with 2 edges connecting the same nodes

If (u, v) ε $\mathcal{E}$ is a directed edge, we say that vertex v is *adjacent* to vertex u. If the graph is undirected, then u is also adjacent to v. In Figure 7-3, A is adjacent to B (but not vice versa); B is adjacent to K *and* K is adjacent to B.

If (u, v) is directed, we say that (u, v) is *incident from* or *leaves* vertex u and is *incident to* or *enters* vertex v. If it is undirected, we say that (u, v) is *incident on* vertices u and v. In either case, we say that u and v are *neighbours*. Thus, two vertices are neighbours if they are connected by an edge, directed or undirected.

In Figure 7.3, the edge (B, A) leaves vertex B and enters vertex A. B is a neighbour of A (and vice versa) even though B is not adjacent to A.

If a graph is directed, the *in-degree* of a vertex is the number of edges *entering* it. The *out-degree* of a vertex is the number of edges *leaving* it. The *degree* of a vertex is the sum of its in-degree and out-degree. This is the same as the number of neighbours of the vertex.

In Figure 7-3, the in-degree of B is 3 and its out-degree is 2; its degree is 5. For A, its in-degree and out-degree are both 1 and its degree is 2. And we have in-degree(N) = 0, out-degree(N) = 2, degree(N) = 2. A vertex with an in-degree of 0 is said to be *isolated*. Thus, N is an isolated vertex.

If a graph is undirected, the *degree* of a vertex is the number of edges incident on it. As in the directed case, this is simply the number of neighbours of the vertex. In Figure 7-1, we have *degree*(A) = 2 and *degree*(B) = 4.

We say there is a *path* from vertex u to vertex v if it is possible to get from u to v by following edges in the graph. More formally, there is a path of length n from u to v if there exists a sequence of vertices u = $v_0, v_1, v_2,..., v_n$ = v such that (v_{i-1}, v_i) ε $\mathcal{E}$, for i = 1, 2, ..., n. The length of the path is the number of edges in the path. If there is a path from u to v, we say that v is *reachable* from u. A path is *simple* if all the vertices in the path are distinct.

In Figure 7-3, the path N → H → B → A from N to A is simple and of length 3. The path N → B → K → B is of length 3 but not simple (B is repeated).

The path $v_0 → v_1 → v_2,... → v_n$ is a *cycle* if $v_0 = v_n$ and there are at least two edges in the path. (Here, we do not include a cycle created by a self-loop, an edge from a vertex to itself.) In other words, a cycle is a path that begins and ends at the same vertex. The cycle is *simple* if $v_1, v_2,..., v_n$ are distinct.

In Figure 7-3, the path A → H → B → A is a simple cycle.

On the other hand, the path A → H → B → K → B → A is a cycle (first and last nodes are the same) but it is not simple (B is repeated).

An *acyclic* graph is one with no cycles. A *directed acyclic graph* is commonly referred to as a *dag*.

An *undirected* graph is *connected* if there is at least one path between any two vertices. A *directed* graph is *strongly connected* if there is at least one path between any two vertices. In other words, 'connected' and 'strongly connected' imply that every vertex is reachable from every other vertex.

The undirected graph in Figure 7-1 is connected. However, the directed graph in Figure 7-3 is not strongly connected since, for instance, N is not reachable from any of the other vertices. However, if we omit N and the edges leaving it, the *subgraph* that remains is strongly connected. We say the subgraph is a *strongly connected component* of the original graph.

A (*free*) *tree* is a connected, acyclic, undirected graph. Figure 7-4 shows a free tree. A free tree with n vertices will necessarily have n-1 edges. We use the term 'free tree' as opposed to a 'rooted tree', the kind we discussed in Chapter 5. We could re-draw Figure 7-4 as a rooted tree (with root A) shown in Figure 7-5. If we wish, we could designate *any* vertex as the root.

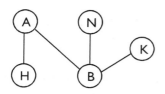
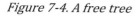

Figure 7-4. A free tree

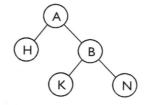

Figure 7-5. A rooted tree

A *weighted* graph is one in which each edge has an associated *weight* or *cost*. For example, each vertex might represent a town and each edge represents a road between two towns. The weight of an edge is the distance between the two towns connected by the edge. The 'weight' can also be the normal time to drive between two towns or the bus fare from one town to the other. As we shall see, weighted graphs are among the most useful kinds of graphs.

7.2 How to Represent a Graph

Consider a graph G(V, E) with |V| = *n* vertices and |E| = *p* edges. To represent G, we must find a way to store the *n* vertices and the *p* edges, including their weights, if any. The two most common ways to represent G are (i) using an n × n *adjacency matrix* and (ii) using n *adjacency lists*. For example, the graph in Figure 7-6 has 7 vertices.

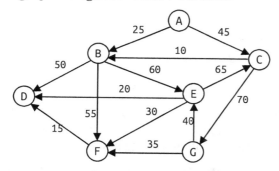

Figure 7-6. A directed graph with 7 vertices

We can represent it using a 7 × 7 adjacency matrix, G, as shown in Figure 7-7.

	1	2	3	4	5	6	7
1	0	25	45	∞	∞	∞	∞
2	∞	0	∞	50	60	55	∞
3	∞	10	0	∞	∞	∞	70
4	∞	∞	∞	0	∞	∞	∞
5	∞	∞	65	20	0	30	∞
6	∞	∞	∞	15	∞	0	∞
7	∞	∞	∞	∞	40	35	0

Figure 7-7. Adjacency matrix representation of a graph

We assign each vertex a unique number from 1 to 7. Here, we assign 1 to A, 2 to B, 3 to C, 4 to D, 5 to E, 6 to F and 7 to G. First, we set G[u, u] to 0 for all u.

Then, if there is an edge of weight w from node u to node v, we set G[u, v] to w. For example, since there is an edge of weight 60 from B to E, we set G[2, 5] = 60. And we set G[6, 4] to 15 since there is an edge of weight 15 from F to D. If there is no edge from u to v, we set G[u, v] = ∞.

In the adjacency list representation, from each vertex u, we keep a linked list of the edges leaving u. For the graph of Figure 7-6, we get the representation shown in Figure 7-8.

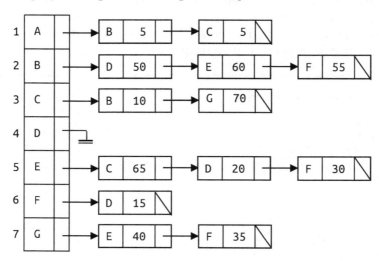

Figure 7-8. Adjacency list representation of a graph

The vertices are shown stored in an array, but any other structure, such as a hash table (next chapter) or a binary search tree, may be used. Each edge-list node consists of three fields: the child vertex, the weight of the edge and a pointer to the next edge node.

Note, for instance, that the edge-list of D is empty since there are no edges leaving D. The nodes of an edge-list can be in any order; we have put them in alphabetical order.

In the edge-list, we have used the *name* of the child vertex for simplicity and clarity. However, in practice, it is usually best to use the *location* of the vertex in whatever data structure is used to hold the vertices. This will give us access to all the other information which may be stored in a vertex, not just the name. We will see more of this later. For now, we store the edge-list by replacing the name of the vertex with its location in the array, giving the representation shown in Figure 7-9 (next page).

As we shall see shortly, this representation is more flexible.

Which representation is better? Adjacency matrix or adjacency list? It depends on the number of edges and the kinds of operations which may need to be performed on the structure.

If there is an edge from each vertex to every other vertex, there will be $n(n-1)$ edges, roughly n^2 edges. If there is a large number of edges (closer to n^2), we say the graph is *dense*. If there are relatively few edges (closer to n, or a small multiple of n), we say the graph is *sparse*.

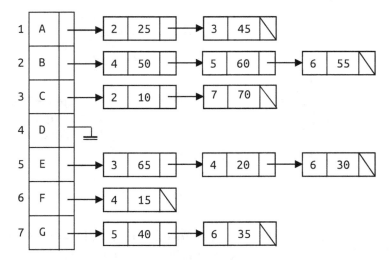

Figure 7-9 Adjacency list representation with node name replaced by node location.

For a dense graph, the matrix representation would be more space-efficient since most of the n^2 entries in the matrix would be non-∞. For a sparse graph, the matrix representation would be inefficient since most of the entries would be ∞. However, the list representation would be better since only the relatively few edges would be stored.

As an exercise, decide which representation is better for each of the following:

- Given two vertices, is there an edge between them?
- Given a vertex, what are the edges leaving the vertex?
- Given a vertex, what are the edges entering the vertex?
- Add a vertex (and associated egdes) to the graph.
- Delete a vertex (and associated edges) from the graph.
- Add an edge to the graph.
- Delete an edge from the graph.
- Change the weight of an edge.
- Process all the edges of a graph.
- Produce a sorted list, by weight, of the edges of the graph.

There are some situations (mainly when the graph is dense) and some operations (such as determining if an edge connects two given vertices) where the matrix representation is decidedly superior. However, for the most part, we will use the list representation since it is generally more space-efficient and allows efficient implementation of the most common operations.

7.3 Build a Graph

We can *describe* the graph of Figure 7-6 with the following data:

```
7
A B C D E F G
A 2 B 25 C 45
```

```
B 3 D 50 E 60 F 55
C 2 B 10 G 70
D 0
E 3 C 65 D 20 F 30
F 1 D 15
G 2 E 40 F 35
```

The first line says there are 7 vertices. The next line gives the names or labels of the vertices. This is followed by 7 more lines, each of which describes the edges leaving a vertex. The first item is the name of a vertex; this is followed by the number of edges, k, leaving the vertex. Next are k pairs of values; each pair describes an edge. For example, the line

```
A 2 B 25 C 45
```

says that vertex A has 2 edges leaving it. They go to B (with a weight of 25) and C (with a weight of 45).

We wish to write a program to read graph data in the above format and build the adjacency list representation of the graph. We will build the representation shown in Figure 7-9.

As shown, each vertex has at least two fields—the name of the vertex and a pointer to the first edge node. Each edge node has three fields—the *location* of the child vertex, the weight of the edge and a pointer to the next edge.

We will need to define two structures—one for the graph vertices and the other for edge nodes. First, we define GVertex and a function to create and return a GVertex structure, given the name of the vertex:

```
typedef struct gEdge {
    int child, weight; //'child' is the location of the child vertex
    struct gEdge *nextEdge;
} GEdge, *GEdgePtr;

GEdgePtr newGEdge(int c, int w) {
//return a pointer to a new GEdge node
    GEdgePtr p = (GEdgePtr) malloc(sizeof (GEdge));;
    p -> child = c;
    p -> weight = w;
    p -> nextEdge = NULL;
    return p;
}
```

Remember, you must precede your program with

```
#include <stdlib.h>
```

in order to use malloc. We will use GVertex and GEdge to write a program to build a graph.

As mentioned, we will store the graph vertices in an array—a GVertex array. We will call the array vertex. We will also need a variable (numV, say) to hold the number of vertices in the graph. We will use vertex[1] to vertex[numV] to hold information for the vertices.

Thus, we can think of vertex and numV as defining the graph. We declare a structure to reflect this:

```
typedef struct graph {
    int numV;
    GVertex vertex[MaxVertices+1];
} *Graph;
```

Note that Graph is declared as a pointer to the structure containing numV and vertex. This will facilitate passing a graph as an argument to a function. It will also allow a function to make changes to a graph and have the changes reflected in the calling function; this would not normally be possible if the graph is passed "by value".

We allocate storage for a graph and set numV with the function newGraph.

```
Graph newGraph(int n) {
    if (n > MaxVertices) {
        printf("\nToo big. Only %d vertices allowed.\n", MaxVertices);
        exit(1);
    }
    Graph p = (Graph) malloc(sizeof(struct graph));
    p -> numV = n;
    return p;
} //end newGraph
```

For example, the statement:

```
Graph G = newGraph(25);
```

will allocate storage for vertex and set numV to 25. We can access these fields with G -> numV and G -> vertex.

Suppose the graph data shown at the start of this section is stored in a file, graph.in. The following code will build and print the graph:

```
#define MaxWordSize 20
#define MaxVertices 50
int main() {
    int numVertices;
    void buildGraph(FILE *, Graph);
    void printGraph(Graph);
    FILE * in = fopen("graph.in", "r");
    fscanf(in, "%d", &numVertices);
    Graph G = newGraph(numVertices);
    buildGraph(in, G);
    printGraph(G);
    fclose(in);
} // end main
```

This reads the number of vertices in the graph and calls buildGraph (see next) to build the graph. It then calls printGraph (see below) to print it.

Here is buildGraph:

```
void buildGraph(FILE * in, Graph G) {
    int numEdges, weight;
    GVertex newGVertex(char[]);
    void addEdge(char[], char[], int, Graph);
    char nodeID[MaxWordSize+1], adjID[MaxWordSize+1];
    for (int h = 1; h <= G -> numV; h++) {
        G -> vertex[h] = newGVertex("");      //create a vertex node
        fscanf(in, "%s", G -> vertex[h].id);   //read the name into id
    }
```

```
    for (int h = 1; h <= G -> numV; h++) {
        fscanf(in, "%s %d", nodeID, &numEdges); //parent and numEdges

        for (int k = 1; k <= numEdges; k++) {
            fscanf(in, "%s %d", adjID, &weight); //child and weight
            addEdge(nodeID, adjID, weight, G);
        }
    }
} //end buildGraph
```

The first for loop reads the names of the vertices and stores them in vertex. The next for loop does the following, using, for example:

C 2 B 10 G 70

- Each pass through the loop processes edge data for one vertex.
- The vertex name, nodeID, and the number of edges, numEdges, are read. Here, nodeID is the parent node C and numEdges is 2.
- On each pass, the inner for loop reads one pair of values—the name of the adjacent (child) vertex and a weight. It passes the edge information—parent, child and weight—to addEdge which adds it to the appropriate list of edges.

Here is addEdge:

```
void addEdge(char X[], char Y[], int weight, Graph G) {
    GEdgePtr newGEdge(int, int);
    //add an edge X -> Y with a given weight
    int h, k;
    //find X in the list of nodes; its location is h
    for (h = 1; h <= G -> numV; h++)
        if (strcmp(X, G -> vertex[h].id) == 0) break;

    //find Y in the list of nodes; its location is k
    for (k = 1; k <= G-> numV; k++)
        if (strcmp(Y, G -> vertex[k].id) == 0) break;

    if (h > G -> numV || k > G -> numV) {
        printf("No such edge: %s -> %s\n", X, Y);
        exit(1);
    }

    GEdgePtr ep = newGEdge(k, weight); //create edge vertex
    // add it to the list of edges, possible empty, from X;
    // it is added so that the list is in order by vertex id
    GEdgePtr prev, curr;
    prev = curr = G -> vertex[h].firstEdge;
    while (curr != NULL &&
            strcmp(Y, G -> vertex[curr -> child].id) > 0) {
        prev = curr;
        curr = curr -> nextEdge;
    }

    if (prev == curr) {
        ep -> nextEdge = G -> vertex[h].firstEdge;
        G -> vertex[h].firstEdge = ep;
    }
```

```
    else {
        ep -> nextEdge = curr;
        prev -> nextEdge = ep;
    }
} //end addEdge
```

The function first searches for the parent vertex, X, in the list of vertices. It then searches for the child vertex, Y, in the list; suppose its location is k. Recall that k, not Y, will be stored in the edge node. A new edge node containing k and the weight of the edge is created. It is then added to the edge list of X so that the edge list is in order by vertex name.

Because of the way addEdge is written, there is some flexibility in the way edge data for the graph is provided. In the sample data used earlier, the edge data was given in the same order the vertices were given, that is, A B C D E F G. And the edge data for a given vertex was given in ascending order by child vertex name (e.g. the edges from B are given in the order D, E, F).

But this is not necessary. The vertices' data can be given in any order and the edge data for a given vertex can be supplied in any order; addEdge will put them in order. So the sample data could have been provided like this:

```
7
A B C D E F G
B 3 F 55 D 50 E 60
G 2 F 35 E 40
D 0
A 2 B 25 C 45
F 1 D 15
C 2 B 10 G 70
E 3 D 20 F 30 C 65
```

Whichever way the data is supplied, buildGraph will build the same graph.

Once the graph is built, we call printGraph to verify that the graph built is indeed the correct one. Here is printGraph:

```
void printGraph(Graph G) {
    for (int h = 1; h <= G -> numV; h++) {
        printf("%s: ", G -> vertex[h].id);
        GEdgePtr p = G -> vertex[h].firstEdge;
        while (p != NULL) {
            printf("%s %d ", G -> vertex[p -> child].id, p -> weight);
            p = p -> nextEdge;
        }
        printf("\n");
    }
} //end printGraph
```

When run with the above data, printGraph prints this:

```
A: B 25 C 45
B: D 50 E 60 F 55
C: B 10 G 70
D:
E: C 65 D 20 F 30
F: D 15
G: E 40 F 35
```

The vertices are printed in the order they were given (on the second line of data) and the edge list for a given vertex is in alphabetical order.

7.4 Traverse a Graph

Consider the problem of traversing a graph by visiting the vertices in some systematic way. We would need to choose one vertex from which to start. Given the following graph, suppose we start from A.

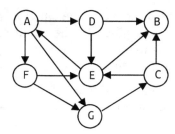

Figure 7-10 A sample graph

One immediate problem is which vertex should we visit next, D or F? In general, if there are several adjacent vertices from which to choose, which one do we choose? The choice is usually arbitrary. Sometimes the choice is forced by the representation of the graph. For example, if the graph is stored using adjacency lists, adjacent vertices will be visited in the order they appear in the edge list. In this graph, we can choose to visit adjacent vertices in alphabetical order.

Suppose we choose D. We would need to remember that F is on hold and we must get back to it at some later time. From D, we must choose B or E. Suppose we choose B. Again, we will need to remember that E is on hold until later. There are no edges leaving B so we have reached a dead-end.

Our traversal method must define a way to proceed on reaching a dead-end. One method is to *backtrack* to the vertex from which we came (D, in this case) and try the next adjacent vertex, if any. In this example, we would try E. If there were no 'next' vertex, we backtrack again, and try the next adjacent vertex, if any. If we backtrack all the way to the start and there is no 'next' vertex to try, our traversal ends.

Suppose we had visited A D B E, in that order. Where do we go from E? Proceeding as before, we will choose the first edge, A. But now we have a problem. We have already visited A so our method must recognize this. If not, we will end up going around in circles with no way out.

One solution is to 'mark' a vertex when it is visited. If traversing an edge would take us to a marked vertex, that edge is not followed. So A will not be chosen. The next adjacent vertex B is also marked (since it has been visited), so B is not chosen. In this case, we backtrack to D and then to A, and try the next vertex from A. This is F, which is unmarked, so it is visited. A common way to mark a vertex is to set some field (visited, say) to false before the vertex is visited and true after it is visited.

In our algorithms, we will use a colour field to mark a vertex. This will give us a little more flexibility, in working with graphs generally, than the two-valued visited field. We will set colour to white before a vertex is visited. After it is visited, its colour can be gray or black, depending on the particular algorithm. A non-white value will mean the vertex has already been seen.

We will see how these three issues—multiple adjacent vertices, reaching a dead- end and not getting caught in a cycle—are handled by the depth-first and breadth-first traversal algorithms.

7.5 Depth-First Traversal

Consider one way of traversing the sample graph of Figure 7-10, starting from A (we assume vertices are marked as they are visited):

- Visit A.
- Follow the first (in alphabetical order) edge and visit D.
- Follow the first edge from D and visit B.
- We have reached a dead-end; backtrack to D and follow the next edge to visit E.
- From E, follow the first edge to A; A is marked, so follow the next edge to B; B is also marked and there are no more edges from E; backtrack to D.
- There are no more edges from D; backtrack to A.
- From A, follow the next edge to visit F.
- From F, follow the first edge to E; E is marked, so follow the next edge to G.
- G is unmarked so visit G and follow its first (and only) edge to C; C is unmarked so visit C.
- From C, follow the first edge to B; B is marked, so follow the next edge to E; E is also marked and there are no more edges from C; backtrack to G.
- There are no more edges from G; backtrack to F.
- There are no more edges from F; backtrack to A.
- From A, follow the next edge to G; G is marked and there are no more edges leaving A; the algorithm ends having visited the vertices in the order: A D B E F G C.

What we have done is visited the vertices in a *depth-first* manner, starting from A. But consider what will happen is we start the traversal from B. We won't go anywhere since there are no edges leaving B. We will visit only B.When we do the traversal of a graph, we will have to arrange things so that all the vertices get visited. One way is to start a new traversal from a vertex that has not yet been visited.

Given a vertex, v, we can do a depth-first traversal starting from v with dfTraverse:

```
void dfTraverse(v) {
    print v.id
    v.colour = gray
    for each edge (v, x)
        if (x.colour == white) dfTraverse(x)
    v.colour = black
} //end dfTraverse
```

When dfTraverse(v) is called, the colour of v is white. Its colour is set to gray to indicate that it has been seen. We then process all the edges leaving v. When that is done, its colour is set to black. So white means "not seen", gray means "being processed" and black means "completely processed".

Note that when we look at an edge (v, x), if x is not white, nothing happens and we simply move on to the next edge, if any.

To ensure that we cover all the vertices in the graph, we can use this:

```
void depthFirstTraversal(G(V, E)) {
    for each vertex v ε V
        v.colour = white
    for each vertex v ε V
        if (v.colour == white) dfTraverse(v)
} //end depthFirstTraversal
```

We first set all the vertices to white. We then call dfTraverse with the first vertex in $\mathcal{V}$ since it is white. When this call returns, we check if any vertex is still white. If we find one, we call dfTraverse with this vertex. This process is repeated until all the vertices in the graph are covered.

In the sample graph, suppose B is designated as the first vertex and A is designated as the second. The call dfTraverse(B) will print B only. On return, the vertex A will still be white so the call dfTraverse(A) is made. This will print A D E F G C. On return, no white vertices remain so the traversal ends. The complete traversal is B A D E F G C.

A depth-first traversal of a graph *defines a depth-first tree*. Consider, again, the depth-first traversal of this graph (same as Figure 7-10):

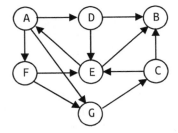

Starting at A, let us identify the edges we followed to visit each of the other vertices D B E F G C in depth-first order:

- To vist D, we followed the edge A → D, so A → D is a tree edge.
- To vist B, we followed the edge D → B, so D → B is a tree edge.
- To vist E, we followed the edge D → E, so D → E is a tree edge.
- To vist F, we followed the edge A → F, so A → F is a tree edge.
- To vist G, we followed the edge F → G, so F → G is a tree edge.
- To vist C, we followed the edge G → C, so G → C is a tree edge.

Those 6 edges define a tree, rooted at A, and connect the 7 vertices. On the left of Figure 7-11, we show only the tree edges. On the right, we draw the tree in the conventional manner. The order of the subtrees (in pre-order) is the order in which they are visited.

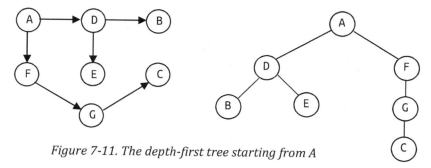

Figure 7-11. The depth-first tree starting from A

But what kind of tree will we get if we started the traversal at B? In this case, we will get 2 trees—a depth-first *forest*. The first tree consists of B only and the second consists of the edges A → D, D → E, A → F, F → G and G → C. This is illustrated in Figure 7-12.

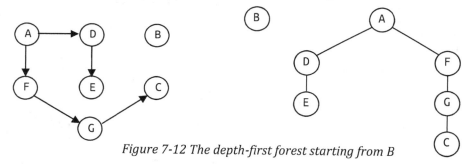

Figure 7-12 The depth-first forest starting from B

In general, a depth-first traversal of a graph will produce a depth-first forest.

7.5.1 Classify Edges By Depth-First Traversal

Consider, again, the edges in the depth-first tree (drawn conventionally on the right) defined by the depth-traversal of the graph (on the left) starting from A:

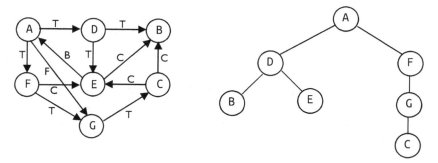

We call these *tree* edges (label T). We now classify the other edges in the graph.

A → G

> In the depth-first tree, this edge connects a vertex, A, to a *descendant*, G, that is not a child. We call such an edge a forward edge (label F). For example, if there were an edge A → E, it would also be a *forward* edge.

E → A

> In the depth-first tree, this edge connects a vertex, E, to an *ancestor*, A. We call such an edge a *back* edge (label B). For example, if there were edges B → D or C → F, these would also be back edges.

E → B

> In the depth-first tree, this edge connects a vertex, E, to a *sibling*, B. We call such an edge a *cross* edge (label C). Any edge that is neither tree, forward nor back is a cross edge.

F → E

> In the depth-first tree, this edge connects a vertex, F, to an unrelated (neither ancestor nor descendant) vertex, E. This is a *cross* edge.

C → B, C → E

> These connect a vertex to an unrelated vertex (in the depth-first tree) and are *cross* edges.

We can easily modify our depth-first traversal algorithm to classify the edges of a graph. In processing the edge v → x:

```
if x is white, then v → x is a tree edge;
if x is gray, then v → x is a back edge;
if x is black, then v → x is either a forward or a cross edge;
```

As you see, tree and back edges are easy to classify. But how do we distinguish between a forward and a cross edge?

To show how, we introduce the notion of *discovery* and *finish* times of a vertex. The discovery time is when the vertex is first encountered. The finish time is when all the edges leaving the vertex have been processed. Remember that dfTraverse(v) is called when we meet v for the first time, when its colour is white. Recall the following:

```
void dfTraverse(v) {
    print v.id
    v.colour = gray
    for each edge (v, x)
        if (x.colour == white) dfTraverse(x)
    v.colour = black
} //end dfTraverse
```

We should set v's discover value when we set its colour to gray. Similarly, we should set its finish value when we set its colour to black (just after processing all its edges). We will initialize a time variable to 0 and increment it each time we need to set a discover or finish time for a vertex. The changes are shown here:

```
void dfTraverse(v) {
    print v.id
    v.colour = gray
    v.discover = ++time;
    for each edge (v, x)
        if (x.colour == white) dfTraverse(x)
    v.colour = black
    v.finish = ++time;
} //end dfTraverse
```

Now we can distinguish between forward and cross edges.

For the edge $v \rightarrow x$:

```
if x is black, then
    if (v.discover < x.discover) v → x is a forward edge
    else v → x is a cross edge
endif
```

Here is dfTraverse which incorporates all the above changes:

```
void dfTraverse(v) {
    print v.id
    v.colour = gray
    v.discover = ++time
    for each edge (v, x)
        if (x.colour == white) {
            (v, x) is a tree edge
            dfTraverse(x)
        }
        else if (x.colour == gray) (v, x) is a back edge
        else if (v.discover < x.discover) (v, x) is a forward edge
             else (v, x) is a cross edge
    endfor
    v.colour = black
    v.finish = ++time
} //end dfTraverse
```

When run on the sample graph, starting from A, we get the results shown in Figure 7-13. We show the discover/finish times separately from the classification of the edges, to reduce the clutter in one diagram:

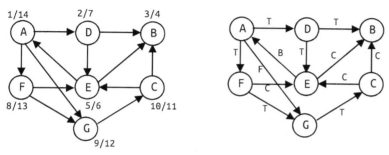

Figure 7-13. Graph with discover/finish times and classified edges

We now trace the call dfTraverse(A) to show how we arrive at these diagrams.

- Set A.discover to 1 and A.colour to gray.
- Follow the first (in alphabetical order) edge to D; D is white, set D.discover to 2 and D.colour to gray.
- Follow the first edge from D to B; B is white, set B.discover to 3 and B.colour to gray.
- There are no edges leaving B; set B.finish to 4, B.colour to black and backtrack to D.
- From D, follow the next edge to E; E is white, set E.discover to 5 and E.colour to gray.
- From E, follow the first edge to A; A is gray so (E, A) is a *back* edge and we follow the next edge to B; B is black and E.discover (5) > B.discover (3) so (E, B) is a *cross* edge; there are no more edges from E so set E.finish to 6, E.colour to black and backtrack to D.
- There are no more edges from D; set D.finish to 7, D.colour to black and backtrack to A.
- From A, follow the next edge to F; F is white, set F.discover to 8 and F.colour to gray.
- From F, follow the first edge to E; E is black and F.discover (8) > E.discover (5) so (F, E) is a *cross* edge; follow the next edge to G.
- G is white, set G.discover to 9, G.colour to gray and follow its first (and only) edge to C; C is white, set C.discover to 10 and C.colour to gray.
- From C, follow the first edge to B; B is black and C.discover (10) > B.discover (3) so (C, B) is a *cross* edge; follow the next edge to E; E is black and C.discover (10) > E.discover (5) so (C, E) is a *cross* edge; there are no more edges from C so set C.finish to 11, C.colour to black and backtrack to G.
- There are no more edges from G; set G.finish to 12, G.colour to black; backtrack to F.
- There are no more edges from F; set F.finish to 13, F.colour to black; backtrack to A.
- From A, follow the next edge to G; G is black and A.discover (1) < G.discover (9) so (A, G) is a *forward* edge; there are no more edges leaving A; set A.finish to 14, A.colour to black and dfTraverse(A) returns.

7.5.2 Implement Depth-First Traversal

We now show how to implement depth-first traversal in a C program. We first define the colour values:

```
#define White 'w'
#define Gray 'g'
#define Black 'b'
```

We write the traversal to compute the discover/finish times. To avoid clutter, we do not classify the edges. If required, this can be easily added. The call

```
depthFirstTraversal(G,1)
```

will perform a depth-first traversal of G starting from vertex 1.

```
void depthFirstTraversal(Graph G, int s) {
//do a depth first traversal of G starting from vertex s
    void dfTraverse(Graph, int);
```

```
    for (int h = 1; h <= G -> numV; h++) {
        G -> vertex[h].colour = White;
        G -> vertex[h].parent = 0;
    }
    printf("\nDepth-first traversal starting from %s\n", G -> vertex[s].id);
    dfTraverse(G, s); //start traversal from s
    //check if any White vertices remain; if so, start another traversal
    for (int h = 1; h <= G -> numV; h++)
        if (G -> vertex[h].colour == White) dfTraverse(G, h);
    printf("\n");
} //end depthFirstTraversal()

void dfTraverse(Graph G, int s) {
    static int time = 0;   //retains its value between calls
    printf("%s ", G -> vertex[s].id);
    G -> vertex[s].colour = Gray;
    G -> vertex[s].discover = ++time;
    GEdgePtr edge = G -> vertex[s].firstEdge;
    while (edge != NULL) {
        if (G -> vertex[edge -> child].colour == White) {
            G -> vertex[edge -> child].parent = s;
            dfTraverse(G, edge -> child);
        }
        edge = edge -> nextEdge;
    }
    G -> vertex[s].colour = Black;
    G -> vertex[s].finish = ++time;
} //end dfTraverse
```

We also keep track of the path to a vertex in the depth-first tree by storing 'parent' information. Initially (in depthFirstTraversal), we set all the parent fields to 0. In dfTraverse, when a white vertex is discovered, its parent field is set. For example, if we follow the edge D → E and E is White, then (D, E) is a tree edge; we set E's parent to D.

Assuming the parent fields have been set, we can print the path to any destination vertex, D, given its string id, with printPath:

```
void printPath(Graph G, char D[]) {
    int h;
    void followPath(Graph, int);
    // find D in the list of nodes (location h)
    for (h = 1; h <= G -> numV; h++)
        if (strcmp(D, G -> vertex[h].id) == 0) break;
    if (h > G -> numV) printf("\nNo such node %s\n", D);
    else {
        printf("\nPath to %s: ", D);
        followPath(G, h);
        printf("\n");
    }
} //end printPath

void followPath(Graph G, int c) {
    if (c != 0) {
        followPath(G, G -> vertex[c].parent);
        printf("%s " , G -> vertex[c].id);
    }
} //end followPath
```

The parent fields link the vertices on the path in reverse order. For example, the path to C from A is: A → F → G → C but the parent fields point the other way, that is: C → G → F → A (the parent of C is G whose parent is F whose parent is A whose parent is none).

Given the destination vertex, followPath simply prints the linked list of vertices in reverse order. For example, the call

```
printPath(G, "C")
```

will print

```
Path to C: A F G C
```

Programming note: For buildGraph (shown earlier) to create the representation of the graph of Figure 7-6, you will need to supply the data as follows:

```
7
A B C D E F G
A 3 D 1 F 1 G 1
B 0
C 2 B 1 E 1
D 2 B 1 E 1
E 2 A 1 B 1
F 2 E 1 G 1
G 1 C 1
```

Since buildGraph expects the weight of the edges to be given, we have used 1 for all the weights. We write Program P7.1 to test our functions.

Program P7.1

```
#include <stdio.h>
#include <stdlib.h>
#include <string.h>

#define MaxWordSize 20
#define MaxVertices 50
#define White 'w'
#define Gray 'g'
#define Black 'b'
typedef struct gEdge {
    int child, weight; //'child' is the location of the child vertex
    struct gEdge *nextEdge;
} GEdge, *GEdgePtr;

typedef struct {
    char id[MaxWordSize+1], colour;
    int parent, cost, discover, finish, inDegree;
    GEdgePtr firstEdge;
} GVertex;

typedef struct graph {
    int numV;
    GVertex vertex[MaxVertices+1];
} *Graph;

int main() {
    int numVertices;
    Graph newGraph(int);
```

```
        void buildGraph(FILE *, Graph), printGraph(Graph), printPath(Graph, char[]);
        void depthFirstTraversal(Graph, int);
        FILE * in = fopen("graph.in", "r");
        fscanf(in, "%d", &numVertices);
        Graph G = newGraph(numVertices);
        buildGraph(in, G);
        printGraph(G);
        depthFirstTraversal(G, 1);
        printPath(G, "C");
        fclose(in);
} // end main

Graph newGraph(int n) {
    if (n > MaxVertices) {
        printf("\nToo big. Only %d vertices allowed.\n", MaxVertices);
        exit(1);
    }
    Graph p = (Graph) malloc(sizeof(struct graph));
    p -> numV = n;
    return p;
} //end newGraph

void buildGraph(FILE * in, Graph G) {
    int numEdges, weight;
    GVertex newGVertex(char[]);
    void addEdge(char[], char[], int, Graph);
    char nodeID[MaxWordSize+1], adjID[MaxWordSize+1];
    for (int h = 1; h <= G -> numV; h++) {
        G -> vertex[h] = newGVertex("");        //create a vertex node
        fscanf(in, "%s", G -> vertex[h].id);    //read the name into id
    }
    for (int h = 1; h <= G -> numV; h++) {
        fscanf(in, "%s %d", nodeID, &numEdges); //parent id and numEdges
        for (int k = 1; k <= numEdges; k++) {
            fscanf(in, "%s %d", adjID, &weight); //get child id and weight
            addEdge(nodeID, adjID, weight, G);
        }
    } //end for
} //end buildGraph

GVertex newGVertex(char name[]) {
    GVertex temp;
    strcpy(temp.id, name);
    temp.firstEdge = NULL;
    return temp;
} //end newGVertex

void addEdge(char X[], char Y[], int weight, Graph G) {
    GEdgePtr newGEdge(int, int);
    //add an edge X -> Y with a given weight
    int h, k;
    //find X in the list of nodes; its location is h
    for (h = 1; h <= G -> numV; h++) if (strcmp(X, G -> vertex[h].id) == 0) break;

    //find Y in the list of nodes; its location is k
    for (k = 1; k <= G-> numV; k++) if (strcmp(Y, G -> vertex[k].id) == 0) break;

    if (h > G -> numV || k > G -> numV) {
        printf("No such edge: %s -> %s\n", X, Y);
        exit(1);
    }
```

```
    GEdgePtr ep = newGEdge(k, weight); //create edge vertex
    // add it to the list of edges, possible empty, from X;
    // it is added so that the list is in order by vertex id
    GEdgePtr prev, curr;
    prev = curr = G -> vertex[h].firstEdge;
    while (curr != NULL && strcmp(Y, G -> vertex[curr -> child].id) > 0) {
        prev = curr;
        curr = curr -> nextEdge;
    }

    if (prev == curr) {
        ep -> nextEdge = G -> vertex[h].firstEdge;
        G -> vertex[h].firstEdge = ep;
    }
    else {
        ep -> nextEdge = curr;
        prev -> nextEdge = ep;
    }
} //end addEdge

GEdgePtr newGEdge(int c, int w) {
//return a pointer to a new GEdge node
    GEdgePtr p = (GEdgePtr) malloc(sizeof (GEdge));;
    p -> child = c;
    p -> weight = w;
    p -> nextEdge = NULL;
    return p;
} //end newGEdge

void printGraph(Graph G) {
    for (int h = 1; h <= G -> numV; h++) {
        printf("%s: ", G -> vertex[h].id);
        GEdgePtr p = G -> vertex[h].firstEdge;
        while (p != NULL) {
            printf("%s %d ", G -> vertex[p -> child].id, p -> weight);
            p = p -> nextEdge;
        }
        printf("\n");
    } //end for
} //end printGraph

void depthFirstTraversal(Graph G, int s) {
//do a depth first traversal of G starting from vertex s
    void dfTraverse(Graph, int);
    for (int h = 1; h <= G -> numV; h++) {
        G -> vertex[h].colour = White;
        G -> vertex[h].parent = 0;
    }
    printf("\nDepth-first traversal starting from %s\n", G -> vertex[s].id);
    dfTraverse(G, s); //start traversal from s
    //check if any White vertices remain; if so, start another traversal
    for (int h = 1; h <= G -> numV; h++)
        if (G -> vertex[h].colour == White) dfTraverse(G, h);
    printf("\n");
} //end depthFirstTraversal()

void dfTraverse(Graph G, int s) {
    static int time = 0;  //retains its value between calls
    printf("%s ", G -> vertex[s].id);
    G -> vertex[s].colour = Gray;
```

```
        G -> vertex[s].discover = ++time;
        GEdgePtr edge = G -> vertex[s].firstEdge;
        while (edge != NULL) {
            if (G -> vertex[edge -> child].colour == White) {
                G -> vertex[edge -> child].parent = s;
                dfTraverse(G, edge -> child);
            }
            edge = edge -> nextEdge;
        }
        G -> vertex[s].colour = Black;
        G -> vertex[s].finish = ++time;
} //end dfTraverse

void printPath(Graph G, char D[]) {
    int h;
    void followPath(Graph, int);
    // find D in the list of nodes (location h)
    for (h = 1; h <= G -> numV; h++)
        if (strcmp(D, G -> vertex[h].id) == 0) break;
    if (h > G -> numV) printf("\nNo such node %s\n", D);
    else {
        printf("\nPath to %s: ", D);
        followPath(G, h);
        printf("\n");
    }
} //end printPath

void followPath(Graph G, int c) {
    if (c != 0) {
        followPath(G, G -> vertex[c].parent);
        printf("%s " , G -> vertex[c].id);
    }
} //end followPath
```

Suppose the file graph.in contains the following data:

```
7
A B C D E F G
A 3 D 1 F 1 G 1
B 0
C 2 B 1 E 1
D 2 B 1 E 1
E 2 A 1 B 1
F 2 E 1 G 1
G 1 C 1
```

Program P7.1 will create the sample graph we've been using. Here it is for easy reference:

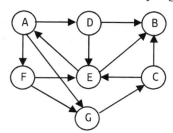

It will then print this:

```
A: D 1 F 1 G 1
B:
C: B 1 E 1
D: B 1 E 1
E: A 1 B 1
F: E 1 G 1
G: C 1

Depth-first traversal starting from A
A D B E F G C

Path to C: A F G C
```

7.6 Topological Sort

There are many situations in which several tasks have to be done and some of these tasks can be done only after others have been completed. For example, in assembling a vehicle, certain parts must be assembled before others can be worked on. The engine cannot be assembled before the parts that go inside it. In teaching a course, several topics may have to be taught and some can be taught only after others have been covered.

In the latter case, we would like to arrange the topics in such an order that if topic A is needed to understand topic B, then A will be taught before B. We will need to do a *topological sort* of the topics.

The topological sorting problem can be stated as follows: given n items, numbered 1 to n, and m requirements of the form $j \rightarrow k$, meaning item j must come before item k, arrange the items in an order such that all requirements are satisfied or determine that no solution is possible.

For example, suppose $n = 9$ and $m = 10$ with the following requirements:

$3 \rightarrow 74 \rightarrow 28 \rightarrow 69 \rightarrow 51 \rightarrow 2$
$6 \rightarrow 52 \rightarrow 57 \rightarrow 88 \rightarrow 11 \rightarrow 9$

Two of the many solutions are:

```
4 3 7 8 6 1 9 2 5
3 7 8 6 1 9 4 2 5
```

If, in addition to the above requirements, we have $5 \rightarrow 8$, there is no solution since $8 \rightarrow 6, 6 \rightarrow 5$, $5 \rightarrow 8$ imply that 8 must come before 5 *and* 5 must come before 8, both of which cannot be satisfied. In this case, we say the requirements are *circular*.

We can solve the 'topological sort' problem by modelling it using a graph. The graph will have n vertices, one for each item. Each requirement $j \rightarrow k$ is represented by a directed edge from vertex j to vertex k. The 10 requirements above will be represented by the following graph:

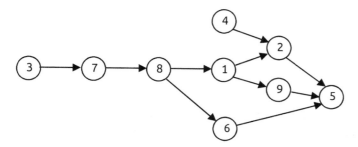

If the graph is acyclic (no cycles) then there is at least one solution to the problem. However, if the graph contains a cycle, there is no solution since this means that the requirements are circular. For example, if there is an edge $5 \rightarrow 8$, then the edges $(8, 6)$, $(6, 5)$ and $(5, 8)$ form a cycle.

We can produce the topological sorted order by doing the following:

```
perform a depth-first traversal of the graph
as each vertex is finished, push it onto a stack, S
when the traversal is done, pop S, and print each item as it is popped
```

For example, starting at vertex 1, the discover/finish times are shown here:

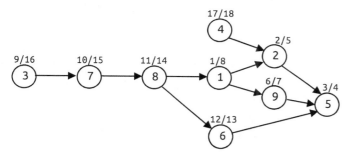

Vertex 5 is the first to finish, so it goes on the stack first. Vertex 4 is the last to finish so it goes on the stack last. In general, vertices go on the stack in the order in which they finish. The topological sort is obtained by listing the vertices *in decreasing order by finish time*. Here, we get the following order which is the first solution, above:

4 3 7 8 6 1 9 2 5

As an exercise, find the solution starting the traversal at vertex 4; repeat for other vertices.

This exercise should make it clear that it does not really matter which vertex we start from; if the problem has a solution, one will be found. However, it is customary to start the traversal from a vertex whose *in-degree* is 0. If a vertex A has an in-degree of 0, it means that there is no edge leading into it. This, in turn, means that there is no requirement that any other item come before it. So we may as well start with A.

We now write `topologicalSort` which performs a depth-first traversal starting from whichever vertex is designated as the first when the graph is built. For the sample problem above, the graph data *could* be supplied as follows:

```
9
1 2 3 4 5 6 7 8 9
3 1 7 1
7 1 8 1
```

```
8 2 1 1 6 1
6 1 5 1
1 2 2 1 9 1
4 1 2 1
2 1 5 1
9 1 5 1
5 0
```

The edge weights, which are not important for solving the problem, are set to 1. Since 1 is designated as the first vertex in the vertex list (the second line of the data), the traversal will start from 1.

A stack will be required for pushing vertices as they are finished. Each stack item will simply be the index of a vertex. For this problem, we define StackData like this:

```
typedef struct {
    int nv; //index of a graph vertex
} StackData;
```

and create the data for a 'stack item' with this:

```
StackData newStackData(int n) {
    StackData temp;
    temp.nv = n;
    return temp;
} //end newStackData
```

We now write topologicalSort.

```
void topologicalSort(Graph G) {
    void dfTopSort(Graph, Stack, int);
    Stack S = initStack();
    for (int h = 1; h <= G -> numV; h++)
        G -> vertex[h].colour = White;

    for (int h = 1; h <= G -> numV; h++)
        if (G -> vertex[h].colour == White) dfTopSort(G, S, h);

    printf("\nTopological sort: ");
    while (!empty(S)) printf("%s ", G -> vertex[pop(S).nv].id);
    printf("\n");
} //end topologicalSort

void dfTopSort(Graph G, Stack S, int s) {
    StackData newStackData(int);
    G -> vertex[s].colour = Gray;
    GEdgePtr edge = G -> vertex[s].firstEdge;
    while (edge != NULL) {
        if (G -> vertex[edge -> child].colour == Gray) {
            printf("\nGraph has a cycle: cannot sort\n");
            exit(1);
        }
        if (G -> vertex[edge -> child].colour == White)
            dfTopSort(G, S, edge -> child);
        edge = edge -> nextEdge;
    }
    G -> vertex[s].colour = Black;
    push(S, newStackData(s));
} //end dfTopSort
```

You are reminded that in order to use the stack routines in <stack.h>, the declaration of StackData must be *followed* by

```
#include <stack.h>
```

Most of the work is done in dfTopSort. This is the usual depth-first traversal except that it checks for back edges. Recall that if the edge (v, x) is being processed and x.colour is Gray, then (v, x) is a back edge. This can happen only if there is a cycle in the graph and, hence, there is no solution.

Note that it is not necessary to record the discover/finish times. As soon as a vertex is finished (after processing all its edges), it is pushed onto the stack. So the vertices go on the stack in *increasing* order by finish time. When we take them off, they will be in *decreasing* order by finish time.

We can perform a topological sort on a graph G with this code:

```
fscanf(in, "%d", &numVertices);
Graph G = newGraph(numVertices);
buildGraph(in, G);
topologicalSort(G);
```

7.6.1 An Improved Topological Sort

The code described in the previous section will solve the topological sort problem. However, it requires us to convert the given requirements into their graph representation. The *description* of this graph is then used as input to buildGraph. A more natural approach would be to input the requirements as given and let the program figure out the graph representation. For instance, the sample problem discussed could be input with the following data:

```
9 10
3 7 4 2 8 6 9 5 1 2
6 5 2 5 7 8 8 1 1 9
```

The first line contains the number of items (9) and the number of requirements (10). This is followed by one or more lines of data containing the requirements. Each requirement $j \to k$ is supplied as the pair of integers j k. For example, the pair 3 7 means there is a requirement that item 3 must come before item 7. The pairs can be supplied in any order with any amount (including all) on one line.

Given that the data is supplied in this format in a file topsort.in, we write Program P7.2 to perform a topological sort.

Program P7.2

```
#include <stdio.h>
#include <stdlib.h>

#define MaxItems 50
#define White 'w'
#define Gray 'g'
#define Black 'b'

typedef struct {
    int nv; //index of a graph vertex
} StackData;
```

```
#include <stack.h>

typedef struct gEdge {
    int child, weight; //'child' is the location of the child vertex
    struct gEdge *nextEdge;
} GEdge, *GEdgePtr;

typedef struct {
    int id, parent, cost, discover, finish, inDegree;
    char colour;
    GEdgePtr firstEdge;
} GVertex;

typedef struct graph {
    int numV;
    GVertex vertex[MaxItems+1];
} *Graph;

int main() {
    int numItems, numRequirements;
    void printRequirements(Graph);
    Graph newGraph(int);
    void buildTopSortGraph(FILE *, Graph, int);
    void topologicalSort(Graph);

    FILE * in = fopen("topsort.in", "r");
    fscanf(in, "%d %d", &numItems, &numRequirements);
    if (numItems > MaxItems) {
        printf("\nToo many items. Only %d allowed.\n", MaxItems);
        exit(1);
    }
    Graph G = newGraph(numItems);
    buildTopSortGraph(in, G, numRequirements);
    printRequirements(G);
    topologicalSort(G);
    fclose(in);
} // end main

Graph newGraph(int n) {
    Graph p = (Graph) malloc(sizeof(struct graph));
    p -> numV = n;
    return p;
} //end newGraph

void buildTopSortGraph(FILE * in, Graph G, int numRequirements) {
    GVertex newGVertex(int);
    void addEdge(int, int, int, Graph);
    int preID, postID;
    for (int h = 1; h <= G -> numV; h++) {
        G -> vertex[h] = newGVertex(-1); //create a vertex node
        G -> vertex[h].id = h;           //IDs run from 1 to h
    }
    for (int h = 1; h <= numRequirements; h++) {
        fscanf(in, "%d %d", &preID, &postID); //get a requirement
        addEdge(preID, postID, 1, G); //set weights to 1
    }
} //end buildTopSortGraph
```

```
 GVertex newGVertex(int name) {
     GVertex temp;
     temp.id = name;
     temp.firstEdge = NULL;
     return temp;
 } //end newGVertex

 void addEdge(int X, int Y, int weight, Graph G) {
     GEdgePtr newGEdge(int, int);
     //add an edge X -> Y with a given weight

     GEdgePtr ep = newGEdge(Y, weight); //create edge vertex
     // add it to the list of edges, possible empty, from X;
     // it is added so that the list is in order by vertex id
     GEdgePtr prev, curr;
     prev = curr = G -> vertex[X].firstEdge;
     while (curr != NULL && Y > G -> vertex[curr -> child].id) {
         prev = curr;
         curr = curr -> nextEdge;
     }

     if (prev == curr) {
         ep -> nextEdge = G -> vertex[X].firstEdge;
         G -> vertex[X].firstEdge = ep;
     }
     else {
         ep -> nextEdge = curr;
         prev -> nextEdge = ep;
     }
 } //end addEdge

GEdgePtr newGEdge(int c, int w) {
//return a pointer to a new GEdge node
    GEdgePtr p = (GEdgePtr) malloc(sizeof (GEdge));;
    p -> child = c;
    p -> weight = w;
    p -> nextEdge = NULL;
    return p;
} //end newGEdge

StackData newStackData(int n) {
    StackData temp;
    temp.nv = n;
    return temp;
} //end newStackData

void topologicalSort(Graph G) {
    void dfTopSort(Graph, Stack, int);
    Stack S = initStack();
    for (int h = 1; h <= G -> numV; h++)
       G -> vertex[h].colour = White;
    for (int h = 1; h <= G -> numV; h++)
       if (G -> vertex[h].colour == White) dfTopSort(G, S, h);
    printf("\nTopological sort: ");
    while (!empty(S))
       printf("%d ", G -> vertex[pop(S).nv].id);
    printf("\n");
} //end topologicalSort
```

```
void dfTopSort(Graph G, Stack S, int s) {
    StackData newStackData(int);
    G -> vertex[s].colour = Gray;
    GEdgePtr edge = G -> vertex[s].firstEdge;
    while (edge != NULL) {
        if (G -> vertex[edge -> child].colour == Gray) {
            printf("\nGraph has a cycle: cannot sort\n");
            exit(1);
        }
        if (G -> vertex[edge -> child].colour == White)
                dfTopSort(G, S, edge -> child);
        edge = edge -> nextEdge;
    }
    G -> vertex[s].colour = Black;
    push(S, newStackData(s));
} //end dfTopSort

void printRequirements(Graph G) {
    printf("The requirements are: \n\n");
    for (int h = 1; h <= G -> numV; h++) {
        int preID = G -> vertex[h].id;
        GEdgePtr p = G -> vertex[h].firstEdge;
        if (p == NULL) continue;
                //no requirement where this item comes first
        while (p != NULL) {
            printf("%d -> %d", preID, G -> vertex[p -> child].id);
            if (p -> nextEdge != NULL) printf(", ");
                //print comma except after last
            p = p -> nextEdge;
        }
        printf("\n");
    }
} //end printRequirements
```

Suppose the file topsort.in contains this:

```
9 10
3 7 4 2 8 6 9 5 1 2
6 5 2 5 7 8 8 1 1 9
```

Program P7.2 produces the following output:

```
The requirements are:

1 -> 2, 1 -> 9
2 -> 5
3 -> 7
4 -> 2
6 -> 5
7 -> 8
8 -> 1, 8 -> 6
9 -> 5

Topological sort: 4 3 7 8 6 1 9 2 5
```

Comments on Program P7.2

- Previously, we have catered for a vertex ID being a string. Here, the items are numbered from 1 to *n*, where *n* is the number of items. Each vertex ID is just an integer. The declaration of GVertex reflects this. Appropriate changes are also made to those functions that use GVertex. Now, for instance, we can compare two vertex IDs using the relational operators rather than strcmp. And we print the IDs using %d rather than %s.

- The function buildTopSortGraph reads the requirements and builds the graph. Note that it is now a bit simpler than the original buildGraph. Given that the vertex IDs are now integers from 1 to *n*, we no longer have to read an ID as a string.

- The function addEdge is also much simpler than before. Previously, we had to search the list of vertices to find the location of a given (string) vertex ID. Now, the integer vertex ID *is* the same as its location in the vertex list. For example, the graph node for item 7 is accessed using G -> vertex[7].

- The requirements are printed using the function printRequirements, a slightly modified version of the previous printGraph.

7.7 Breadth-First Traversal

We now look at the other common way of traversing a graph—breadth-first traversal. This is similar to level-order traversal for a (binary) tree. We perform a breadth-first traversal of the following graph, starting from A:

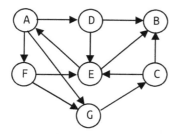

Assume that edges of a vertex are processed in alphabetical order.

- From A, there are edges to D, F and G and these will be visited in that order.
- From D, there are edges to B and E and these will be visited in that order.
- From F, there are edges to E and G; these have been met before so there is nothing to do.
- From G, there is an edge to C and this is visited.
- From B, there is no edge so there is nothing to do.
- From E, there are edges to A and B; these have been met before so there is nothing to do.
- From C, there are edges to B and E; these have been met before so there is nothing to do.

There are no more vertices to process so the traversal ends, having visited the vertices in the order A D F G B E C.

The traversal may be easier to follow if we draw the graph in a tree-like manner, like this:

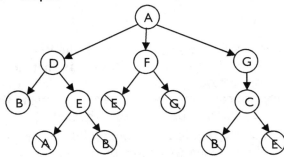

Using this diagram, the breadth-first traversal is a little more obvious. Essentially, it reduces to a level-order traversal: traverse vertices from left to right, from top to bottom. If you meet a vertex that has already been seen, ignore it. This is indicated by a line across the vertex.

Like the level-order traversal of a tree, we can perform a breadth-first traversal of a graph using a queue. The gist of the algorithm is as follows:

```
initialize a queue, Q
set the colour of all vertices to White and parent fields to 0
enqueue the start vertex, s
s.colour = gray
while (Q is not empty) {
    let p = Q.dequeue
    visit p
    for each edge (p, x)
        if (x.colour is white) {
            x.colour = gray
            x.parent = p
            enqueue x
        }
    endfor
    p.colour = black
}
```

We trace the algorithm with the sample graph starting from A. Vertices are visited as they are taken off the queue.

- A is put on Q with A.colour set to gray and we enter while loop.
- Q is not empty; p is set to A; we process the edges (A, D), (A, F) and (A, G); the colour of D, F and G is set to gray, their parent is set to A and they are put on Q. Q now contains D F G (D at the head, G at the tail).
- A.colour is set to black and we go back to the top of the while loop.
- Q is not empty; p is set to D; we process the edges (D, B) and (D, E); the colour of B and E is set to gray, their parent is set to D and they are put on Q. Q now contains F G B E.
- D.colour is set to black and we go back to the top of the while loop.
- Q is not empty; p is set to F; we process the edges (F, E) and (F, G); the colour of E and G is not white so there is nothing to do. Q contains G B E.
- F.colour is set to black and we go back to the top of the while loop.

- Q is not empty; p is set to G; we process the edge (G, C); the colour of C is set to gray, its parent is set to G and it is put on Q. Q contains B E C.
- G.colour is set to black and we go back to the top of the while loop.
- Q is not empty; p is set to B; there are no edges leaving B so there is nothing to do. Q contains E C.
- B.colour is set to black and we go back to the top of the while loop.
- Q is not empty; p is set to E; we process the edges (E, A) and (E, B); the colour of A and B is not white so there is nothing to do. Q contains C.
- E.colour is set to black and we go back to the top of the while loop.
- Q is not empty; p is set to C; we process the edges (C, B) and (C, E); the colour of B and E is not white so there is nothing to do. Q is empty.
- C.colour is set to black and we go back to the top of the while loop.
- Q is empty so the algorithm terminates.

Using the queue header file defined in chapter 4, we will write a function to implement breadth-first traversal. Each queue item is just the index of a vertex. We define QueueData as follows:

```
typedef struct {
    int nv; //index of a graph vertex
} QueueData;
```

and create the data for a 'queue item' with this:

```
QueueData newQueueData(int n) {
    QueueData temp;
    temp.nv = n;
    return temp;
} //end newQueueData
```

Here is breadthFirstTraversal; it closely follows the algorithm given above. It prints the names of the vertices in breadth-first order.

```
void breadthFirstTraversal(Graph G, int s) {
//do a breadth first traversal of G starting from vertex[s]
    QueueData newQueueData(int);

    for (int h = 1; h <= G -> numV; h++) {
        G -> vertex[h].colour = White;
        G -> vertex[h].parent = 0;
    }
    G -> vertex[s].colour = Gray;
    G -> vertex[s].parent = 0;
    Queue Q = initQueue();
    enqueue(Q, newQueueData(s));
    printf("\nBreadth-first traversal starting from %s\n", G->vertex[s].id);
    while (!empty(Q)) {
        int aParent = dequeue(Q).nv;
        printf("%s ", G -> vertex[aParent].id);
        GEdgePtr edge = G -> vertex[aParent].firstEdge;
```

```
    while (edge != NULL) {
        if (G -> vertex[edge -> child].colour == White) {
            G -> vertex[edge -> child].colour = Gray;
            G -> vertex[edge -> child].parent = aParent;
            enqueue(Q, newQueueData(edge -> child));
        }
        edge = edge -> nextEdge;
    } //end while
    G -> vertex[aParent].colour = Black;
  } //end while (!empty(Q))
  printf("\n");
} //end breadthFirstTraversal
```

Programming note: If you are writing a program in which you need to use both stacks and queues, you will need to rename some of the items in one of the headers (queue.h, say) to avoid duplicate names. For example, instead ofnode, Node, NodePtr and empty (also defined in stack.h), you can use Qnode, QNode, QNodePtr and Qempty.

Suppose we wish to get from one vertex, S, to another vertex, D, by following the fewest number of edges. We could do a breadth-first traversal from S and stop when D is first encountered. We could then reconstruct the path using the parent fields.

7.8 Shortest Paths: Dijkstra's Algorithm

In what we have done so far (traversals and topological sort), we did not need to use the weights of the edges in the graph. Now we consider the problem of finding the shortest path from a source node, S, to a destination node, D, where 'shortest' is defined as the lowest sum of weights of the edges on a path from S to D. We use the terms *least-cost* path, *minimum-weight* path and *shortest* path to mean the same thing.

Consider this graph:

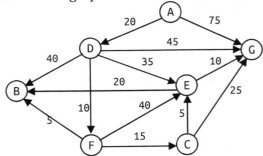

Suppose we wish to find the shortest path from A to E. There are several ways to get to E:

```
A → D → E           (with a cost of 20 + 35 = 55)
A → D → F → E       (with a cost of 20 + 10 + 40 = 70)
A → D → F → C → E   (with a cost of 20 + 10 + 15 + 5 = 50)
```

Of these, the last is the *least-cost* path.

While we may be interested in finding the shortest path from one vertex to another specific vertex, it turns out that it is no easier to solve this problem than to find the shortest paths from the source vertex to *all* other vertices.

We will find these shortest paths using an algorithm due to E. W. Dijkstra.

This algorithm assumes that *the edge weights are non-negative*. We will see the need for this condition shortly. We first show how Dijkstra's algorithm finds the shortest paths from vertex A to all other vertices in the above graph. We assume that

- V.cost holds the current cost of a path from A to a vertex V.
- V.parent holds the parent of V on the current shortest path from A to V.

Initially, we set all the parent fields to nil (meaning "no parent") and the cost fields to infinity (∞), indicating that no path to the vertex has yet been found.

vertex	A	B	C	D	E	F	G
parent	nil	nil	nil	nil	nil	nil	nil
cost	0	∞	∞	∞	∞	∞	∞

We will also need a priority queue, Q, which holds the vertices based on their current cost. Initially, we will put all the vertices on Q. Vertex A, with a cost of 0, will be at the head:

Q: A_0 B_∞ C_∞ D_∞ E_∞ F_∞ G_∞ (head is on the left)

- We take A off the queue and look at the edges leaving A. We will process edges in alphabetical order but any order will work. The edge (A, D) gives us a path to D at a cost of 20. This is lower than the current cost to D (∞) so we update the cost to 20, set the parent of D to A and adjust D's position in Q.
- The edge (A, G) gives us a path to G at a cost of 75. This is lower than the current cost to G (∞) so we update the cost to 75, set the parent of G to A and adjust G's position in Q. We have the following:

vertex	A	B	C	D	E	F	G
parent	nil	nil	nil	A	nil	nil	A
cost	0	∞	∞	20	∞	∞	75

Q: D_{20} G_{75} B_∞ C_∞ E_∞ F_∞

- We take D (the vertex with the lowest cost) off the queue. *Whenever we take a vertex off the queue, we have found the shortest path to that vertex.* So we can conclude that the mininum cost to D (from A) is 20. Why is this so? Well, if there were a shorter path to D, it will have to go through G (there is no other edge leaving A). But the cost to G is 75. The only way to get a shorter path to D via G is for edges to have negative weights (for example, if there was an edge G → D with weight -60). Since we do not allow negative weights, this cannot happen.
- We process the edges leaving D. The edge (D, B) gives us a path to B at a cost of $20 + 40 = 60$ (the cost to D plus the weight of (D, B)). This is lower than the current cost to B (∞) so we update the cost to 60, set the parent of B to D and adjust B's position in Q.

- The edge (D, E) gives us a path to E at a cost of $20 + 35 = 55$ (the cost to D plus the weight of (D, E)). This is lower than the current cost to E (∞). We update the cost to 55, set the parent of E to D and adjust E's position in Q.

- The edge (D, F) gives us a path to F at a cost of $20 + 10 = 30$ (the cost to D plus the weight of (D, F)). This is lower than the current cost to F (∞) so we update the cost to 30, set the parent of F to D and adjust F's position in Q.

- The edge (D, G) gives us a path to G at a cost of $20 + 45 = 65$ (the cost to D plus the weight of (D, G)). This is lower than the current cost to G (75) so we update the cost to 65, change G's parent to D and adjust G's position in Q. We have the following:

vertex	A	B	C	D	E	F	G
parent	nil	D	nil	A	D	D	D
cost	0	60	∞	20	55	30	65

Q: F_{30} E_{55} B_{60} G_{65} C_∞

- We take F off the queue and process the edges leaving F. The edge (F, B) gives us a path to B at a cost of $30 + 5 = 35$ (the cost to F plus the weight of (F, B)). This is lower than the current cost to B (60) so we update the cost to 35, change B's parent to F and adjust B's position in Q.

- The edge (F, C) gives us a path to C at a cost of $30 + 15 = 45$ (the cost to F plus the weight of (F, C)). This is lower than the current cost to C (∞) so we update the cost to 45, change C's parent to F and adjust C's position in Q.

- The edge (F, E) gives us a path to E at a cost of $30 + 40 = 70$ (the cost to F plus the weight of (F, E)). This is higher than the current cost to E (55) so we leave E as it is. We now have this:

vertex	A	B	C	D	E	F	G
parent	nil	F	F	A	D	D	D
cost	0	35	45	20	55	30	65

Q: B_{35} C_{45} E_{55} G_{65}

- We take B off the queue and process the edges leaving B. But there are none, so nothing changes except Q, which now contains this:

Q: C_{45} E_{55} G_{65}

- We take C off the queue and process the edges leaving C. The edge (C, E) gives us a path to E at a cost of $45 + 5 = 50$ (the cost to C plus the weight of (C, E)). This is lower than the current cost to E (55). We update the cost to 50, change E's parent to C and adjust E's position in Q.

- The edge (C, G) gives us a path to G at a cost of $45 + 25 = 70$ (the cost to C plus the weight of (C, G)). This is higher than the current cost to G (65) so we leave G as it is. We now have this:

vertex	A	B	C	D	E	F	G
parent	nil	F	F	A	C	D	D
cost	0	35	45	20	50	30	65

Q: E_{50} G_{65}

- We take E off the queue and process the only edge leaving E. The edge (E, G) gives us a path to G at a cost of 50 + 10 = 60 (the cost to E plus the weight of (E, G)). This is lower than the current cost to G (65) so we update the cost to 60, change G's parent to E and adjust G's position in Q. We have the following:

vertex	A	B	C	D	E	F	G
parent	nil	F	F	A	C	D	D
cost	0	35	45	20	50	30	60

Q: G_{60}

- We take G off the queue and process the edges leaving G. But there are none, so nothing changes except Q, which is now empty.

- Since Q is empty, the algorithm terminates, with the following results:

```
Cost to B: 35, Path: A → D → F → B
Cost to C: 45, Path: A → D → F → C
Cost to D: 20, Path: A → D
Cost to E: 50, Path: A → D → F → C → E
Cost to F: 30, Path: A → D → F
Cost to G: 60, Path: A → D → F → C → E → G
```

The path to any vertex can be found by following the parent pointers. For example, the parent of B is F, the parent of F is D and the parent of D is A. So the path from A to B is A → D → F → B. We formulate Dijkstra's algorithm as follows:

```
Dijkstra(G, W, s)
//find minimum-cost paths from s to every other vertex
//assumes that W(p, x), the weight of the edge (p, x), >= 0
// Q is a priority queue
    initSingleSource(G, s)  //see below
    add all the vertices of G to Q
    while not empty(Q) do
        p = Q.extract-min()
        if (p.cost == ∞) break; //no paths to other vertices via p
        for each edge (p, x)    //for each edge leaving p
            if (p.cost + W(p, x) < x.cost) then // better path found
                x.cost = p.cost + W(p, x)
                x.parent = p
                adjust x's position in Q
            endif
        endfor
    endwhile
    for each vertex v in G
        print v.cost and the path to get to v from s
end Dijkstra

initSingleSource(G, s)
    for each vertex v in G
        v.cost = ∞
        v.parent = nil
    endfor
    s.cost = 0
end initSingleSource
```

7.8.1 Implement Dijkstra's Algorithm

We can implement Dijkstra's algorithm in a fairly straightforward manner, as shown below:

```
void Dijkstra(Graph G, int s) {
    void initSingleSource(Graph, int);
    void siftDown(Graph, int, int[], int, int, int[]);
    void siftUp(Graph, int[], int, int[]);
    void printCostPath(Graph);
    int heap[MaxVertices + 1], heapLoc[MaxVertices + 1];
    //heapLoc[i] gives the position in heap of vertex i
    //if heapLoc[i] = k, then heap[k] contains i

    initSingleSource(G, s);
    for (int i = 1; i <= G -> numV; i++) heap[i] = heapLoc[i] = i;
    heap[1] = s; heap[s] = 1; heapLoc[s] = 1; heapLoc[1] = s;
    int heapSize = G -> numV;
    while (heapSize > 0) {
        int u = heap[1];
        if (G -> vertex[u].cost == Infinity) break; //no paths to other vertices
        //reorganize heap after removing top item
        siftDown(G, heap[heapSize], heap, 1, heapSize-1, heapLoc);
        GEdgePtr p = G -> vertex[u].firstEdge;
        while (p != NULL) {
            if (G -> vertex[u].cost + p -> weight < G -> vertex[p -> child].cost) {
                G -> vertex[p -> child].cost = G -> vertex[u].cost + p -> weight;
                G -> vertex[p -> child].parent = u;
                siftUp(G, heap, heapLoc[p -> child], heapLoc);
            }
            p = p -> nextEdge;
        }
        --heapSize;
    } //end while

    printCostPath(G);
} //end Dijkstra

void initSingleSource(Graph G, int s) {
    for (int i = 1; i <= G -> numV; i++) {
        G -> vertex[i].cost = Infinity;
        G -> vertex[i].parent = 0;
    }
    G -> vertex[s].cost = 0;
} //end initSingleSource

void printCostPath(Graph G) {
    void followPath(Graph, int);
    for (int i = 1; i <= G -> numV; i++) {
        printf("Cost to %s: %d, Path: ", G -> vertex[i].id, G -> vertex[i].cost);
        followPath(G, i);
        printf("\n");
    }
} //end printCostPath
```

```
void followPath(Graph G, int c) {
    if (c != 0) {
        followPath(G, G -> vertex[c].parent);
        if (G -> vertex[c].parent != 0) printf(" -> "); //do not print -> for source
        printf("%s " , G -> vertex[c].id);
    }
} //end followPath
```

If G is a Graph, we call the function with this:

Dijkstra(G, s)

where s is the index of the source vertex in the order that the vertices were supplied when the graph was built. For example, suppose the order was

A B C D E F G

then

Dijkstra(G, 1)

will find minimum-cost paths from A (vertex 1) and

Dijkstra(G, 6)

will find minimum-cost paths from F (vertex 6).

The code closely follows the algorithm above. The priority queue is implemented using a min-heap (item with the *lowest* cost is at the root). The items in the array heap are the vertex numbers (1, 2, 3, etc.). So, for instance, if vertex 4 has the current lowest cost then heap[1] will contain 4.

We will need to keep track of where a vertex is in the heap. This is necessary to be able to adjust the position of a vertex in the heap when its path cost is lowered. For example, suppose vertex[2].cost is 60 and heap[3] = 2 (meaning that vertex 2 is stored in location 3). If vertex[2].cost changes to 35, we will have to adjust the position of vertex 2 in the heap based on its new cost. But we can only do so if we know where it is.

We use the array heapLoc to keep track of the location of a vertex in heap. In this example, we will have heapLoc[2] = 3, meaning that vertex 2 is stored in heap[3]. Suppose, as a result of its cost changing to 35, vertex 2 must be moved to heap[1]. This would also mean that whatever was in heap[1] (vertex 5, say) must be moved to heap[3]. These changes would be reflected in heapLoc. So heapLoc[2] will become 1 (meaning that vertex 2 is in heap[1]) and heapLoc[5] will become 3 (meaning that vertex 5 is in heap[3]).

The following statements initialize the heap.

```
for (int i = 1; i <= G -> numV; i++)
    heap[i] = heapLoc[i] = i;
heap[1] = s; heap[s] = 1; heapLoc[s] = 1; heapLoc[1] = s;
```

The for loop puts vertex i in heap[i]. The other statements ensure that the source vertex s is placed at the root of the heap, by swapping it with vertex 1. Of course, if the start vertex *is* 1, these statements have no effect.

Reorganizing the heap is done using slightly modified versions of siftUp and siftDown from Chapter 6. These are shown as part of Program P7.3, a program which tests our implementation of Dijkstra's algorithm.

Program P7.3

```
#include <stdio.h>
#include <stdlib.h>
#include <string.h>

#define MaxWordSize 20
#define MaxVertices 50
#define White 'w'
#define Gray 'g'
#define Black 'b'
#define Infinity 99999

typedef struct gEdge {
    int child, weight; //'child' is the location of the child vertex
    struct gEdge *nextEdge;
} GEdge, *GEdgePtr;

typedef struct {
    char id[MaxWordSize+1], colour;
    int parent, cost, discover, finish, inDegree;
    GEdgePtr firstEdge;
} GVertex;

typedef struct graph {
    int numV;
    GVertex vertex[MaxVertices+1];
} *Graph;

int main() {
    int numVertices;
    Graph newGraph(int);
    void buildGraph(FILE *, Graph);
    void printGraph(Graph);
    void depthFirstTraversal(Graph, int);
    void Dijkstra(Graph, int);
    FILE * in = fopen("dijkstra.in", "r");

    fscanf(in, "%d", &numVertices);
    Graph G = newGraph(numVertices);
    buildGraph(in, G);
    printGraph(G);
    Dijkstra(G, 1);
    fclose(in);
} // end main

void Dijkstra(Graph G, int s) {
    void initSingleSource(Graph, int);
    void siftDown(Graph, int, int[], int, int, int[]);
    void siftUp(Graph, int[], int, int[]);
    void printCostPath(Graph);
    int heap[MaxVertices + 1], heapLoc[MaxVertices + 1];
    //heapLoc[i] gives the position in heap of vertex i
    //if heapLoc[i] = k, then heap[k] contains i

    initSingleSource(G, s);
    for (int i = 1; i <= G -> numV; i++) heap[i] = heapLoc[i] = i;
    heap[1] = s; heap[s] = 1; heapLoc[s] = 1; heapLoc[1] = s;
    int heapSize = G -> numV;
```

```
    while (heapSize > 0) {
        int u = heap[1];
        if (G -> vertex[u].cost == Infinity) break; //no paths to other vertices
        //reorganize heap after removing top item
        siftDown(G, heap[heapSize], heap, 1, heapSize-1, heapLoc);
        GEdgePtr p = G -> vertex[u].firstEdge;
        while (p != NULL) {
            if (G -> vertex[u].cost + p -> weight < G -> vertex[p -> child].cost) {
                G -> vertex[p -> child].cost = G -> vertex[u].cost + p -> weight;
                G -> vertex[p -> child].parent = u;
                siftUp(G, heap, heapLoc[p -> child], heapLoc);
            }
            p = p -> nextEdge;
        } //end while
        --heapSize;
    } //end while

    printCostPath(G);
} //end Dijkstra

void initSingleSource(Graph G, int s) {
    for (int i = 1; i <= G -> numV; i++) {
        G -> vertex[i].cost = Infinity;
        G -> vertex[i].parent = 0;
    }
    G -> vertex[s].cost = 0;
} //end initSingleSource

void printCostPath(Graph G) {
    void followPath(Graph, int);
    for (int i = 1; i <= G -> numV; i++) {
        printf("Cost to %s: %2d, Path: ", G -> vertex[i].id, G -> vertex[i].cost);
        followPath(G, i);
        printf("\n");
    }
} //end printCostPath

void followPath(Graph G, int c) {
    if (c != 0) {
        followPath(G, G -> vertex[c].parent);
        if (G -> vertex[c].parent != 0) printf(" -> ");
        printf("%s ", G -> vertex[c].id);
    }
} //end followPath

void siftUp(Graph G, int heap[], int n, int heapLoc[]) {
//sifts up heap[n] so that heap[1..n] contains a heap based on cost
    int siftItem = heap[n];
    int child = n;
    int parent = child / 2;
    while (parent > 0) {
        if (G->vertex[siftItem].cost >= G->vertex[heap[parent]].cost) break;
        heap[child] = heap[parent]; //move down parent
        heapLoc[heap[parent]] = child;
        child = parent;
        parent = child / 2;
    }
    heap[child] = siftItem;
    heapLoc[siftItem] = child;
} //end siftUp
```

```
void siftDown(Graph G, int key, int heap[], int root, int last, int heapLoc[]) {
    int smaller = 2 * root;
    while (smaller <= last) { //while there is at least one child
        if (smaller < last) //there is a right child as well; find the smaller
            if (G->vertex[heap[smaller+1]].cost < G->vertex[heap[smaller]].cost)
                smaller++;
        //'smaller' holds the index of the smaller child
        if (G -> vertex[key].cost <= G -> vertex[heap[smaller]].cost) break;
        //cost[key] is bigger; promote heap[smaller]
        heap[root] = heap[smaller];
        heapLoc[heap[smaller]] = root;
        root = smaller;
        smaller = 2 * root;
    } //end while
    heap[root] = key;
    heapLoc[key] = root;
} //end siftDown

Graph newGraph(int n) {
    if (n > MaxVertices) {
        printf("\nToo big. Only %d vertices allowed.\n", MaxVertices);
        exit(1);
    }
    Graph p = (Graph) malloc(sizeof(struct graph));
    p -> numV = n;
    return p;
} //end newGraph

void buildGraph(FILE * in, Graph G) {
    int numEdges, weight;
    GVertex newGVertex(char[]);
    void addEdge(char[], char[], int, Graph);
    char nodeID[MaxWordSize+1], adjID[MaxWordSize+1];
    for (int h = 1; h <= G -> numV; h++) {
        G -> vertex[h] = newGVertex("");        //create a vertex node
        fscanf(in, "%s", G -> vertex[h].id);    //read the name into id
    }
    for (int h = 1; h <= G -> numV; h++) {
        fscanf(in, "%s %d", nodeID, &numEdges); //parent id and numEdges
        for (int k = 1; k <= numEdges; k++) {
            fscanf(in, "%s %d", adjID, &weight); //get child id and weight
            addEdge(nodeID, adjID, weight, G);
        }
    }
} //end buildGraph

GVertex newGVertex(char name[]) {
    GVertex temp;
    strcpy(temp.id, name);
    temp.firstEdge = NULL;
    return temp;
}

void addEdge(char X[], char Y[], int weight, Graph G) {
    GEdgePtr newGEdge(int, int);
    //add an edge X -> Y with a given weight
    int h, k;
    //find X in the list of nodes; its location is h
    for (h = 1; h <= G -> numV; h++) if (strcmp(X, G -> vertex[h].id) == 0) break;
```

```
    //find Y in the list of nodes; its location is k
    for (k = 1; k <= G-> numV; k++) if (strcmp(Y, G -> vertex[k].id) == 0) break;

    if (h > G -> numV || k > G -> numV) {
        printf("No such edge: %s -> %s\n", X, Y);
        exit(1);
    }

    GEdgePtr ep = newGEdge(k, weight); //create edge vertex
    // add it to the list of edges, possible empty, from X;
    // it is added so that the list is in order by vertex id
    GEdgePtr prev, curr;
    prev = curr = G -> vertex[h].firstEdge;
    while (curr != NULL && strcmp(Y, G -> vertex[curr -> child].id) > 0) {
        prev = curr;
        curr = curr -> nextEdge;
    }

    if (prev == curr) {
        ep -> nextEdge = G -> vertex[h].firstEdge;
        G -> vertex[h].firstEdge = ep;
    }
    else {
        ep -> nextEdge = curr;
        prev -> nextEdge = ep;
    }
} //end addEdge

GEdgePtr newGEdge(int c, int w) {
//return a pointer to a new GEdge node
    GEdgePtr p = (GEdgePtr) malloc(sizeof (GEdge));;
    p -> child = c;
    p -> weight = w;
    p -> nextEdge = NULL;
    return p;
} //end newGEdge

void printGraph(Graph G) {
    for (int h = 1; h <= G -> numV; h++) {
        printf("%s: ", G -> vertex[h].id);
        GEdgePtr p = G -> vertex[h].firstEdge;
        while (p != NULL) {
            printf("%s %d ", G -> vertex[p -> child].id, p -> weight);
            p = p -> nextEdge;
        }
        printf("\n");
    } //end for
    printf("\n");
} //end printGraph
```

Suppose the file dijkstra.in contains the following, a description of the sample graph used in this section:

```
7
A B C D E F G
A 2 D 20 G 75
```

```
B 0
C 2 E 5 G 25
D 4 B 40 E 35 F 10 G 45
E 2 B 20 G 10
F 3 B 5 C 15 E 40
G 0
```

When Program P7.3 is run, it produces the following output:

```
A: D 20 G 75
B:
C: E 5 G 25
D: B 40 E 35 F 10 G 45
E: B 20 G 10
F: B 5 C 15 E 40
G:

Cost to A:  0, Path: A
Cost to B: 35, Path: A  -> D  -> F  -> B
Cost to C: 45, Path: A  -> D  -> F  -> C
Cost to D: 20, Path: A  -> D
Cost to E: 50, Path: A  -> D  -> F  -> C  -> E
Cost to F: 30, Path: A  -> D  -> F
Cost to G: 60, Path: A  -> D  -> F  -> C  -> E  -> G
```

7.9 Shortest Paths: Bellman-Ford Algorithm

The Bellman-Ford algorithm finds the shortest paths from a given source vertex to all other vertices. However, it does not require that the weights of the edges be non-negative, as in Dijkstra's algorithm. It will find shortest paths for graphs with negative-weight edges. However, if the graph contains a *negative-weight* cycle, then there is no solution and the algorithm detects this.

To illustrate the last point, consider this graph:

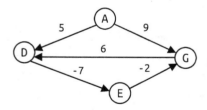

What is the cost of a path from A to G? The path A → G gives a cost of 9. But the path A → G → D → E → G gives a cost of 6. Further, each time we traverse the path G → D → E → G we reduce the cost by 3 since G → D → E → G is a negative-weight cycle with a cost of -3. In other words, we can reduce the cost of the path from A to G to any value we wish by traversing the cycle an appropriate number of times. Hence, there is no "minimum-cost" to the path.

On the other hand, if the weight of D → E were -3, say, there would be no negative-weight cycle and the minimum cost from A to G would be 9. So negative-weight *edges* are not a problem but a negative-weight *cycle* is.

Suppose the graph has *n* vertices. Bellman-Ford will first make *n*-1 passes over all the edges. Given an edge *p* → *x*, it checks to see if there is a better path to *x* via *p*. If there is no path to *p* as yet (its cost is infinite) there is nothing to do for this edge.

If p.cost is finite, the cost to *x* via *p* is

p.cost + weight(p → x)

If this cost is less than the current cost to *x* (x.cost), the algorithm updates x.cost to this new value and sets x.parent to *p*. This 'processing' is sometimes called *relaxing the edge*. We can express this as follows:

```
relax(W, p, x)
    if (p.cost != ∞ && p.cost + W(p, x) < x.cost) {
        x.cost = p.cost + W(p, x)
        x.parent = p
    endif
end relax
```

After the first *n*-1 passes, a final pass is made. If the cost to any vertex can be further reduced, then the graph contains a negative-weight cycle and there is no solution. Otherwise, v.cost gives the minimum cost to *v* for all vertices *v* and the parent fields define the paths. We express these ideas in the following algorithm:

```
boolean Bellman-Ford(G, W, s)
//find minimum-cost paths from s to every other node
//W(p, x) is the weight of the edge p → x
//return false if there is no solution; true, otherwise
    initSingleSource(G, s)
    for pass = 1 to n - 1      //n is the number of vertices
        for each edge p → x
            relax(W, p, x)
    endfor
    //make a final pass to check for negative-weight cycles
    for each edge p → x
        if (p.cost != ∞ && p.cost + W(p, x) < x.cost) {
            print "Graph contains a negative-weight cycle: no solution"
            return false
        endif
    endfor
    for each vertex v in G
        print v.cost and the path to get to v from s
    return true
end Bellman-Ford
```

We illustrate how the algorithm works by finding minimum-cost paths from A in the following graph:

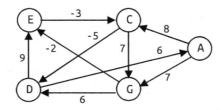

Initially, we have this:

vertex	A	C	D	E	G
parent	nil	nil	nil	nil	nil
cost	0	∞	∞	∞	∞

We will relax the edges in the order (A, C), (A, G), (C, D), (C, G), (D, A), (D, E), (E, C), (G, D) and (G, E). We note that *any* order will give the same result after all the passes.

1st pass

- Relaxing (A, C) changes C.cost to 8 and C.parent to A.
- Relaxing (A, G) changes G.cost to 7 and G.parent to A.
- Relaxing (C, D) changes D.cost to 3 and D.parent to C.
- Relaxing (C, G) changes nothing.
- Relaxing (D, A) does nothing.
- Relaxing (D, E) changes E.cost to 12 and E.parent to D.
- Since E.cost is 12, relaxing (E, C) does nothing since C.cost has a lower value 8.
- Relaxing (G, D) changes nothing.
- Relaxing (G, E) changes E.cost to 5 and E.parent to G.

We have this:

vertex	A	C	D	E	G
parent	nil	A	C	G	A
cost	0	8	3	5	7

2nd pass

- Relaxing (A, C), (A, G), (C, D), (C, G), (D, A) and (D, E) changes nothing.
- Relaxing (E, C) changes C.cost to 2 and C.parent to E.
- Relaxing (G, D) and (G, E) changes nothing.

We now have this:

vertex	A	C	D	E	G
parent	nil	E	C	G	A
cost	0	2	3	5	7

3rd pass

- Relaxing (A, C) and (A, G) does nothing.
- Relaxing (C, D) changes D.cost to -3 and its parent remains C.
- Relaxing (C, G), (D, A), (D, E), (E, C), (G, D) and (G, E) changes nothing.

We have this:

vertex	A	C	D	E	G
parent	nil	E	C	G	A
cost	0	2	-3	5	7

4th pass

- Nothing changes on this pass. All the costs remain the same from the third pass.

Final pass

- Final pass: as we would expect, nothing changes here; no vertex cost is reduced, so we have a solution, as follows:

```
Cost to A:   0, Path: A
Cost to C:   2, Path: A → G → E → C
Cost to D:  -3, Path: A → G → E → C → D
Cost to E:   5, Path: A → G → E
Cost to G:   7, Path: A → G
```

Note, for instance, that if the edge (D, E) had a weight of 7 (instead of 9), the graph would have a negative-weight cycle (E → C → D → E) of -1. The algorithm will report that there is no solution.

As an exercise, run the Bellman-Ford algorithm on the following graph, with A as the source vertex. Try processing the edges in different orders.

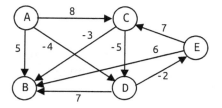

7.9.1 Implement Bellman-Ford Algorithm

We can implement the Bellman-Ford algorithm as follows:

```
int BellmanFord(Graph G, int s) {
    int u, v, pass;
    void initSingleSource(Graph, int);
    void printCostPath(Graph);
    void relax(Graph, int, int, int);

    initSingleSource(G, s);
```

```
    for (pass = 1; pass < G -> numV; pass++) {
        for (int h = 1; h <= G -> numV; h++) {
            if (G -> vertex[h].cost != Infinity) {
                GEdgePtr p = G -> vertex[h].firstEdge;
                while (p != NULL) {
                    relax(G, h, p -> child, p -> weight);
                    p = p -> nextEdge;
                }
            } //end if
        } //end for h
    } //end for pass
    //make final pass to check for negative weight cycles
    for (int h = 1; h <= G -> numV; h++) {
        GEdgePtr p = G -> vertex[h].firstEdge;
        while (p != NULL) {
            if (G -> vertex[h].cost + p -> weight < G -> vertex[p -> child].cost) {
                printf("\nNo solution: graph has negative weight cycle\n");
                return 1;
            }
            p = p -> nextEdge;
        } //end while
    } //end for
    printCostPath(G);
    return 0;
} //end BellmanFord

void relax(Graph G, int u, int v, int weight) {
//relax the edge (vertex[u], vertex[v])
    if (G -> vertex[u].cost + weight < G -> vertex[v].cost) {
        G -> vertex[v].cost = G -> vertex[u].cost + weight;
        G -> vertex[v].parent = u;
    }
} //end relax
```

relax does not need to check if vertex[u].cost is Infinity; this is done before relax is called.

If G is a Graph, we call the function with this:

BellmanFord(G, s)

where s is the *position* of the source vertex in the order that the vertices were supplied when the graph was built. For example, suppose we have a graph with 5 vertices given in the following order:

A C D E H

The call

BellmanFord(G, 1)

will find minimum-cost paths from A (vertex 1) and the call

BellmanFord(G, 4)

will find minimum-cost paths from E (vertex 4).

The edges are processed in the order in which they appear in the adjacency-list representation. The order of the vertices is the order given when the graph was built. And, for each vertex, the children are processed in ascending order.

7.10 Minimum-Cost Spanning Trees

Given an undirected graph, G, a *spanning tree* of G is a subgraph of G containing all the vertices but only those edges of G that are necessary to form a (free) tree. For example, given the graph:

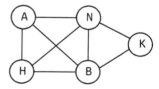

the following are two possible spanning trees for it:

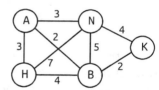

Recall that a tree of *n* vertices will necessarily have *n*-1 edges.

If the graph is *weighted*, the *cost* of a spanning tree is the sum of the weights of its edges. For example, given this graph:

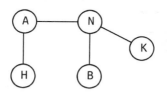

the cost of this spanning tree

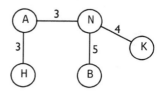

is 3 + 3 + 4 + 5 = 15.

And the cost of this one

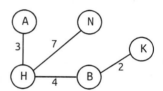

is 2 + 3 + 4 + 7 = 16.

A *minimum-cost spanning tree* (MST) is one with the lowest cost of all possible spanning trees. There may be more than one MST for a given graph. The MST for the above graph is this:

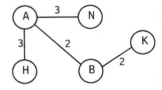

Its cost is 10.

Minimum-cost spanning trees have useful applications. For example, it may be required to connect several computers using a minimum of cabling. If we model the network using a graph where the computers are the vertices and the weight of an edge (P, X) is the length of cable required to connect computers P and X, then an MST of the graph gives the required answer.

7.10.1 Prim's Algorithm

Prim's algorithm starts off with any vertex as the first vertex in the tree and grows the tree one vertex at a time. We illustrate the method using the following graph:

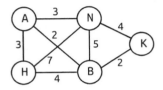

Suppose we start with H. We look at the neighbours of H and note the connection cost of each neighbour. Here, the cost of connecting A is 3, the cost of connecting B is 4 and the cost of connecting N is 7. These neighbours are placed in a priority queue. We can record this information as follows:

vertex	A	B	H	K	N
parent	H	H	nil	nil	H
cost	3	4	0	∞	7

Q: A₃ B₄ N₇

Next, we remove the item at the head of the queue and 'process' it. Here, we remove A and add it to the growing MST which now consists of H and A connected by an edge of weight 3.

We *process* A by looking at its neighbours which are *not* in the MST. The first is B. The cost of connecting B to the tree via A is 2. The current cost of B is 4. We have a better connection for B so we set its cost to 2 and its parent to A.

The next neighbour of A is H but H is already in the MST. The next neighbour is N. The cost of connecting N to the tree via A is 3. The current cost of N is 7. We have a better connection for N so we set its cost to 3 and its parent to A. So far, we have this (items in bold are in the MST):

vertex	A	B	H	K	N
parent	H	A	nil	nil	A
cost	3	2	0	∞	3

Q: B_2 N_3

Next, we remove B from the queue and process it by looking at its neighbours not in the MST. Neighbours A and H are in the MST so we look at the next neighbour N. The cost of connecting N to the tree via B is 5. The current cost of N is 3 which is better so we leave things as they are.

The next neighbour is K. The cost of connecting K to the tree via B is 2. The current cost of K is ∞. We have a better connection for K so we set its cost to 2 and its parent to B. We now have this (items in bold are in the MST):

vertex	A	B	H	K	N
parent	H	A	nil	B	A
cost	3	2	0	2	3

Q: K_2 N_3

Next, we remove K from the queue and process it by looking at its neighbours not in the MST. The only such neighbour is N. The cost of connecting N to the tree via K is 4. The current cost of N is 3 which is better so we leave things as they are. At this stage, we have this (items in bold are in the MST):

vertex	A	B	H	K	N
parent	H	A	nil	B	A
cost	3	2	0	2	3

Q: N_3

Finally, we remove N from the queue. All its neighbours are already in the MST so nothing further happens. The algorithm ends and the parent fields define the minimum-cost spanning tree.

From the diagram, we can see that the cost fields add up to 10 and that the edges (H, A), (A, B), (B, K) and (A, N) form the tree.

As an exercise, work through the algorithm using K as the starting vertex.

The alert reader will recognize that Prim's algorithm is very similar to Dijkstra's. Both algorithms keep track of the "current cost" of a vertex; this determines its position in a priority queue. In both algorithms, when we take a vertex off the queue, that vertex is "finished"—either the minimum cost to get to it from the source vertex has been found or it is added to the MST.

We then process the neighbours of the "finished" vertex, P. In Dijkstra's, we ask what is the *cost of the path from the source to a neighbour* via P. In Prim's, we ask what is *the cost of connecting a neighbour* to the spanning tree via P. We should expect the implementation of Prim's to be similar to that of Dijkstra's.

In processing the neighbours of a vertex, Prim's algorithm needs to know if a neighbour is already in the MST. We will use the colour property of a vertex for this. All vertices are set to White, initially. When one is added to the MST, its colour is set to Black. We can formulate Prim's algorithm as follows:

```
Prim(G, W, s)
//construct minimum-cost spanning tree starting with vertex s
// Q is a priority queue
    initPrim(G, s)  //see below
    add all the vertices of G to Q
    while not empty(Q) do
        p = Q.extract-min()
        if (p.cost == ∞) break; //remaining vertices unreachable from p
        p.colour = Black //this vertex is added to the MST
        for each edge (p, x)    //for each edge leaving p
            if (W(p, x) < x.cost) then // lower connection cost found
                x.cost = W(p, x)
                x.parent = p
                adjust x's position in Q
            endif
        endfor
    endwhile
    for each vertex v in G
        if (v != s)    print edge (v.parent, v) and v.cost
end Prim
```

We write initPrim as follows:

```
initPrim(G, s)
    for each vertex v in G
        v.cost = ∞
        v.parent = nil
        v.colour = White
    endfor
    s.cost = 0
end initPrim
```

7.10.2 Implement Prim's Algorithm

We can implement Prim's algorithm as shown in Program P7.4. The program reads the description of a graph from a file prim.in and finds the minimum-cost spanning tree. For example, suppose we are given this graph:

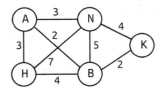

We store the following data in prim.in:

```
5
A B H K N
A 3 B 2 H 3 N 3
B 4 A 2 H 4 K 2 N 5
H 3 A 3 B 4 N 7
N 4 A 3 B 5 H 7 K 4
K 2 B 2 N 4
```

The program will construct the MST starting with vertex H. Since H is the third vertex (in the list given on the second line of the data), this is accomplished by the statement:

`Prim(G, 3);`

The methods `siftUp` and `siftDown` are the same as for Dijkstra's. We print the MST using `printMST`. When run, Program P7.4 produces the following output:

```
The edges/weights in the MST are

(H, A): 3
(A, B): 2
(B, K): 2
(A, N): 3

Cost of tree: 10
```

Program P7.4

```c
#include <stdio.h>
#include <stdlib.h>
#include <string.h>

#define MaxWordSize 20
#define MaxVertices 50
#define White 'w'
#define Gray 'g'
#define Black 'b'
#define Infinity 99999

typedef struct gEdge {
    int child, weight; //'child' is the location of the child vertex
    struct gEdge *nextEdge;
} GEdge, *GEdgePtr;

typedef struct {
    char id[MaxWordSize+1], colour;
    int parent, cost, discover, finish, inDegree;
    GEdgePtr firstEdge;
} GVertex;

typedef struct graph {
    int numV;
    GVertex vertex[MaxVertices+1];
} *Graph;
```

```
int main() {
    int numVertices;
    Graph newGraph(int);
    void buildGraph(FILE *, Graph);
    void Prim(Graph, int);

    FILE * in = fopen("prim.in", "r");

    fscanf(in, "%d", &numVertices);
    Graph G = newGraph(numVertices);
    buildGraph(in, G);
    Prim(G, 3);
    fclose(in);
} // end main

void Prim(Graph G, int s) {
//perform Prim's algorithm on G starting with vertex s
    void initPrim(Graph, int);
    void siftDown(Graph, int, int[], int, int, int[]);
    void siftUp(Graph, int[], int, int[]);
    void printMST(Graph, int);
    int heap[MaxVertices + 1], heapLoc[MaxVertices + 1];
    initPrim(G, s);
    for (int h = 1; h <= G -> numV; h++) heap[h] = heapLoc[h] = h;
    heap[1] = s; heap[s] = 1; heapLoc[s] = 1; heapLoc[1] = s;
    int heapSize = G -> numV;
    while (heapSize > 0) {
        int u = heap[1];
        if (G -> vertex[u].cost == Infinity) break;
        G -> vertex[u].colour = Black;
        //reorganize heap after removing top item
        siftDown(G, heap[heapSize], heap, 1, heapSize-1, heapLoc);
        GEdgePtr p = G -> vertex[u].firstEdge;
        while (p != NULL) {
            if (G -> vertex[p -> child].colour == White &&
                p -> weight < G -> vertex[p -> child].cost) {
                G -> vertex[p -> child].cost = p -> weight;
                G -> vertex[p -> child].parent = u;
                siftUp(G, heap, heapLoc[p -> child], heapLoc);
            }
            p = p -> nextEdge;
        } //end while
        --heapSize;
    } //end while

    printMST(G, s);
} //end Prim

void initPrim(Graph G, int s) {
    for (int h = 1; h <= G -> numV; h++) {
        G -> vertex[h].cost = Infinity;
        G -> vertex[h].parent = 0;
        G -> vertex[h].colour = White; //to Black when vertex is added to MST
    }
    G -> vertex[s].cost = 0;
} //end initPrim

void printMST(Graph G, int s) {
    printf("\nThe edges/weights in the MST are\n\n");
    int costMST = 0;
```

```
    for (int h = 1; h <= G -> numV; h++)
        if (h != s) {
            printf("(%s, %s): %d\n",
                    G -> vertex[G -> vertex[h].parent].id,
                    G -> vertex[h].id, G -> vertex[h].cost);
            costMST += G -> vertex[h].cost;
        }
    printf("\nCost of tree: %d\n", costMST);
} //end printMST

void siftUp(Graph G, int heap[], int n, int heapLoc[]) {
//sifts up heap[n] so that heap[1..n] contains a heap based on cost
    int siftItem = heap[n];
    int child = n;
    int parent = child / 2;
    while (parent > 0) {
        if (G->vertex[siftItem].cost >= G->vertex[heap[parent]].cost) break;
        heap[child] = heap[parent]; //move down parent
        heapLoc[heap[parent]] = child;
        child = parent;
        parent = child / 2;
    }
    heap[child] = siftItem;
    heapLoc[siftItem] = child;
} //end siftUp

void siftDown(Graph G, int key, int heap[], int root,
              int last, int heapLoc[]) {
    int smaller = 2 * root;
    while (smaller <= last) { //while there is at least one child
        if (smaller < last) //there is a right child; find the smaller
            if (G->vertex[heap[smaller+1]].cost <
                G->vertex[heap[smaller]].cost) smaller++;
        //'smaller' holds the index of the smaller child
        if (G -> vertex[key].cost <= G -> vertex[heap[smaller]].cost)
            break;
        //cost[key] is bigger; promote heap[smaller]
        heap[root] = heap[smaller];
        heapLoc[heap[smaller]] = root;
        root = smaller;
        smaller = 2 * root;
    } //end while
    heap[root] = key;
    heapLoc[key] = root;
} //end siftDown

Graph newGraph(int n) {
    if (n > MaxVertices) {
        printf("\nToo big. Only %d vertices allowed.\n", MaxVertices);
        exit(1);
    }
    Graph p = (Graph) malloc(sizeof(struct graph));
    p -> numV = n;
    return p;
} //end newGraph

void buildGraph(FILE * in, Graph G) {
    int numEdges, weight;
    GVertex newGVertex(char[]);
    void addEdge(char[], char[], int, Graph);
```

```
        char nodeID[MaxWordSize+1], adjID[MaxWordSize+1];
        for (int h = 1; h <= G -> numV; h++) {
            G -> vertex[h] = newGVertex("");        //create a vertex node
            fscanf(in, "%s", G -> vertex[h].id); //read the name into id
        }
        for (int h = 1; h <= G -> numV; h++) {
            fscanf(in, "%s %d", nodeID, &numEdges); //parent id and numEdges
            for (int k = 1; k <= numEdges; k++) {
                fscanf(in, "%s %d", adjID, &weight); //get child id and weight
                addEdge(nodeID, adjID, weight, G);
            }
        }
} //end buildGraph

GVertex newGVertex(char name[]) {
    GVertex temp;
    strcpy(temp.id, name);
    temp.firstEdge = NULL;
    return temp;
}

void addEdge(char X[], char Y[], int weight, Graph G) {
    GEdgePtr newGEdge(int, int);
    //add an edge X -> Y with a given weight
    int h, k;
    //find X in the list of nodes; its location is h
    for (h = 1; h <= G -> numV; h++)
        if (strcmp(X, G -> vertex[h].id) == 0) break;

    //find Y in the list of nodes; its location is k
    for (k = 1; k <= G-> numV; k++)
        if (strcmp(Y, G -> vertex[k].id) == 0) break;

    if (h > G -> numV || k > G -> numV) {
        printf("No such edge: %s -> %s\n", X, Y);
        exit(1);
    }

    GEdgePtr ep = newGEdge(k, weight); //create edge vertex
    // add it to the list of edges, possible empty, from X;
    // it is added so that the list is in order by vertex id
    GEdgePtr prev, curr;
    prev = curr = G -> vertex[h].firstEdge;
    while (curr != NULL &&
            strcmp(Y, G -> vertex[curr -> child].id) > 0) {
        prev = curr;
        curr = curr -> nextEdge;
    }

    if (prev == curr) {
        ep -> nextEdge = G -> vertex[h].firstEdge;
        G -> vertex[h].firstEdge = ep;
    }
    else {
        ep -> nextEdge = curr;
        prev -> nextEdge = ep;
    }
} //end addEdge
```

```
GEdgePtr newGEdge(int c, int w) {
//return a pointer to a new GEdge node
    GEdgePtr p = (GEdgePtr) malloc(sizeof (GEdge));;
    p -> child = c;
    p -> weight = w;
    p -> nextEdge = NULL;
    return p;
} //end newGEdge
```

As an exercise, construct the MST for this graph:

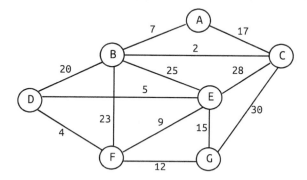

7.10.3 Kruskal's Algorithm

Kruskal's algorithm for constructing an MST is one of those algorithms that is easy to describe but not so easy to implement. First, the description:

```
Kruskal's algorithm for G(V, E)
    for each v in V, create a tree consisting of v only
    sort the edges of E by non-decreasing weight
    for each edge (u, v) in E, in order by non-decreasing weight
        if u and v belong to different trees, connect them with the edge (u, v)
end Kruskal
```

We illustrate the method with the following graph:

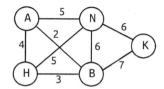

First, we create 5 trees consisting of one vertex each:

Next, we sort the edges in order by weight, giving this:

(A, B, 2)

```
(B, H, 3)
(A, H, 4)
(A, N, 5)
(H, N, 5)
(B, N, 6)
(K, N, 6)
(B, K, 7)
```

If two or more edges have the same weight, their relative order does not matter. We now 'step through' the edges, in order:

- **(A, B, 2)**: A and B are in different trees, so we connect them with this edge and we have the following trees:

- **(B, H, 3)**: B and H are in different trees, so we connect them with this edge:

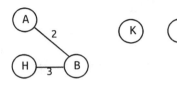

- (A, H, 4): A and H are in the same tree, so we disregard this edge.
- **(A, N, 5)**: A and N are in different trees, so we connect them with this edge:

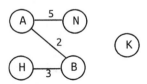

- (H, N, 5): H and N are in the same tree, so we disregard this edge.
- (B, N, 6): B and N are in the same tree, so we disregard this edge.
- **(K, N, 6)**: K and N are in different trees, so we connect them with this edge:

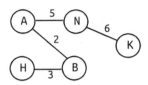

- (B, K, 7): B and K are in the same tree, so we disregard this edge.

All the edges have been processed and we have a minimum-cost spanning tree with a cost of 16. This is not the only one. The following is another MST with a cost of 16.

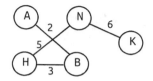

Here, we processed *all* the edges. However, we could keep track of how many edges have been used to join trees and stop when *n*-1 edges have been used (if there are *n* vertices).

7.10.4 Implement Kruskal's Algorithm

A key issue in implementing Kruskal's algorithm is how to determine if two vertices are in different trees and, if they are, how to join the two trees. The fact that the vertices are in *trees* is not important. All we need to know is whether two vertices are in the same set and, if they are not, how to join the two sets. For now, we will discuss a very simplistic method for representing and manipulating *disjoint* sets.

Suppose there are 8 vertices numbered 1, 2, 3, 4, 5, 6, 7, 8. Initially, each vertex is in its own set. We use an array P[1..8] and represent this information as follows:

P

0	0	0	0	0	0	0	0
1	2	3	4	5	6	7	8

Now suppose we want to join {2} and {5}. We can do this by setting P[2] to 5 or by setting P[5] to 2). If we then want to join {2, 5} and {7}, we can do so by setting P[5] to 7 or P[7] to 5—either one will work; we use the former. At this stage, we have this:

P

0	5	0	0	7	0	0	0
1	2	3	4	5	6	7	8

Now, we have the following sets: {1}, {2, 5, 7}, {3}, {4}, {6} and{8}.

We introduce the notion of a *set identifier*; this is a chosen member of the set which will be returned in answer to the query "To which set does a given vertex belong?"

For single-member sets, the set identifier is the member. If a set has more than one member, we follow P values from any member until P[i] is 0; i is the set identifier. For example, to answer "To what set does 2 belong?", we look at P[2], this is 5. We then look at P[5]; this is 7. We look at P[7]; this is 0 so the set identifier is 7. We get the same answer if we ask to what set does 5 or 7 belong.

Of course, for a single-member set (3, say), we have P[3] = 0 so 3 identifies its own set.

In general, if x is a member, we can write getSetID(x) to return the set identifier of the set to which x belongs:

```
int getSetID(int P[], int x) {
    while (P[x] != 0) x = P[x];
    return x;
} //end getSetID
```

How do we join two sets containing members x and y, respectively? We first find

xi = getSetID(x)

and

yi = getSetID(y)

We then set P[xi] to yi. We could also set P[yi] to xi. Either way will work.

For example, to join {1} and {8}, we set P[1] to 8, and we have this:

P

8	5	0	0	7	0	0	0
1	2	3	4	5	6	7	8

We could draw the sets represented by **P** as follows:

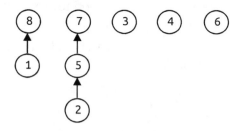

Each set is represented by a tree. We can think of P[x] as the "parent" of x in the tree representation. From this, we can see that the "set identifier" is simply the root of the tree representing the set. To join two sets, we set the root of one tree to point to the root of the other.

Suppose we want to join the "set containing 1" with the "set containing 5", that is, the sets {1, 8} and {2, 5, 7}. We find getSetID(1) (which is 8) and getSetID(5) (which is 7). We set P[8] to 7 and we have the following:

P

8	5	0	0	7	0	0	7
1	2	3	4	5	6	7	8

These values represent the following trees (sets):

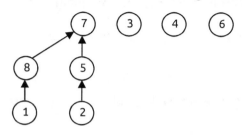

We can "union" the set containing x and the set containing y with the function union:

```
void union(int P[], int x, int y) {
    int xi = getSetID(P, x);
    int yi = getSetID(P, y);
    if (xi != yi) P[xi] = yi; //if x, y are not already in the same set
} //end union
```

To facilitate sorting of the edges, we store them in an array edgeList. Each element of edgeList is of type UndirectedEdge, defined as:

```
typedef struct {
    int parent, child, weight;
} UndirectedEdge;
```

and we create an UndirectedEdge structure with this:

```
UndirectedEdge newUndirectedEdge(int p, int c, int w) {
    UndirectedEdge temp;
    temp.parent = p;
    temp.child = c;
    temp.weight = w;
    return temp;
} //end newUndirectedEdge
```

We will implement Kruskal's algorithm as a function, Kruskal. We let MaxEdges represent the maximum number of edges in the graph; the actual number could be less than MaxEdges.

We declare edgeList like this:

```
UndirectedEdge edgeList[MaxEdges];
```

and store all the edges of the graph in it. This could be done with code such as this:

```
for (int h = 1; h <= G -> numV; h++) {
    GEdgePtr p = G -> vertex[h].firstEdge;
    while (p != NULL) {
        if (!inEdgeList(h, p -> child, list, numEdges)) {
            if (numEdges == MaxEdges) {
                printf("\nToo many edges; exceeds %d\n", MaxEdges);
                exit(1);
            }
            list[numEdges] = newUndirectedEdge(h, p -> child, p -> weight);
            numEdges++;
        }
        p = p -> nextEdge;
    } //end while
} //end for
```

Keep in mind that, in the representation of an undirected graph, each edge appears twice. For instance, the edge connecting A and H appears as (A, H) and (H, A); H appears on the list of A and A appears on the list of H. Even though the program will work if an edge is processed twice (once as (A, H) and once as (H, A)), we prefer to store and process it once.

So before storing an edge, we check the list to see if it is already there. We use a sequential search, as shown in the function inEdgeList:

```
int inEdgeList(int u, int v, UndirectedEdge list[], int n) {
//search for edge (u, v) in list[0..n-1]
    for (int h = 0; h < n; h++)
        if (u == list[h].child && v == list[h].parent) return 1;
    return 0; //edge not found
} //end inEdgeList
```

Note that if the edge (A, H) is already stored, when we meet (H, A), we must check for it by reversing its vertices. If we simply check for (H, A), we will not find it. In inEdgeList, u is the parent and v is the child of the edge we are searching for. We compare u with the *child* of a stored edge and v with its *parent*.

Once the edges are stored in edgeList, we can sort them using any sorting method; our program uses *insertion sort*. For the sample graph, if we print the edges in the format "(parent, child): weight", we will get this order:

```
(A, B): 2
(B, H): 3
(A, H): 4
(A, N): 5
(H, N): 5
(B, N): 6
(K, N): 6
(B, K): 7
```

The order of edges with the same weight does not matter.

We now write Kruskal and all the supporting functions as part of Program P7.5. It assumes that the data for the graph is stored in the file kruskal.in. For the sample graph, the file will contain the following:

```
5
A B H K N
A 3 B 2 H 4 N 5
B 4 A 2 H 3 K 7 N 6
H 3 A 4 B 3 N 5
N 4 A 5 B 6 H 5 K 6
K 2 B 7 N 6
```

As each edge in the MST is found (when it is used to join two trees), we store it in the array MST. At the end, we print the edges which make up the MST as well as the cost of the tree. For the sample graph, we get the following output:

```
The edges/weights in the MST are

(A, B): 2
(B, H): 3
(A, N): 5
(K, N): 6

Cost of tree: 16
```

Program P7.5

```c
#include <stdio.h>
#include <stdlib.h>
#include <string.h>

#define MaxWordSize 20
#define MaxVertices 50
#define MaxEdges 100
#define White 'w'
#define Gray 'g'
#define Black 'b'
#define Infinity 99999

typedef struct gEdge {
    int child, weight; //'child' is the location of the child vertex
    struct gEdge *nextEdge;
} GEdge, *GEdgePtr;

typedef struct {
    char id[MaxWordSize+1], colour;
    int parent, cost, discover, finish, inDegree;
    GEdgePtr firstEdge;
} GVertex;

typedef struct graph {
    int numV;
    GVertex vertex[MaxVertices+1];
} *Graph;

typedef struct {
    int parent, child, weight;
} UndirectedEdge;
int main() {
    int numVertices;
    Graph newGraph(int);
    void buildGraph(FILE *, Graph);
    void Kruskal(Graph);

    FILE * in = fopen("kruskal.in", "r");

    fscanf(in, "%d", &numVertices);
    Graph G = newGraph(numVertices);
    buildGraph(in, G);
    Kruskal(G);
    fclose(in);
} // end main

void Kruskal(Graph G) {
    int getSortedEdges(Graph, UndirectedEdge[], int);
    int getSetID(int[], int);
    void setUnion(int[], int, int);
    void printKruskalMST(Graph, UndirectedEdge[], int);
    UndirectedEdge edgeList[MaxEdges];
    int P[MaxVertices+1]; //P used to implement disjoint subsets

    for (int h = 1; h <= G -> numV; h++) P[h] = 0;

    int numEdges = getSortedEdges(G, edgeList, MaxEdges);
    UndirectedEdge MST[MaxEdges];
```

```
        int t = 0; //used to index MST
        for (int h = 0; h < numEdges; h++) {
            int xRoot = getSetID(P, edgeList[h].parent);
            int yRoot = getSetID(P, edgeList[h].child);
            if (xRoot != yRoot) {
                MST[t++] = edgeList[h];
                setUnion(P, xRoot, yRoot);
            } //end if
        } //end for
        printKruskalMST(G, MST, t);
} //end Kruskal

void printKruskalMST(Graph G, UndirectedEdge MST[], int n) {
//print the n edges in the MST and the total cost
    int cost = 0;
    printf("\nThe edges/weights in the MST are\n\n");
    for (int h = 0; h < n; h++) {
        printf("(%s, %s): %d\n", G -> vertex[MST[h].parent].id,
                    G -> vertex[MST[h].child].id, MST[h].weight);
        cost += MST[h].weight;
    }
    printf("\nCost of tree: %d\n", cost);
} //end printKruskalMST

int getSetID(int P[], int x) {
    while (P[x] != 0) x = P[x];
    return x;
} //end getSetID

void setUnion(int P[], int x, int y) {
    int xi = getSetID(P, x);
    int yi = getSetID(P, y);
    if (xi != yi) P[xi] = yi;
} //end setUnion

int getSortedEdges(Graph G, UndirectedEdge list[], int max) {
    int inEdgeList(int, int, UndirectedEdge[], int);
    UndirectedEdge newUndirectedEdge(int, int, int);
    void sortEdges(UndirectedEdge[], int);
    int numEdges = 0;

    for (int h = 1; h <= G -> numV; h++) {
        GEdgePtr p = G -> vertex[h].firstEdge;
        while (p != NULL) {
            if (!inEdgeList(h, p -> child, list, numEdges)) {
                if (numEdges == max) {
                    printf("\nToo many edges; exceeds %d\n", max);
                    exit(1);
                }
                list[numEdges] = newUndirectedEdge(h, p -> child,
                                                    p -> weight);
                numEdges++;
            } //end if
            p = p -> nextEdge;
        } //end while
    } //end for
    sortEdges(list, numEdges);
    return numEdges;
} //end getSortedEdges
```

```
UndirectedEdge newUndirectedEdge(int p, int c, int w) {
    UndirectedEdge temp;
    temp.parent = p;
    temp.child = c;
    temp.weight = w;
    return temp;
} //end newUndirectedEdge

int inEdgeList(int u, int v, UndirectedEdge list[], int n) {
//search for edge (u, v) in list[0..n-1]
    for (int h = 0; h < n; h++)
        if (u == list[h].child && v == list[h].parent) return 1;
    return 0; //edge not found
} //end inEdgeList

void sortEdges(UndirectedEdge list[], int n) {
//sort list[0] to list[n-1] by increasing weight
    int i, j;
    for (i = 1; i < n; i++) {
        UndirectedEdge hold = list[i];
        j = i - 1;
        while (j >= 0 && hold.weight < list[j].weight) {
            list[j+1] = list[j];
            j = j - 1;
        }
        list[j+1] = hold;
    } //end for
} //end sortEdges

Graph newGraph(int n) {
    if (n > MaxVertices) {
        printf("\nToo big. Only %d vertices allowed.\n", MaxVertices);
        exit(1);
    }
    Graph p = (Graph) malloc(sizeof(struct graph));
    p -> numV = n;
    return p;
} //end newGraph

void buildGraph(FILE * in, Graph G) {
    int numEdges, weight;
    GVertex newGVertex(char[]);
    void addEdge(char[], char[], int, Graph);
    char nodeID[MaxWordSize+1], adjID[MaxWordSize+1];
    for (int h = 1; h <= G -> numV; h++) {
        G -> vertex[h] = newGVertex("");      //create a vertex node
        fscanf(in, "%s", G -> vertex[h].id);//read the name into id
    }
    for (int h = 1; h <= G -> numV; h++) {
        fscanf(in, "%s %d", nodeID, &numEdges); //parent id and numEdges
        for (int k = 1; k <= numEdges; k++) {
            fscanf(in, "%s %d", adjID, &weight);//get child and weight
            addEdge(nodeID, adjID, weight, G);
        }
    }
} //end buildGraph
```

```
GVertex newGVertex(char name[]) {
    GVertex temp;
    strcpy(temp.id, name);
    temp.firstEdge = NULL;
    return temp;
} //end newGVertex

void addEdge(char X[], char Y[], int weight, Graph G) {
    GEdgePtr newGEdge(int, int);
    //add an edge X -> Y with a given weight
    int h, k;
    //find X in the list of nodes; its location is h
    for (h = 1; h <= G -> numV; h++)
        if (strcmp(X, G -> vertex[h].id) == 0) break;

    //find Y in the list of nodes; its location is k
    for (k = 1; k <= G-> numV; k++)
        if (strcmp(Y, G -> vertex[k].id) == 0) break;

    if (h > G -> numV || k > G -> numV) {
        printf("No such edge: %s -> %s\n", X, Y);
        exit(1);
    }

    GEdgePtr ep = newGEdge(k, weight); //create edge vertex
    // add it to the list of edges, possible empty, from X;
    // it is added so that the list is in order by vertex id
    GEdgePtr prev, curr;
    prev = curr = G -> vertex[h].firstEdge;
    while (curr != NULL &&
            strcmp(Y, G -> vertex[curr -> child].id) > 0) {
        prev = curr;
        curr = curr -> nextEdge;
    }

    if (prev == curr) {
        ep -> nextEdge = G -> vertex[h].firstEdge;
        G -> vertex[h].firstEdge = ep;
    }
    else {
        ep -> nextEdge = curr;
        prev -> nextEdge = ep;
    }
} //end addEdge

GEdgePtr newGEdge(int c, int w) {
//return a pointer to a new GEdge node
    GEdgePtr p = (GEdgePtr) malloc(sizeof (GEdge));;
    p -> child = c;
    p -> weight = w;
    p -> nextEdge = NULL;
    return p;
} //end newGEdge
```

EXERCISES 7

1. Write functions which, given the name of a node, returns the in-degree and out-degree of the node.

2. Write a non-recursive function for performing depth-first traversal on a graph.

3. When a depth-first traversal is performed on an undirected graph, all edges will be classified as either *tree* or *back* only. Verify this. Write a function to perform a depth-first traversal and classify the edges of an undirected graph.

4. You are given the following graph:

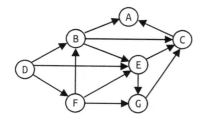

   (a) Give the depth-first and breadth-first traversals of the graph starting at D. Edges of a node are processed *in alphabetical order*.

   (b) Assume that a depth-first traversal is performed starting at D and that *edges of a node are processed in alphabetical order*. Indicate the discovery and finish times for each node and label each edge with T (tree edge), B (back edge), F (forward edge) or C (cross edge), according to its type.

5. On a map there are *n* cities numbered 1 to *n*. The map shows the highways leaving each city to neighbouring cities and their respective distances. Highways run in both directions and do not intersect each other.

   (a) Write an algorithm to determine the set of highways, with smallest total distance, that connect all cities.

   (b) Given the city numbers *c1* and *c2*, write a function to print the shortest travel route from *c1* to *c2*.

6. A maze has a single entry point and a single exit point. On each corridor there is an item with a known value. If you walk along a corridor, you can pick up the item. However, you cannot retrace your steps and you can walk along a corridor only in the direction of an arrow painted on the floor.

   (a) Devise a method for representing the maze.

   (b) Write a program which, given a map of the maze, advises which path to take to collect the most valuable treasure.

7. You are given the following graph:

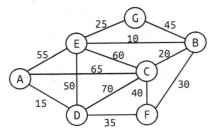

(a) Give the adjacency matrix and list representation of the graph.

(b) Give the depth-first and breadth-first traversals starting at A. Edges of a node are processed in alphabetical order.

(c) Starting at A, derive and draw the minimum-cost spanning trees obtained using Prim's and Kruskal's algorithms.

(d) Derive the minimal-cost paths from C to every other node using Dijkstra's algorithm. For each node, give the cost and the path to get to the node.

8. The following is the adjacency matrix representation of a directed graph, G, with 5 nodes, assumed numbered 1 to 5 from left to right.

```
 0   5   8  -4   ∞
-2   0   ∞   ∞   ∞
 ∞  -3   0   9   ∞
 ∞   7   ∞   0   2
 6   ∞   7   ∞   0
```

The Bellman-Ford algorithm is to be used to find the shortest paths from node 5 to all other nodes. Show the distance and parent values after each of the first 4 passes. (One pass processes *all* the edges of the graph.) The edges are to be processed in the order left to right, top to bottom.

9. When a depth-first traversal is performed on an undirected graph, all edges will be classified as either *tree* or *back* only. Verify this. Write a function to perform a depth-first traversal and classify the edges of an undirected graph.

10. A telephone network is represented by an undirected graph. Each vertex represents a switching station and each edge represents a communication line with a given bandwidth. The bandwidth on a path between two stations is the lowest bandwidth on the path. Write functions for the following:

(a) Given a station S, find the set of stations which can be reached from S using no more than 3 lines.

(b) Given two stations, find the maximum bandwidth among all paths between the two stations.

CHAPTER 8

■ ■ ■

Hashing

In this chapter, we will explain:

- The fundamental ideas on which hashing is based
- How to solve the search and insert problem using hashing
- How to delete an item from a hash table
- How to resolve collisions using linear probing
- How to resolve collisions using quadratic probing
- How to resolve collisions using chaining
- How to resolve collisions using linear probing with double hashing
- How to link items in order using arrays

8.1 Hashing Fundamentals

Searching for an item in a (large) table is a common operation in many applications. In this chapter, we discuss *hashing*, a fast method for performing this search. The main idea behind hashing is to use the key of an item (for example, the vehicle registration number of a vehicle record) to determine *where* in the table (the *hash table*) the item is stored. The key is first converted to a number (if it is not already one), and this number is mapped (we say *hashed*) to a table location. The method used to convert a key to a table location is called the *hash function*.

It is entirely possible, of course, for two or more keys to hash to the same location. When this happens, we say we have a *collision*, and we must find a way to resolve the collision. The efficiency (or otherwise) of hashing is determined to a large extent by the method used to resolve collisions. Much of the chapter is devoted to a discussion of these methods.

8.1.1 The Search and Insert Problem

The classical statement of the search and insert problem is as follows:

> *Given a list of items (the list may be empty initially), search for a given item in the list. If the item is not found, insert it in the list.*

Items can be things such as numbers (student, account, employee, vehicle, and so on), names, words, or strings in general. For example, suppose we have a set of integers, not necessarily distinct, and we want to find out how many distinct integers there are.

We start with an empty list. For each integer, we look for it in the list. If it is not found, it is added to the list and counted. If it is found, there is nothing to do.

In solving this problem, a major design decision is how to search the list, which, in turn, will depend on how the list is stored and how a new integer is added. The following are some possibilities:

1. The list is stored in an array, and a new integer is placed in the next available position in the array. This implies that a sequential search must be used to look for an incoming integer. This method has the advantages of simplicity and easy addition, but searching takes longer as more numbers are put in the list.

2. The list is stored in an array, and a new integer is added in such a way that the list is always in order. This may entail moving numbers that have already been stored so that the new number may be slotted in the right place.

   However, since the list is in order, a binary search can be used to search for an incoming integer. For this method, searching is faster, but insertion is slower than in the previous method. Since, in general, searching is done more frequently than inserting, this method might be preferable to the previous method.

   Another advantage here is that, at the end, the integers will be in order, if this is important. If method 1 is used, the numbers will have to be sorted.

3. The list is stored as an unsorted linked list so must be searched sequentially. Since the entire list must be traversed if an incoming number is not present, the new number can be added at the head or tail; both are equally easy.

4. The list is stored as a sorted linked list. A new number must be inserted "in place" to maintain the order. Once the position is found, insertion is easy. The entire list does not have to be traversed if an incoming number is not present, but we are still restricted to a sequential search.

5. The list is stored in a binary search tree. Searching is reasonably fast provided the tree does not become too unbalanced. Adding a number is easy—it's only a matter of setting a couple links. An in-order traversal of the tree will give the numbers in sorted order, if this is required.

Yet another possibility is the method called *hashing*. As we will see, this has the advantages of extremely fast search times and easy insertion.

8.2 Hashing: Solve Search/Insert Problem

We illustrate how hashing works by solving the "search and insert" problem for a list of integers. The list will be stored in an array num[0] to num[n-1]. In our example, we assume n is 12.

num

Initially, there are no numbers in the list. Suppose the first incoming number is 52. The idea behind hashing is to convert 52 (usually called the *key*) into a valid table location (k, say). Here, the valid table locations are 0 to 11.

If there is no number in num[k], then 52 is stored in that location. If num[k] is occupied by another key, we say a *collision* has occurred, and we must find another location in which to try and place 52. This is called *resolving the collision*.

The method used to convert a key to a table location is called the *hash function* (H, say). Any calculation that produces a valid table location (array subscript) can be used, but, as we shall see, some functions give better results than others.

For example, we could use the following:

H1(key) = key % 10

In other words, we simply take the last digit of the key. Thus, 52 would hash to 2. Note that H1 produces locations between 0 and 9 only. If the table had 100 locations, say, the function would be *valid*, but it may not be a *good* function to use since all the keys would hash to the same few locations (0 to 9), with many collisions.

Another function is this:

H2(key) = key % 12

The expression key % 12 (the remainder when we divide by 12) produces a value between 0 and 11. In general, key % n produces values between 0 and n-1, inclusive. We will use this function in our example.

H2(52) = 52 % 12 = 4

We say, "52 hashes to location 4." Since num[4] is empty, we place 52 in num[4].

Suppose, later, we are searching for 52. We first apply the hash function, and we get 4. We compare num[4] with 52; they match, so we find 52 with just one comparison.

Now suppose the following keys come in the order given:

52 33 84 43 16 59 31 23 61

- 52 is placed in num[4].
- 33 hashes to 9; num[9] is empty, so 33 is placed in num[9].
- 84 hashes to 0; num[0] is empty, so 84 is placed in num[0].
- 43 hashes to 7; num[7] is empty, so 43 is placed in num[7].

At this stage, we have the following:

num

84				52			43		33		
0	1	2	3	4	5	6	7	8	9	10	11

- 16 hashes to 4; num[4] is occupied and not by 16—we have a collision. To resolve the collision, we must find another location in which to put 16. One obvious choice is to try the very next location, 5; num[5] is empty, so 16 is placed in num[5].
- 59 hashes to 11; num[11] is empty, so 59 is placed in num[11].
- 31 hashes to 7; num[7] is occupied and not by 31—we have a collision. We try the next location, 8; num[8] is empty, so 31 is placed in num[8].

The array num has now become this:

num

84				52	16		43	31	33		59
0	1	2	3	4	5	6	7	8	9	10	11

- 23 hashes to 11; num[11] is occupied and not by 23—we have a collision. We must try the next location, but what is the next location here? We pretend that the table is "circular" so that location 0 follows location 11. However, num[0] is occupied and not by 23. So, we try num[1]; num[1] is empty, so 23 is placed in num[1].
- Finally, 61 hashes to 1; num[1] is occupied and not by 61—we have a collision. We try the next location, 2; num[2] is empty, so 61 is placed in num[2].

The following shows the array after all the numbers have been inserted:

num

84	23	61		52	16		43	31	33		59
0	1	2	3	4	5	6	7	8	9	10	11

Note that if a number is already in the array, the method would find it. For example, suppose we are searching for 23.

- 23 hashes to 11.
- num[11] is occupied and not by 23.
- We try the next location, 0; num[0] is occupied and not by 23.
- We next try num[1]; num[1] is occupied by 23—we find it.

Suppose we are searching for 33; 33 hashes to 9, and num[9] contains 33—we find it immediately.

As an exercise, determine the state of num after the previous numbers have been added using the following hash function:

H1(key) = key % 10

We can summarize the process described with the following algorithm:

```
//find or insert 'key' in the hash table, num[0..n-1]
loc = H(key)
while (num[loc] is not empty && num[loc] != key) loc = (loc + 1) % n
if (num[loc] is empty) { //key is not in the table
    num[loc] = key
    add 1 to the count of distinct numbers
}
else print key, " found in location ", loc
```

Note the expression for going to the next location:

```
(loc + 1) % n
```

If loc+1 *is less than* n, the expression simply evaluates to loc+1. If loc+1 *is equal to* n, the expression evaluates to 0, the location which comes after location n-1. In either case, loc takes on the value of the next location.

Alert readers will realize that we exit the while loop when either num[loc] is empty or it contains the key. What if neither happens so the while loop never exits? This situation will arise if the table is completely full (no empty locations) and does not contain the key we are searching for.

However, *in practice*, we never allow the hash table to become completely full. We always ensure that there are a few "extra" locations that are not filled by keys so that the while statement *will* exit at some point. In general, the hash technique works better when there are more free locations in the table.

How does the algorithm tell when a location is "empty"? We will need to initialize the array with some value that indicates "empty." For instance, if the keys are positive integers, we can use 0 or -1 as the empty value.

Let's write Program P8.1, which reads integers from a file, numbers.in, and uses a hash technique to determine the number of distinct integers in the file.

Program P8.1

```
#include <stdio.h>
#include <stdlib.h>
#define MaxNumbers 20
#define N 23
#define Empty 0
int main() {
    FILE * in = fopen("numbers.in", "r");
    int key, num[N];
    for (int h = 0; h < N; h++) num[h] = Empty;
    int distinct = 0;
    while (fscanf(in, "%d", &key) == 1) {
        int loc = key % N;
        while (num[loc] != Empty && num[loc] != key) loc = (loc + 1) % N;

        if (num[loc] == Empty) { //key is not in the table
            if (distinct == MaxNumbers) {
                printf("\nTable full: %d not added\n", key);
                exit(1);
            }
```

```
        num[loc] = key;
        distinct++;
    } //end if
  } //end while
  printf("\nThere are %d distinct numbers\n", distinct);
  fclose(in);
} //end main
```

If numbers.in contains the following:

25 28 29 23 26 35 22 31 21 26 25 21 31 32 26 20 36 21 27 24

Program P8.1 prints

There are 14 distinct numbers

Notes on Program P8.1

- MaxNumbers (20) is the maximum amount of distinct numbers catered for.
- N (23) is the hash table size, a little bigger than MaxNumbers so that there is always at least 3 free locations in the table.
- The hash table occupies num[0] to num[N-1].
- If key is not in the table (an empty location is encountered), we first check if the number of entries has reached MaxNumbers. If it has, we declare the table full and do not add key. Otherwise, we put key in the table and count it.
- If key is found, we simply go on to read the next number.

8.2.1 The Hash Function

In the previous section, we saw how an integer key can be "hashed" to a table location. It turns out that the "remainder" operation (%) often gives good results for such keys. But what if the keys were non-numeric, for example, words or names?

The first task is to convert a non-numeric key to a number and then apply the "remainder." Suppose the key is a word. Perhaps the simplest thing to do is add up the *numeric value* of each letter in the word. If the word is stored in a character array, word, properly terminated by \0, we can do this as follows:

```
int h = 0, wordNum = 0;
while (word[h] != '\0') wordNum += word[h++];
loc = wordNum % n; //loc is assigned a value from 0 to n-1
```

This method will work, but one objection is that words that contain the same letters would hash to the same location. For example, *mate*, *meat*, and *team* will all hash to the same location. In hashing, we must try to avoid *deliberately* hashing keys to the same location. One way around this is to assign a weight to each letter depending on its position in the word.

We can assign weights arbitrarily—the main goal is to avoid hashing keys with the same letters to the same location. For instance, we can assign 3 to the first position, 5 to the second position, 7 to the third position, and so on. The following shows how:

```
int h = 0, wordNum = 0;
int w = 3;
while (word[h] != '\0') {
    wordNum += w * word[h++];
    w = w + 2;
}
loc = wordNum % n; //loc is assigned a value from 0 to n-1
```

The same technique will work if a key contains arbitrary characters.

In hashing, we want the keys to be scattered all over the table. If, for instance, keys are hashed to one area of the table, we can end up with an unnecessarily high number of collisions. To this end, we should try to use *all* of the key. For example, if the keys are alphabetic, it would be unwise to map all keys beginning with the same letter to the same location. Put another way, we should avoid systematically hitting the same location.

And since hashing is meant to be fast, the hash function should be relatively easy to calculate. The speed advantage will be diminished if we spend too much time computing the hash location.

8.2.2 Delete an Item from a Hash Table

Consider, again, the array after all the sample numbers have been inserted:

num

84	23	61		52	16		43	31	33		59
0	1	2	3	4	5	6	7	8	9	10	11

Recall that 43 and 31 both hashed initially to location 8. Suppose we want to delete 43. The first thought might be to set its location to empty. Assume we did this (set num[7] to empty) and were now looking for 31. This will hash to 7; but since num[7] is empty, we will conclude, wrongly, that 31 is not in the table. So, we cannot delete an item simply by setting its location to empty since other items may become unreachable.

The simplest solution is to set its location to a deleted value—some value that cannot be confused with empty or a key. In this example, if the keys are positive integers, we can use 0 for empty and -1 for deleted.

Now, when searching, we still check for the key or an empty location; deleted locations are ignored. A common error is to stop the search at a deleted location; doing so would lead to incorrect conclusions.

If our search reveals that an incoming key is not in the table, the key can be inserted in an empty location or a deleted one, if one was encountered along the way. For example, suppose we had deleted 43 by setting num[7] to -1. If we now search for 55, we will check locations 7, 8, 9, and 10. Since num[10] is empty, we conclude that 55 is not in the table.

We can, if we want, set num[10] to 55. But we could write our algorithm to remember the deleted location at 7. If we do, we can then insert 55 in num[7]. This is better since we will find 55 faster than if it were in num[10]. We would also be making better use of our available locations by reducing the number of deleted locations.

What if there are several deleted locations along the way? It is best to use the first one encountered since this will reduce the search time for the key. With these ideas, we can rewrite our search/insert algorithm as follows:

```
//find or insert 'key' in the hash table, num[0..n-1]
loc = H(key)
deletedLoc = 0
while (num[loc] != Empty && num[loc] != key) {
    if (deletedLoc == 0 && num[loc] == Deleted) deletedLoc = loc
    loc = (loc + 1) % n
}
if (num[loc] == Empty) { //key not found
    if (deletedLoc != 0) loc = deletedLoc
    num[loc] = key
}
else print key, " found in location ", loc
```

Note that we still search until we find an empty location or the key. If we meet a deleted location and deletedLoc is 0, this means it's the first one. Of course, if we *never* meet a deleted location and the key is not in the table, it will be inserted in an empty location.

8.3 Resolve Collisions

In Program P8.1, we resolve a collision by looking at the next location in the table. This is, perhaps, the simplest way to resolve a collision. We say we resolve the collision using *linear probing*, and we will discuss this in more detail in the next section. After this, we will take a look at more sophisticated ways of resolving collisions. Among these are *quadratic probing, chaining,* and *double hashing*.

8.3.1 Linear Probing

Linear probing is characterized by the statement

loc = loc + 1

Consider, again, the state of num after the nine numbers have been added:

num

84	23	61		52	16		43	31	33		59
0	1	2	3	4	5	6	7	8	9	10	11

As you see, the chances of hashing a new key to an empty location decrease as the table fills up.

Suppose a key hashes to location 11. It will be placed in num[3] after trying locations 11, 0, 1, and 2. In fact, any new key that hashes to 11, 0, 1, 2, or 3 will end up in num[3]. When that happens, we will have a long, unbroken chain of keys from location 11 to location 5. Any new key hashing to this chain will end up in num[6], creating an even longer chain.

This phenomenon of *clustering* is one of the main drawbacks of linear probing. Long chains tend to get longer since the probability of hashing to a long chain is usually greater than that of hashing to a short chain. It is also easy for two short chains to be joined, creating a longer chain that, in turn, will tend to get longer. For example, any key that ends up in num[6] will create a long chain from locations 4 to 9.

We define two types of clustering.

1. *Primary clustering* occurs when keys that hash to different locations trace the same sequence in looking for an empty location. Linear probing exhibits primary clustering since a key that hashes to 5, say, will trace 5, 6, 7, 8, 9, and so on, and a key that hashes to 6 will trace 6, 7, 8, 9, and so on.

2. *Secondary clustering* occurs when keys that hash to the same location trace the same sequence in looking for an empty location. Linear probing exhibits secondary clustering since keys that hash to 5, say, will trace the same sequence 5, 6, 7, 8, 9, and so on.

Methods of resolving collisions that hope to improve on linear probing will target the elimination of primary and/or secondary clustering.

You may wonder if using loc = loc + k where k is a constant greater than 1 (for example, 3) will give any better results than loc = loc + 1. As it turns out, this will not alter the clustering phenomenon since groups of k-apart keys will still be formed.

In addition, it can even be worse than when k is 1 since it is possible that not all locations will be generated. Suppose the table size is 12, k is 3, and a key hashes to 5. The sequence of locations traced will be 5, 8, 11, 2 ((11 + 3) % 12), 5, and the sequence repeats itself. By comparison, when k is 1, all locations are generated.

However, this is not really a problem. If the table size is m and k is "relatively prime" to m (their only common factor is 1), then all locations are generated. Two numbers will be relatively prime if one is a prime and the other is not a multiple of it, such as 5 and 12. But being prime is not a necessary condition. The numbers 21 and 52 (neither of which is prime) are relatively prime since they have no common factors other than 1.

If k is 5 and m is 12, a key hashing to 5 will trace the sequence 5, 10, 3, 8, 1, 6, 11, 4, 9, 2, 7, 0—all locations are generated. A key hashing to any other location will also generate all locations.

In any case, being able to generate all locations is academic since if we had to trace many locations to find an empty one, the search would be too slow, and we would probably need to use another method.

Notwithstanding what we've just said, it turns out that loc = loc + k, where k *varies* with the key, gives us one of the best ways to implement hashing. We will see how in Section 8.3.4.

So, how fast is the linear method? We are interested in the average *search length*, that is, the number of locations that must be examined to find or insert a given key. In the previous example, the search length of 33 is 1, the search length of 61 is 2, and the search length of 23 is 3.

The search length is a function of the *load factor*, *f*, of the table, where:

f = fraction of table filled and is calculated as follows:

$$\frac{number\ of\ entries\ in\ table}{number\ of\ table\ locations}$$

For a successful search, the average number of comparisons is

$$\frac{1}{2}\left(1 + \frac{1}{1-f}\right)$$

and for an unsuccessful search, the average number of comparisons is

$$\frac{1}{2}\left(1 + \frac{1}{(1-f)^2}\right)$$

Note that the search length depends only on the fraction of the table filled, *not* on the table size.

The following table shows how the search length increases as the table fills up:

f	successful search length	unsuccessful search length
0.25	1.2	1.4
0.50	1.5	2.5
0.75	2.5	8.5
0.90	5.5	50.5

At 90% full, the average successful search length is a reasonable 5.5. However, it can take quite long (50.5 probes) to determine that a new key is not in the table. If linear probe is being used, it would be wise to ensure that the table does not become more than about 75% full. This way, we can guarantee good performance with a simple algorithm.

8.3.2 Quadratic Probing

In this method, suppose an incoming key collides with another at location loc; we go forward $ai + bi^2$ where a, b are constants and i takes on the value 1 for the first collision, 2 if there is a second collision, 3 if there is a third collision, and so on. For example, if we let $a = 1$ and $b = 1$, we go forward $i + i^2$ from location loc. Suppose the initial hash location is 7 and there is a collision.

We calculate $i + i^2$ with $i = 1$; this gives 2, so we go forward by 2 and check location $7 + 2 = 9$.

If there is still a collision, we calculate $i + i^2$ with $i = 2$; this gives 6, so we go forward by 6 and check location $9 + 6 = 15$.

If there is still a collision, we calculate $i + i^2$ with $i = 3$; this gives 12, so we go forward by 12 and check location $15 + 12 = 27$.

And so on. Each time we get a collision, we increase i by 1 and recalculate how much we must go forward this time. We continue this way until we find the key or an empty location.

If, at any time, going forward takes us beyond the end of the table, we wrap around to the beginning. For example, if the table size is 25 and we go forward to location 27, we wrap to location 27 − 25, that is, location 2.

For the next incoming key, if there is a collision at the initial hash location, we set i to 1 and continue as explained above. It is worth noting that, for each key, the sequence of "increments" will be 2, 6, 12, 20, 30.... We can, of course, get a different sequence by choosing different values for *a* and *b*.

We can summarize the process just described with the following algorithm:

```
//find or insert 'key' in the hash table, num[1..n]
loc = H(key)
i = 0
while (num[loc] != Empty && num[loc] != key) {
    i = i + 1
    loc = loc + a * i + b * i * i
    if (loc >= n) loc = loc % n
}
if (num[loc] == Empty) num[loc] = key
else print key, " found in location ", loc
```

With quadratic probing, keys that hash to different locations trace different sequences; hence, primary clustering is eliminated. However, keys that hash to the same location will trace the same sequence, so secondary clustering remains.

Here are some other points to note:

- If *n* is a power of 2, that is, $n = 2^m$ for some *m*, this method explores only a small fraction of the locations in the table and is, therefore, not very effective.

- If *n* is prime, the method can reach half the locations in the table; this is usually sufficient for most practical purposes.

8.3.3 Chaining

In this method, all items which hash to the same location are held on a linked list. One way to implement this is to let the hash table contain "top of list" pointers. For instance, if hash[0..n-1] is the hash table, then hash[k] will point to the linked list of all items which hash to location k. An item can be added to a linked list at the head, at the tail or in a position such that the list is in order.

To illustrate the method, suppose the items are integers. Each linked list item will consist of an integer value and a pointer to the next item. We define the following structure:

```
typedef struct node {
    int num;
    struct node *next;
} Node, *NodePtr
```

We create a new node containing n with this:

```
Node newNode(int n) {
    Node temp;
    temp.num = n;
    temp.next = NULL;
    return temp;
}
```

We can now define hash as follows:

```
NodePtr hash[MaxItems]; //MaxItems is a symbolic constant
```

We initialize it with this:

```
for (int h = 0; h < MaxItems; h++) hash[h] = NULL;
```

Suppose an incoming key, inKey, hashes to location k. We must search the linked list pointed to by hash[k] for inKey. If it is not found, we must add it to the list. In our program, we will add it such that the list is in ascending order.

We write Program P8.2 to count the number of distinct integers in the input file, chaining.in. The program uses "hashing with chaining". At the end, we print the list of numbers which hash to each location.

Program P8.2

```c
#include <stdio.h>
#include <stdlib.h>
#define N 13
#define Empty 0

typedef struct node {
    int num;
    struct node *next;
} Node, *NodePtr;

NodePtr newNode(int n) {
    NodePtr p = (NodePtr) malloc(sizeof(Node));
    p -> num = n;
    p -> next = NULL;
    return p;
} //end newNode

int main() {
    int key, search(int, NodePtr[], int);
    void printList(NodePtr);
    FILE * in = fopen("chaining.in", "r");
    NodePtr hash[N];
    for (int h = 0; h < N; h++) hash[h] = NULL;
    int distinct = 0;
    while (fscanf(in, "%d", &key) == 1)
        if (!search(key, hash, N)) distinct++;

    printf("\nThere are %d distinct numbers\n\n", distinct);
    for (int h = 0; h < N; h++)
        if (hash[h] != NULL) {
            printf("hash[%d]:   ", h);
            printList(hash[h]);
        }
    fclose(in);
} //end main

int search(int inKey, NodePtr hash[], int n) {
//return 1 if inKey is found; 0, otherwise
//insert a new key in its appropriate list so list is in order
    NodePtr newNode(int);
    int k = (inKey + 1) % n;
    NodePtr curr = hash[k];
    NodePtr prev = NULL;
    while (curr != NULL && inKey > curr -> num) {
        prev = curr;
        curr = curr -> next;
    }
```

```
        if (curr != NULL && inKey == curr -> num) return 1; //found
        //not found; inKey is a new key; add it so list is in order
        NodePtr np = newNode(inKey);
        np -> next = curr;
        if (prev == NULL) hash[k] = np;
        else prev -> next = np;
        return 0;
} //end search

void printList(NodePtr top) {
    while (top != NULL) {
        printf("%2d ", top -> num);
        top = top -> next;
    }
    printf("\n");
} //end printList
```

If chaining.in contains the following numbers:

```
24 57 35 37 31 98 85 47 60 32 48 82 16 96 87 46 53 92 71 56
73 85 47 46 22 40 95 32 54 67 31 44 74 40 58 42 88 29 78 87
45 13 73 29 84 48 85 29 66 73 87 17 10 83 95 25 44 93 32 39
```

Program P8.2 produces the following output:

```
There are 43 distinct numbers

hash[0]: 25
hash[1]: 13 39 78
hash[2]: 40 53 66 92
hash[3]: 54 67 93
hash[4]: 16 29 42
hash[5]: 17 56 82 95
hash[6]: 31 44 57 83 96
hash[7]: 32 45 58 71 84
hash[8]: 46 85 98
hash[9]: 47 60 73
hash[10]: 22 35 48 74 87
hash[11]: 10 88
hash[12]: 24 37
```

If m keys have been stored in the linked lists and there are n hash locations, the average length of a list is m/n, and since we must search the lists sequentially, the average successful search length is $m/2n$. The search length can be reduced by increasing the number of hash locations.

Another way to implement "hashing with chaining" is to use a single array and use array subscripts as links. We can use these declarations:

```
typedef struct node {
    int num;    //key
    int next;   //array subscript of the next item in the list
} Node;

Node hash[MaxItems+1];
```

The first part of the table, hash[1..n], say, is designated as the hash table and the remaining locations are used as an *overflow* table, as in Figure 8-1.

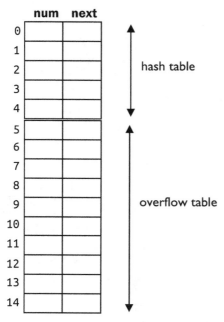

Figure 8-1. Array implementation of chaining

Here, hash[1..5] is the hash table and hash[6..15] is the overflow table.

Suppose key hashes to location k in the hash table:

- If hash[k].num is empty (0, say), we set it to key and set hash[k].next to -1, say, to indicate a null pointer.

- If hash[k].num is not 0, we must search the list starting at k for key. If it is not found, we put it in the next free location (f, say) in the overflow table and link it to the list starting at hash[k]. One way to link it is as follows:

```
hash[f].next = hash[k].next;
hash[k].next = f;
```

- Another way to link the new key is to add it at the end of the list. If L is the location of the last node in the list, this could be done with the following:

```
hash[L].next = f;
hash[f].next = -1; //this is now the last node
```

If deletions are possible, we need to decide what to do with deleted locations. One possibility is to keep a list of all available locations in the overflow table. When one is needed to store a key, it is retrieved from the list. When an item is deleted, its location is returned to the list.

Initially, we link all the items in the overflow table as shown in Figure 8-2 (next page) and let the variable free point to the first item in the list; here, free = 5. Item 5 points to item 6 which points to item 7 and so on with item 14 at the end of the list.

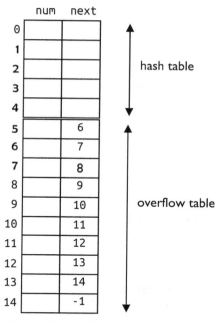

Figure 8-2. Link items in overflow table to form "free list"

Suppose 37 hashes to location 2. This is empty, so 37 is stored in hash[2].num. If another number (24, say) hashes to 2, it must be stored in the overflow table. First we must get a location from the "free list." This can be done with the following:

```
f = free;
free = hash[free].next;
return f;
```

Here, 6 is returned, and free is set to 7. The number 24 is stored in location 6, and hash[2].next is set to 6. At this stage, we have free = 7, with the tables having the values shown here.

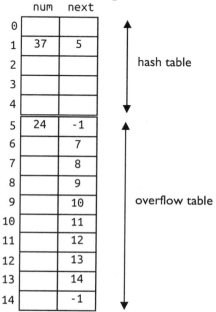

Now, consider how an item may be deleted. There are two cases to consider:

1. If the item to be deleted is in the hash table (at k, say), we can delete it with this:

```
if (hash[k].next == -1) set hash[k].num to Empty
//only item in list
else { //copy an item from the overflow table to the hash table
    h = hash[k].next;
    hash[k] = hash[h]; //copy info at location h to location k
    return h to the free list    //see next
}
```

    We can return a location (h, say) to the free list with this:

```
hash[h].next = free;
free = h;
```

2. If the item to be deleted is in the overflow table (at curr, say) and prev is the location of the item which points to the one to be deleted, then:

```
hash[prev].next = hash[curr].next;
return curr to the free list
```

Now consider how an incoming key might be processed. Suppose free is 8 and the number 52 hashes to location 1. We search the list starting at 1 for 52. It is not found, so 52 is stored in the next free location, 8. Location 5 contains the last item in the list so hash[5].next is set to 8 and hash[8].next is set to -1.

In general, we can perform a search for key and, if not found, insert it at the end of the list with this:

```
k = H(key)    //H is the hash function
if (hash[k].num == Empty) {
    hash[k].num = key
    hash[k].next = -1
}
else {
    curr = k
    prev = -1
    while (curr != -1 && hash[curr].num != key) {
        prev = curr
        curr = hash[curr].next
    }
    if (curr != -1) key is in the list at location curr
    else {  //key is not present
        hold = hash[free].next //save the next free location, if any
        hash[free].num = key
        hash[free].next = -1 //new item placed at end of list
        hash[prev].next = free
        free = hold
    } //end else
} //end else
```

8.3.4 Linear Probing with Double Hashing

This technique is also called *open addressing with double hashing*.

In Section 8.3.1, we saw that using loc = loc + k, where k is a constant greater than 1, does not give us a better performance than when k is 1. However, by letting k vary with the key, we can get excellent results since, unlike linear and quadratic probing, keys that hash to the same location will probe different sequences of locations in searching for an empty one.

The most natural way to let k vary with the key is to use a second hash function. The first hash function will generate the initial table location. If there is a collision, the second hash function will generate the increment, k. If the table locations run from 1 to n, we can use the following:

```
convert key to a numeric value, num (if it is not already numeric)
loc = num % n //this gives the initial hash location
k = num % (n - 2) + 1 //this gives the increment for this key
```

We mentioned before that it is wise to choose *n* (the table size) as a prime number. In this method, we get even better results if *n*-2 is also prime. In this case, *n* and *n*-2 are called *twin primes*, for example 103/101, 1021/1019.

Apart from the fact that k is not fixed, the method is the same as linear probing. We describe it in terms of two hash functions, H1 and H2. H1 produces the initial hash location, a value between 0 and *n*-1, inclusive. H2 produces the increment, a value between 1 and *n*-1 that is relatively prime to *n*. This is desirable so that, if required, many locations will be probed. As discussed earlier, if *n* is prime, any value between 1 and *n*-1 will be relatively prime to it.

In the example above, the second hash function produces a value between 1 and *n*-2, inclusive, so this value will be relatively prime to *n*. Here is the algorithm:

```
//find or insert 'key' using "linear probing with double hashing"
loc = H1(key)
k = H2(key)
while (hash[loc] != Empty && hash[loc] != key) {
    loc = loc + k
    if (loc >= n) loc = loc % n
}
if (hash[loc] == Empty) hash[loc] = key
else print key, " found in location ", loc
```

As before, to ensure that the while loop exits at some point, we do not allow the table to become completely full. If we want to cater for MaxItems, say, we declare the table size to be bigger than MaxItems. In general, the more free locations in the table, the better the hash technique works.

However, with double hashing, we do not need as many free locations as with normal linear probe to guarantee good performance. This is because double hashing eliminates both primary and secondary clustering.

Primary clustering is eliminated since keys that hash to different locations will generate different sequences of locations. Secondary clustering is eliminated since different keys that hash to the same location will generate different sequences. This is so since, in general, different keys will generate different increments (k, in the algorithm). It would be a rare coincidence indeed for two different keys to be hashed to the same values by both H1 and H2.

In practice, the performance of any hashing application can be improved by keeping information on how often each key is accessed. If we have this information beforehand, we can simply load the hash table with the most popular items first and the least popular last. This will lower the average access time for all keys.

If we do not have this information beforehand, we can keep a counter with each key and increment it each time the key is accessed. After some predefined time (a month, say), we reload the table with the most popular items first and the least popular last. We then reset the counters and garner statistics for the next month. This way we can ensure that the application remains fine-tuned since different items may become popular in the next month.

8.4 Word Frequency Count

Consider, once again, the problem of writing a program to do a frequency count of the words in a passage. Output consists of an alphabetical listing of the words with their frequencies. Now, we will store the words in a hash table using "linear probing with double hashing".

Each element in the table consists of three fields—word, freq and next. We will use the following structure for items to be stored in the table:

```
typedef struct {
    char word[MaxWordSize + 1];
    int freq, next;
} WordInfo;
```

We declare and initialize the table with this (Empty is a symbolic constant):

```
WordInfo wordTable[N+1]; //N - table size
for (int h = 0; h < N; h++) strcpy(wordTable[h].word, Empty);
```

The table is searched for each incoming word. If the word is not found, it is added to the table and its frequency count is set to 1. If the word is found, then its frequency count is incremented by 1.

In addition, when a word is added to the table, we set links such that we maintain a linked list of the words in alphabetical order. The variable first points to the first word in order. For example, suppose five words have been stored in the hash table. We link them, via next, as shown in Figure 8-3, with first = 5:

	word	freq	next
0	for	2	6
1			
2	wife	4	-1
3	man	1	2
4			
5	boy	1	0
6	girl	2	3

Figure 8-3. Words linked in alphabetical order (first = 5)

Thus, the first word is boy which points to for (0), which points to girl (6), which points to man (3), which points to wife (2), which does not point to anything (-1). The words are linked in alphabetical order: boy for girl man wife. Note that the linking works no matter where the hash algorithm places a word.

The hash algorithm first places the word. Then, regardless of where it is placed, that location is linked to maintain the words in order. For example, suppose, the new word kid hashes to location 1. Then the link of kid will be set to 3 (to point to man) and the link of girl will be set to 1 (to point to kid), as shown in Figure 8-4.

	word	freq	next
0	for	2	6
1	kid	1	3
2	wife	4	-1
3	man	1	2
4			
5	boy	1	0
6	girl	2	1

Figure 8-4. Words after kid has been added

We print the alphabetical listing by traversing the linked list. Program P8.3 shows all the details.

Program P8.3

```
#include <stdio.h>
#include <ctype.h>
#include <string.h>
#define MaxWordSize 20
#define MaxWords 30
#define N 31
#define Empty ""
typedef struct {
    char word[MaxWordSize + 1];
    int freq, next;
} WordInfo;

int main() {
    int getWord(FILE *, char[]);
    void printResults(FILE *, WordInfo [], int);
    int search(WordInfo [], char []);
    int addToTable(WordInfo [], char [], int, int);
    char word[MaxWordSize+1];
    WordInfo wordTable[N]; //N - table size

    for (int h = 0; h < N; h++) strcpy(wordTable[h].word, Empty);

    FILE * in = fopen("wordFreqHash.in", "r");
    FILE * out = fopen("wordFreqHash.out", "w");

    int first = -1; //points to first word in alphabetical order
    int numWords = 0;
```

```
        while (getWord(in, word) != 0) {
            int loc = search(wordTable, word);
            if (strcmp(wordTable[loc].word, word) == 0) //word found
                wordTable[loc].freq++;
            else //this is a new word
                if (numWords < MaxWords) { //if table is not full
                    first = addToTable(wordTable, word, loc, first);
                    ++numWords;
                }
                else fprintf(out, "'%s' not added to table\n", word);
        }
        printResults(out, wordTable, first);
        fclose(in);
        fclose(out);
} // end main

int getWord(FILE * in, char str[]) {
// stores the next word, if any, in str; word is converted to lowercase
// returns 1 if a word is found; 0, otherwise
    char ch;
    int n = 0;
    // read over non-letters
    while (!isalpha(ch = getc(in)) && ch != EOF) ; //empty while body
    if (ch == EOF) return 0;
    str[n++] = tolower(ch);
    while (isalpha(ch = getc(in)) && ch != EOF)
        if (n < MaxWordSize) str[n++] = tolower(ch);
    str[n] = '\0';
    return 1;
} // end getWord

int search(WordInfo table[], char key[]) {
//search for key in table; if found, return its location;
//if not, return the location in which it must be inserted
    int convertToNumber(char []);
    int keyNum = convertToNumber(key);
    int loc = (keyNum + 1) % N;
    int k = keyNum % (N - 2) + 1;

    while ((strcmp(table[loc].word, Empty) != 0) &&
                (strcmp(table[loc].word, key) != 0)) {
        loc = loc + k;
        if (loc >= N) loc = loc % N;
    }
    return loc;
} // end search

int convertToNumber(char key[]) {
    int h = 0, keyNum = 0, w = 3;
    while (key[h] != '\0') {
        keyNum += w * key[h++];
        w = w + 2;
    }
    return keyNum;
} //end convertToNumber

int addToTable(WordInfo table[], char key[], int loc, int head) {
//stores key in table[loc] and links it in alphabetical order
    strcpy(table[loc].word, key);
    table[loc].freq = 1;
```

```
        int curr = head;
        int prev = -1;
        while (curr != -1 && (strcmp(key, table[curr].word) > 0)) {
            prev = curr;
            curr = table[curr].next;
        }
        table[loc].next = curr;
        if (prev == -1) return loc; //new first item
        table[prev].next = loc;
        return head; //first item did not change
} //end addToTable

void printResults(FILE *out, WordInfo table[], int head) {
    fprintf(out, "\nWords          Frequency\n\n");
    while (head != -1) {
        fprintf(out, "%-15s %2d\n", table[head].word, table[head].freq);
        head = table[head].next;
    }
} //end printResults
```

Using a table size of 31 and MaxWords set to 30, Program P8.3 was run with the following data (from the song *Let It Be* by *The Beatles*) in wordFreqHash.in:

```
When I find myself in times of trouble
Mother Mary comes to me
Speaking words of wisdom, let it be
And in my hour of darkness
She is standing right in front of me
Speaking words of wisdom, let it be
Let it be, let it be
Let it be, let it be
Whisper words of wisdom, let it be
```

It sent the following output to the file wordFreqHash.out:

Words	Frequency
and	1
be	7
comes	1
darkness	1
find	1
front	1
hour	1
i	1
in	3
is	1
it	7
let	7
mary	1
me	2
mother	1
my	1
myself	1
of	6

right	1
she	1
speaking	2
standing	1
times	1
to	1
trouble	1
when	1
whisper	1
wisdom	3
words	3

EXERCISES 8

1. Integers are inserted into a hash table H[0..10] using the primary hash function

   h1(k) = k mod 11

   Show the state of the array after inserting the following keys:

   10, 22, 31, 4, 15, 28, 17, 88, 58

   using (a) linear probing (b) quadratic probing with probe function $i + i^2$ and (c) double hashing with h2(k) = 1 + k % 9.

2. Integers are inserted in an integer hash table list[0] to list[n-1] using "linear probe with double hashing". Assume that the function h1 produces the initial hash location and the function h2 produces the increment. An available location has the value Empty and a deleted location has the value Deleted.

   Write a function to search for a given value key. If found, the function returns the location containing key. If not found, the function inserts key in the first deleted location encountered (if any) in searching for key, or an Empty location, and returns the location in which key was inserted. You may assume that list contains room for a new integer.

3. In a hashing application, the key consists of a string of letters. Write a hash function which, given a key and an integer max, returns a hash location between 1 and max, inclusive. Your function must use all of the key and should not deliberately return the same value for keys consisting of the same letters.

4. A hash table of size *n* contains two fields—an integer data field and an integer link field—called data and next. The next field is used to link data items in the hash table in ascending order. A value of -1 indicates the end of the list. The variable top (initially set to -1) indicates the location of the smallest data item.

   Integers are inserted in the hash table using hash function h1 and linear probing. The data field of an available location has the value Empty and no item is ever deleted from the table. Write programming code to search for a given value key. If found, do nothing. If not found, insert key in the table and link it in its ordered position. You may assume that the table contains room for a new integer.

5. In a certain application, keys which hash to the same location are held on a linked list. The hashtable location contains a pointer to the first item on the list and a new key is placed at the end of the list. Each item in the linked list consists of an integer key, an integer count and a pointer to the next element in the list. Storage for a linked list item is allocated as needed. Assume that the hash table is of size *n* and the call H(key) returns a location from 0 to *n*-1, inclusive.

    (a) Write programming code to initialize the hash table.

    (b) Write a function which, given the key nkey, searches for it. If not found, add nkey in its appropriate position and set count to 0. If found, add 1 to count; if count reaches 10, delete the node from its current postion, place it at the head of its list and set its count to 0.

6. Write a program to read and store a thesaurus as follows:

    Data for the program consists of lines of input. Each line contains a (variable) number of distinct words, all of which are synonyms. You may assume that words consist of letters only and are separated by one or more blanks. Words may be spelt using any combination of upper and lower case letters. All words are to be stored in a hash table using "open addressing with double hashing". A word can appear on more than one line, but each word must be inserted only once in the table. If a word appears on more than one line then all words on those lines are synonyms. This part of the data is terminated by a line containing the word EndOfSynonyms.

    The data structure must be organized such that, given any word, all synonyms for that word can be quickly found.

    The next part of the data consists of several commands, one per line. A valid command is designated by P, A, D or E.

    P *word* prints, in alphabetical order, all synonyms of *word*.

    A *word1 word2* adds *word1* to the list of synonyms for *word2*.

    D *word* deletes *word* from the thesaurus.

    E, on a line by itself, indicates the end of the data.

7. Write a program to compare quadratic probing, linear probing with double hashing and chaining. Data consists of an English passage and you are required to store all the distinct words in the hash tables. For each word and each method, record the number of probes required to insert the word in the hash table.

    Cater for 100 words. For quadratic probing and double hashing, use a table size of 103. For chaining, use two table sizes—23 and 53. For each of the four methods, use the same basic hash function.

    Print an alphabetical listing of the words and the number of probes for each of the four methods. For each method, give the average number of probes for all the words. Organize your output so that the performance of the methods can be easily compared.

CHAPTER 9

■ ■ ■

Working with Matrices

In this chapter, we will explain:

- How the elements of one- and two-dimensional arrays are stored
- How to conserve storage for matrices with special properties
- How to store triangular matrices to save storage
- How to store symmetric and skew-symmetric matrices to save storage
- How to store band matrices to save storage
- How to store sparse matrices to save storage

9.1 Store Large Matrices

There are many applications in which large matrices are needed. Examples are common in engineering and mathematics. The bigger the matrix, the more storage is required to store it. In some cases, the storage requirement of a program is dominated by that of the matrices it needs to manipulate. In this chapter, we look at ways to take advantage of special properties a matrix may have in order to reduce the amount of memory needed to store it.

9.1.1 Store 1-D and 2-D Arrays

In previous chapters, we worked with trees and graphs and saw how we could write programs to manipulate these non-linear structures. In all of this, it is useful to remember that the computer's memory (primary storage) has a linear structure. Typically, *memory addresses* range from 0 to some number *n* where *n* depends on how much memory our computer has.

When we need to store a graph, say, in memory, we must find a way to translate this non-linear structure into the linear arrangement of a computer's memory. Of course, if our data structure is linear to begin with (like a one-dimensional array), the translation is easier. In this section, we consider how 1-D arrays (linear) and 2-D arrays (non-linear) are stored in memory.

Consider the declaration:

```
int A[100];
```

The array A contains 100 elements, A[0] to A[99], stored somewhere in memory. Each element is an integer. When we use statements like these:

```
A[i] = 25;
int c = A[i] -3;
```

how does the computer know where to find A[i]?

Suppose each element occupies 4 bytes. When the array is declared, the compiler requests 400 bytes of storage for the array. The address of the first byte of storage is usually called the *base address*, BA. This address is stored as one of the properties of A. Other properties would include the size and the type. Thus,

- A[0] is stored at memory location BA.
- A[1] is stored at memory location BA + 4.
- A[2] is stored at memory location BA + 8.
- A[3] is stored at memory location BA + 12.

In general,

- A[i] is stored at memory location BA + 4i.

When your program references A[i], the value of i is determined and this value is used to calculate where A[i] is stored. Similar remarks apply if the subscript is an expression.

For 1-D arrays of other types, the situation is similar. If each element occupies k bytes, then A[i] is stored in location BA + k * i.

Consider now the case of a 2-D array:

```
int A[4][5];
```

This array has 4 rows and 5 columns—a total of 20 elements. As before, the compiler requests storage (80 bytes) to store this array and is given the base address where the array can be stored. We can think of the array as follows:

$A_{0,0}$	$A_{0,1}$	$A_{0,2}$	$A_{0,3}$	$A_{0,4}$
$A_{1,0}$	$A_{1,1}$	$A_{1,2}$	$A_{1,3}$	$A_{1,4}$
$A_{2,0}$	$A_{2,1}$	$A_{2,2}$	$A_{2,3}$	$A_{2,4}$
$A_{3,0}$	$A_{3,1}$	$A_{3,2}$	$A_{3,3}$	$A_{3,4}$

The problem here is how to arrange the elements in a linear order to store them in memory. The two obvious choices are to store them in row order (*row-major* order) or column order (*column-major* order). We will use row order. The following holds:

- A[0][0] is stored at memory location BA;

- A[0][1] is stored at memory location BA + 4;
- A[0][2] is stored at memory location BA + 8;
- A[0][3] is stored at memory location BA + 12;
- A[0][4] is stored at memory location BA + 16;
- A[1][0] is stored at memory location BA + 20;

and so on, until

- A[3][4] is stored at memory location BA + 76.

Where is A[i][j] stored? We can work out the answer as follows:

- Each row occupies 20 bytes.
- There are i rows before the row in which A[i][j] is stored; these rows occupy $20i$ bytes.
- There are j elements before A[i][j] in its own row; these elements occupy $4j$ bytes.
- Hence the total number of bytes before A[i][j] is $20i + 4j$.
- Hence A[i][j] is stored at location BA + $20i + 4j$.

Using this formula, we see that A[3][4] is stored at BA + 76.

Given the more general declaration:

```
int A[m][n]; // m, n are constants
```

We can use a similar argument to show that A[i][j] is stored at this location:

```
BA + 4(ni + j)
```

And, if each element occupies k bytes, A[i][j] is stored at

```
BA + k(ni + j)
```

9.2 Store Matrices with Special Properties

There are many applications in mathematics and engineering, among others, which use large two-dimensional matrices. An $m \times n$ matrix (m rows, n columns) consists of mn elements. If each element occupies k bytes, the amount of storage required to store the matrix is kmn bytes.

However, many times, such matrices have special properties which a programmer can exploit to reduce the amount of storage required. In this section, we will discuss triangular, symmetric, skew-symmetric, band and sparse matrices.

9.2.1 Triangular Matrices

An $n \times n$ lower-triangular matrix is one in which the non-zero elements are all found *on or below* the main diagonal, in the "lower triangle". All elements *above* the main diagonal are zero. The following shows a 5×5 lower-triangular matrix:

$A_{1,1}$	0	0	0	0
$A_{2,1}$	$A_{2,2}$	0	0	0
$A_{3,1}$	$A_{3,2}$	$A_{3,3}$	0	0
$A_{4,1}$	$A_{4,2}$	$A_{4,3}$	$A_{4,4}$	0
$A_{5,1}$	$A_{5,2}$	$A_{5,3}$	$A_{5,4}$	$A_{5,5}$

Note that the matrix must be *square*—the number of rows is the same as the number of columns. In keeping with the usual mathematical treatment of matrices, we assume that the rows and columns are numbered starting from 1.

An element $A_{i,j}$ *above* the main diagonal has the property that $i < j$; *on* the main diagonal, $i = j$; *below* the main diagonal, $i > j$.

In order to conserve storage, we will store the lower triangle elements in a one-dimensional array, $B[1..m]$, where m is $n(n+1)/2$, the number of elements in the lower triangle. We will not store the zero elements. We will not use $B[0]$. If you need to use $B[0]$, a minor adjustment to our formula below will be necessary.

The number of elements to store is derived by noting that we store 1 element from the first row, 2 elements from the second row, and so on, until we store n elements from the nth row. This gives a total of

$1 + 2 + 3 + \ldots + n = \frac{1}{2} n(n+1)$

We need to decide the order in which we will store the elements in B. We will use row-major order, that is, we store the elements from the first row, followed by the elements from the second row, and so on, until we store the elements from the last row. So, for the sample matrix, we will store the elements in this order:

$A_{1,1}$	$A_{2,1}$	$A_{2,2}$	$A_{3,1}$	$A_{3,2}$	$A_{3,3}$	$A_{4,1}$	$A_{4,2}$	$A_{4,3}$	$A_{4,4}$	$A_{5,1}$	$A_{5,2}$	$A_{5,3}$	$A_{5,4}$	$A_{5,5}$
1	2	3	4	5	6	7	8	9	10	11	12	13	14	15

There are 5*6/2 = 15 elements to store. We store them in $B[1]$ to $B[15]$.

Given that the values are stored in B, how can we work out the value of $A_{i,j}$? We know that if i is less than j, the value is not stored and hence it is zero. If the value *is* stored, we can work out its position in B as follows:

- There are $(i-1)$ rows before the ith row.

- There are $1 + 2 + ... + (i\text{-}1) = \frac{1}{2} i(i - 1)$ elements in these rows.
- There are j elements up to $A_{i,j}$ in the ith row.
- Hence, the number of elements up to, and including, $A_{i,j}$ is $\frac{1}{2} i(i - 1) + j$.

Thus, $A_{i,j}$ is stored in $B[\frac{1}{2} i(i - 1) + j]$. For example, $A_{4,3}$ is stored in $B[4.3/2 + 3]$, that is, $B[9]$.

We can write a function which, given i and j, accesses B and returns the value of $A_{i,j}$. We assume that the values in the matrix are of type double.

```
double A(double B[], int i, int j) {
    if (i < j) return 0.0;
    return B[i * (i - 1) / 2 + j];
}
```

By naming the function A, we can work with the matrix in pretty much the same way as if we had stored all the elements. Instead of the array notation A[i][j], we now use the function call A(i,j).

As an exercise, write the function assuming the elements in the lower triangle are stored in column-major order.

We can treat an *upper-triangular* matrix in a similar manner. A 5×5 upper-triangular matrix would look like this:

$A_{1,1}$	$A_{1,2}$	$A_{1,3}$	$A_{1,4}$	$A_{1,5}$
0	$A_{2,2}$	$A_{2,3}$	$A_{2,4}$	$A_{2,5}$
0	0	$A_{3,3}$	$A_{3,4}$	$A_{3,5}$
0	0	0	$A_{4,4}$	$A_{4,5}$
0	0	0	0	$A_{5,5}$

Here, an element $A_{i,j}$ is zero if $i > j$; it is in the upper triangle if $i \le j$. As an exercise, devise a scheme for storing the upper-triangular elements in a one-dimensional array and write an appropriate access function to return $A_{i,j}$.

9.2.2 Symmetric and Skew-Symmetric Matrices

A *symmetric* matrix, A, is one in which $A_{i,j} = A_{j,i}$. If we think of the main diagonal as a mirror, elements which are reflections of each other have the same value. We can take advantage of this property by storing the elements in the lower triangle, say. When we need a value from the upper triangle, we can retrieve its "reflection" from the lower triangle. For instance, if we need $A_{2,4}$ (not stored) we simply retrieve $A_{4,2}$ (stored).

We can write the access function for $A_{i,j}$ based on the following:

- If $A_{i,j}$ is in the lower triangle ($i \geq j$), retrieve it from B[½ i(i-1) + j].
- If it is in the upper triangle, reverse the subscripts and retrieve B[½ j(j-1) + i].

Here is the function:

```
double A(double B[], int i, int j) {
    if (i >= j) return B[i * (i - 1) / 2 + j];
    return B[j * (j - 1) / 2 + i];
} //end A
```

A *skew-symmetric* matrix, A, is one in which $A_{i,j} = -A_{j,i}$. This impiles that the diagonal elements are zero. (If we want to allow the diagonal elements to be non-zero, we can say $A_{i,j} = -A_{j,i}$, $i \neq j$.) We can picture this as follows:

0	$A_{1,2}$	$A_{1,3}$	$A_{1,4}$	$A_{1,5}$
$A_{2,1}$	0	$A_{2,3}$	$A_{2,4}$	$A_{2,5}$
$A_{3,1}$	$A_{3,2}$	0	$A_{3,4}$	$A_{3,5}$
$A_{4,1}$	$A_{4,2}$	$A_{4,3}$	0	$A_{4,5}$
$A_{5,1}$	$A_{5,2}$	$A_{5,3}$	$A_{5,4}$	0

Since the diagonal elements are zero, we do not need to store them. And since the elements in the upper triangle can be derived from those in the lower triangle, we do not need to store them.

We store the elements in the strictly lower triangle in a one-dimensional array, B, with $A_{2,1}$ in B[1], $A_{3,1}$ in B[2], $A_{3,2}$ in B[3], and so on, with $A_{5,4}$ in B[10]. The sample matrix will be stored as follows:

$A_{2,1}$	$A_{3,1}$	$A_{3,2}$	$A_{4,1}$	$A_{4,2}$	$A_{4,3}$	$A_{5,1}$	$A_{5,2}$	$A_{5,3}$	$A_{5,4}$
1	2	3	4	5	6	7	8	9	10

Based on this, we derive the access formula for $A_{i,j}$ as follows:

- There are (i-1) rows before the ith row.
- There are $0 + 1 + 2 + ... + (i\text{-}2) = ½ (i - 1)(i - 2)$ elements in these rows.
- There are j elements up to, and including, $A_{i,j}$ in the ith row.
- Hence, the number of elements up to, and including, $A_{i,j}$ is ½ $(i - 1)(i - 2) + j$.

Thus, $A_{i,j}$ is stored in B[$(i - 1)(i - 2)/2 + j$]. For example, $A_{4,3}$ is stored in B[3.2/2 + 3], that is, B[6].

We can write the access function for $A_{i,j}$ based on the following:

- If $A_{i,j}$ is on the main diagonal, return 0.
- If $A_{i,j}$ is in the lower triangle ($i > j$), retrieve B[½$(i - 1)(i - 2) + j$].

- If $A_{i,j}$ is in the upper triangle ($i < j$), reverse the subscripts and retrieve the negative of $B[\frac{1}{2}(j - 1)(j - 2) + i]$.

Here is the function:

```
double A(double B[], int i, int j) {
    if (i == j) return 0.0;
    if (i > j) return B[(i - 1) * (i - 2) / 2 + j];
    return -B[(j - 1) * (j - 2) / 2 + i];
} //end A
```

9.2.3 Band Matrices

A *band* matrix, A, is one in which all the non-zero elements are on a band which includes the main diagonal and subdiagonals on both sides. For example, the following shows a 6×6 *tri-diagonal* matrix (band of width 3):

$A_{1,1}$	$A_{1,2}$	0	0	0	0
$A_{2,1}$	$A_{2,2}$	$A_{2,3}$	0	0	0
0	$A_{3,2}$	$A_{3,3}$	$A_{3,4}$	0	0
0	0	$A_{4,3}$	$A_{4,4}$	$A_{4,5}$	0
0	0	0	$A_{5,4}$	$A_{5,5}$	$A_{5,6}$
0	0	0	0	$A_{6,5}$	$A_{6,6}$

Note that for those elements $A_{i,j}$ on the band, we have $|i - j| \le 1$ and for those elements off the band, we have $|i - j| > 1$.

In general, if for some integer m, we have $A_{i,j} = 0$ when $|i - j| > m$, then A is a band matrix with a band width of $2m + 1$. When $m = 1$, A is tri-diagonal.

Clearly, we can save a lot of storage if we store the elements on the band only.

Consider the case of an $n \times n$ tri-diagonal matrix. Except for the first and last rows, each row has 3 elements on the band. The first and last rows have two each. This gives a total of $3n - 2$ elements on the band.

We will store these elements in a one-dimensional array B[1..3n-2]. We can choose to store them in row order, column order or even by diagonals. We will use row order.

Thus, we will store $A_{1,1}$ in B[1], $A_{1,2}$ in B[2], $A_{2,1}$ in B[3], and so on, with $A_{n,n}$ in B[3n-2]. For the sample 6×6 matrix, we will store the band elements as follows:

$A_{1,1}$	$A_{1,2}$	$A_{2,1}$	$A_{2,2}$	$A_{2,3}$	$A_{3,2}$	$A_{3,3}$	$A_{3,4}$	$A_{4,3}$	$A_{4,4}$	$A_{4,5}$	$A_{5,4}$	$A_{5,5}$	$A_{5,6}$	$A_{6,5}$	$A_{6,6}$
1	2	3	4	5	6	7	8	9	10	11	12	13	14	15	16

Given this arrangement, we can derive the access formula for $A_{i,j}$ as follows:

- We work out how many elements there are *before* $A_{i,i}$.
- There are $(i\text{-}1)$ rows before the *i*th row, all with 3 elements except the first.
- If we imagine $A_{i,i-1}$ being added to the first row, which has 2 elements, we get $3(i$ - $1)$ elements *before* $A_{i,i}$. Adding 1 takes us to $A_{i,i}$. Thus, $A_{i,i}$ is stored in position $3(i$ - $1) + 1 = 3i - 2$.
- Next, consider $j - i$. For elements on the band, this is either -1, 0 or +1. These are exactly the 'offsets' we must add to the position of $A_{i,i}$ to get the positions of $A_{i,i-1}$, $A_{i,i}$ and $A_{i,i+1}$, respectively.
- Hence $A_{i,j}$ is stored in position $3i - 2 + j - i = 2(i$ - $1) + j$.

For example, $A_{4,5}$ is stored in position $2(4 - 1) + 5 = 11$.

We must check whether our formula works for elements in the first row since it was derived based on "rows before the *i*th row" and there are no rows before the first. But when i is 1, the formula reduces to j, which gives the correct position. Hence the formula is valid for all band elements.

We can write the access function for $A_{i,j}$ as follows:

```
double A(double B[], int i, int j) {
    if (abs(i - j) > 1) return 0.0;
    return B[2 * (i - 1) + j];
} //end A
```

Here, abs(a), the absolute value of a, can be defined as follows:

```
#define abs(a) ((a) < 0) ? -(a) : (a)
```

As an exercise, work out the access function for a matrix with a band width of 5.

9.2.4 Sparse Matrices

While there is no precise definition of a sparse matrix, we think of it as one with many more zeroes than non-zeroes. A useful guide is to think of a matrix as sparse if less than 20% of its elements are non-zero.

The following is an example of a 5×6 sparse matrix:

	1	2	3	4	5	6
1	0.0	0.0	2.9	0.0	3.7	0.0
2	5.1	0.0	0.0	0.0	0.0	2.2
3	0.0	0.0	0.0	3.1	0.0	0.0
4	0.0	0.0	0.0	0.0	0.0	0.0
5	0.0	0.0	4.3	0.0	7.6	0.0

Note also that whereas the previous matrices were *required* to be square, that is not the case for a sparse matrix. In general, we will think of it as an $m{\times}n$ matrix.

There are several ways to store a sparse matrix to minimize storage. Some are discussed below.

9.2.4.1 Hash Table

We use the (i, j) subscripts of the non-zero elements as the key and store the subscripts and the value in the hash table. We need to store the subscripts since two different pairs of subscripts may hash to the same location.

If each matrix value requires 8 bytes (double) and each subscript occupies 2 bytes, this gives a total of 12 bytes for each non-zero value. Storing the matrix normally would take up $8mn$ bytes. If there are k non-zero values, we would save storage if $12k$ is less than $8mn$.

The percentage savings would be

$(8mn - 12k)/8mn \times 100$

For example, if there are 20% non-zeroes, then $k/mn = 0.2$ and the savings is 70%.

9.2.4.2 Linked Lists

In this method, we store the non-zero elements of each row (or column) in a linked list. If there are 5 rows, we use an array (row, say) of size 5; row[i] points to the first non-zero element in the ith row. If all the elements of the ith row are zero, row[i] is set to null.

The following shows how the above matrix can be stored by rows:

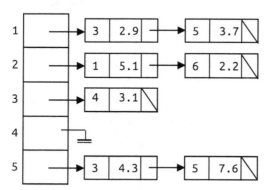

Each item in the list contains the column number and the value. It is natural to store the row elements in increasing order by column number. But this can be changed, if necessary.

The amount of storage required by this method can be easily calculated. Suppose there are m rows and k non-zero elements. Assume that a pointer value occupies 4 bytes, a column number occupies 2 bytes and a matrix value occupies 8 bytes. The array takes up $4m$ bytes and the list elements take up $14k$ bytes for a total of $4m + 14k$ bytes.

Retrieving element $A_{i,j}$ requires you to search the list starting at row[i] for a column value of j. If found, the value is returned; if not found, the value is 0.

Suppose a linked list element is a Node structure defined as follows:

```
typedef struct node {
    int column;
    double value;
    struct node *next;
} Node, *NodePtr;
```

We can write the access function like this:

```
double A(NodePtr row[], int i, int j) {
    NodePtr curr = row[i];
    while (curr != NULL && j > curr -> column) curr = curr -> next;
    if (curr == NULL || j < curr -> column) return 0.0;
    return curr -> value;
} //end A
```

This method is efficient if A will be accessed primarily by rows; for example, if we need to calculate the matrix product A × B. It is also easy to accommodate changes to matrix values. A value which goes from non-zero to 0 just has to be deleted from the appropriate list and one which goes from 0 to non-zero just has to be added. Both these operations are simple and efficient with a linked list.

Some matrix operations require that rows be interchanged. This is almost trivial to do here; to interchange rows *i* and *j*, all we need to do is swap row[i] and row[j].

But suppose we need the matrix product B × A? Now we will need to access A by columns. In this case, it is better to store A by columns, rather than rows. If there are *n* columns, we can use an array (col, say) of size *n* such that col[j] points to the list of non-zero elements in the *j*th column.

What if we need A by both rows and columns? We can combine the two representations using row and col pointers; row[i] points to elements in the *i*th row and col[j] points to elements in the *j*th column. Now, however, each list element will contain a row number, a column number, a pointer to the next non-zero element in the same row and a pointer to the next non-zero element in the same column.

Other variations are possible. Depending on how the matrix is to be processed, we can, for instance, have pointers to previous elements in the same row or column.

9.2.4.3 Arrays

Instead of linked lists, we can use arrays to store the matrix by rows or columns. Suppose we want to store the non-zero values in the sample matrix by columns. We first store the values in column-major order; with each value, we store the row in which it appears (we will explain item 1 shortly):

value	0.0	5.1	2.9	4.3	3.1	3.7	7.6	2.2
row	1	2	1	5	3	1	5	2
	1	2	3	4	5	6	7	8

Thus, 5.1 is in row 2, 2.9 is in row 1, 4.3 is in row 5, and so on. Let's assume this array is called B; B[i].value and B[i].row refer to the value and row at position i.

Next, we must fill in "access arrays" which tell us *where* in B the elements of each column are located. Since there are 6 columns, we will need an array (col, say) of size 6. Each element will have two fields—start and end; col[j].start is the location of the first element of column *j* in B and col[j].end is the location of the last element of column *j* in B. Here are the values for the sample matrix:

start	2	1	3	5	6	8
end	2	1	4	5	7	8
	1	2	3	4	5	6

For example, there are 2 non-zero elements in column 5. They are stored in B[6] and B[7]. Hence, col[5].start is set to 6 and col[5].end is set to 7.

Of particular interest is column 2. This is a column of all zeroes. Instead of having to do something special for zero columns, we choose to store a single zero in B[1] and set start and end to 1 for any column that contains all zeroes. Doing so will enable zero columns to be processed in the same way as non-zero columns.

In effect, we are saying that a zero column contains one "non-zero" element, stored in B[1]; this happens to be 0. This is a small penalty to pay for simpler processing.

This method is very efficient if we need to process the matrix by columns or if we need to interchange two columns. To interchange columns *j* and *k*, we just swap the values in col[j] and col[k].

If there are *k* non-zero values and *n* columns, the amount of storage required by this method is $10(k + 1) + 4n$ bytes.

If we need the matrix by rows, a similar scheme can be employed.

One of the big advantages of storing a sparse matrix this way is that some kinds of processing are speeded up greatly. Consider the matrix product C × A where C is *m×p* and A is *p×n*. Conventionally, we multiply, pairwise, each row of C by each column of A. The product (T, say) is an *m×n* matrix. The following pseudocode shows how:

```
for i = 1 to m
    for j = 1 to n
        //multiply row i of C by column j of A; this give T[i, j]
        T[i, j] = 0
        for k = 1 to p
            T[i, j] += C[i, k] * A[k, j]
```

This gives a total of *mpn* multiplications. (There are also *mpn* additions.)

But suppose a column of A has only one non-zero element. Since we *know* that, except for this one element, all the other multiplications involving this column will give 0, we need perform only one multiplication when multiplying by this column. Hence, the number of multiplications involving this column is reduced from *mp* to *m*. The following shows how to do the multiplication assuming A is stored as above:

```
for i = 1 to m
    for j = 1 to n
        //multiply row i of C by column j of A; this give T[i, j]
        T[i, j] = 0
        for u = col[j].start to col[j].end
            T[i, j] += C[i, B[u].row] * B[u].value
```

Here, we ensure that only the non-zero elements of A are multiplied by the corresponding elements in C.

In general, if there are *k* non-zero elements in A, the number of multiplications is reduced from *mpn* to *mk*.

For example, if $m = p = n = 1000$ and *k* is 100000 (10% non-zeroes), the number of multiplications is reduced from one billion (10^9) to 100 million (10^8), a savings of 900 million. Put another way, storing A as sparse will perform the matrix multiplication in about one-tenth of the time that it would take than if A were stored normally.

9.2.5 Other Special Types of Matrices

Sometimes a matrix is defined by some special relation among its elements. For example,

$A_{i,j} = A_{u,v}$ if $i + j = u + v$

As the following shows, elements on the diagonals going from south-west to north-east are equal since their subscripts add up to the same value:

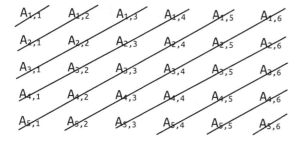

There are at most 10 distinct values in the matrix. Another way to look at it is that the sum of subscripts ranges from 2 to 11, a range of 10 values. In general, for an $m \times n$ matrix, there will be at most $m + n - 1$ distinct values.

For such a matrix, all we need is an array `B[1..m+n-1]`. We store values starting from $A_{1,1}$, going across the first row then down the last column, like this:

$A_{1,1}$	$A_{1,2}$	$A_{1,3}$	$A_{1,4}$	$A_{1,5}$	$A_{1,6}$	$A_{2,6}$	$A_{3,6}$	$A_{4,6}$	$A_{5,6}$
1	2	3	4	5	6	7	8	9	10

The access function is almost trivial:

```
double A(double B[], int i, int j) {
    return B[i + j - 1];
}
```

As an exercise, write the access function for a matrix A where

(a) $A_{i,j} = A_{u,v}$ if $i - j = u - v$

(b) $A_{i,j} = A_{u,v}$ if $|i - j| = |u - v|$

EXERCISES 9

1. The elements in the lower triangle of a lower-triangular matrix, A, are stored in column-major order in a one-dimensional array, B. Write a function which, given i and j, accesses B and returns the value of $A_{i,j}$.

2. The elements on the band of a tri-diagonal matrix are stored as follows: the upper diagonal, followed by the main diagonal, followed by the lower diagonal. Write the access function for $A_{i,j}$.

3. The elements in the upper triangle of an upper-triangular matrix, A, are stored in column-major order in a one-dimensional array, B.

    (a) Write a function which, given i and j, accesses B and returns the value of $A_{i,j}$.

    (b) Write the function if the elements are stored in row-major order.

4. Show how to store a sparse matrix by columns using linked lists.

5. A sparse matrix is stored by rows using linked lists. Write code to print the matrix in its normal form.

6. Write code to read the non-zero values of a sparse matrix (each element is supplied as *row, column, value*) and create the linked list representation (i) by rows (ii) by columns (iii) by rows and columns.

7. Write code to read the non-zero values of a sparse matrix (each element is supplied as *row, column, value*) and create the array representation (i) by rows (ii) by columns.

8. An $n \times n$ matrix A is used to store the rate per minute for telephone calls between any two of n towns. A[i,j] is the rate per minute for calling from town i to town j and vice versa. Within a town, calls are free. Devise a scheme to store the information in A in a one-dimensional array B, conserving storage as much as possible.

    (a) Write a function which, given i and j, accesses B and returns the value of A[i,j].

    (b) Using the function from (a), write another function which, given i, returns the town with the highest rate of calling from town i. Assume there is only one such town.

9. For any pair $(i, j, i \neq j)$ taken from n persons, it is known whether person i is younger than, older than or the same age as person j.

    (a) Explain how this information can be represented using an $n \times n$ matrix, A. State any special properties of the matrix.

    (b) Explain how the information in A can be stored in a one-dimensional array B, conserving storage as much as possible.

    (c) Write a function which, given i and j, accesses B and returns -1, 0 or 1 depending on whether person i is younger, same age as, or older than person j, respectively.

10. An $n \times n$ matrix A is used to store the points obtained in football matches among n teams. A team gets 3 points for a win, 1 point for a draw and 0 points for a loss. A[i,j] is set to 3 if team i beats team j, to 1 if the match is drawn and to 0 if team i loses to team j. In order to conserve storage, the values in the (strictly) lower triangle of A are stored in an array B[1..m] in row order.

    (a) What is the value of m?

    (b) Write a function which, given i and j, accesses B and returns the value of A[i,j]. If i or j is invalid, the function returns -1.

11. A is an $m \times n$ sparse matrix. B is an $n \times n$ tri-diagonal matrix. It is required to find the product ABA^T.

    (a) Devise schemes for storing A and B, conserving storage as much as possible.

    (b) Using your schemes, write code to find ABA^T.

Index

Index

Index

CPSIA information can be obtained
at www.ICGtesting.com
Printed in the USA
LVHW101224200120
644156LV00008B/300